MIRACLES

MIRACLES

CAMBRIDGE STUDIES
IN THEIR
PHILOSOPHY AND HISTORY

Edited by

C. F. D. MOULE

LONDON
A. R. MOWBRAY & CO LTD

© A. R. Mowbray & Co Ltd, 1965

Printed in Great Britain by
A. R. Mowbray & Co Ltd in the City of Oxford
5120

Dedication

To the members of the New Testament Seminar these essays are gratefully dedicated, and especially to Geoffrey Styler, whose skill and devoted service as Secretary have made it what it is, and to the memory of Barry Mackay, a fastidious scholar full of promise.

CONTENTS

(Appointments are held in the University of Cambridge except where otherwise stated)

PAGE

vii

1

INTRODUCTION

BY

C. F. D. MOULE

INTRODUCTION

THE CAMBRIDGE New Testament Seminar has a distinguished lineage, including among its former chairmen F. C. Burkitt and C. H. Dodd. There were giants in those days, both in the chair and round the table. But I am not prepared to say that there are not one or two giants round the table even now, and, I suspect, also some incipient giants: for the number of young students—Research Students and a few others doing advanced courses—has, I think, increased of latter years, in proportion to the already established scholars; and I shall be surprised if some of their names are not well known in the world of scholarship in a few years' time. However, it is not a working Seminar, in the sense of one which plans or expects to achieve solid research or to record findings. It is too large and mixed a body for that to be possible or desirable. Instead, it provides, I like to think, a forum in which matters of New Testament scholarship can be discussed freely and with the utmost informality. Sometimes they are matters of great moment, sometimes they are of almost purely academic interest; sometimes the wildest theories are ventilated, sometimes there is a most realistic discussion. It is, to me, a weekly occasion of academic luxury, when I need not stop to ask: Is this important? Will anything come of it? Is there not something more urgent to do? but need only ask: Is it interesting?

It is not surprising, in such circumstances, if nothing has hitherto been published as the work of the Seminar itself. A considerable number of papers in learned journals have found their first hearing at it, and a few books may have been conceived or, at any rate, nurtured in its atmosphere. But its only collective record hitherto has been the minutes, kept with monumental skill, accuracy, fulness, and wit for many years, during my chairmanship, by the Reverend G. M. Styler.

3

The present symposium on miracles, therefore, represents a departure from precedent. The session on miracle produced a larger number of contributions from Seminar members and invited readers than I have ever known on any one subject before; and, although the Seminar, collectively and individually, is well aware that these represent scattered materials for a work on miracle rather than a unified or considered statement, it nevertheless seems worthwhile to give them to a wider public. In most of the recent books on miracle, little or no attention is paid to the comparative study of ancient writers on the subject outside the Bible, or even to a comparative study of the Old Testament alongside of the New. It is hoped, therefore, that this collection, which includes a number of sketches for such a comparative study, may be a step in the right direction. In this connexion we are specially indebted to Dr. A. H. McDonald who graciously consented to come in as a guest from another Faculty to make a contribution from the angle of a Classical scholar; and to the other guest-reader, Dr. Mary Hesse, who provides a welcome comment from the side of an expert in the philosophy of science.

Regrettably, one or two of the contributions have had to be omitted, either because they were, in one way or another, already committed to publication elsewhere, or because they did not fit the pattern of this collection. In the first category is an original paper, soon to be published in a journal, by another of our guest-participants, the Reverend J. C. Hindley, of Serampore College, whom it was a great pleasure to welcome.

My own contributions were of an extremely incidental and ephemeral type; but I am exercising the editor's prerogative of putting some of my material into this short introductory essay, and some of it into excursus at the end.

This introduction cannot hope to offer a comprehensive statement binding all the contributions together, because the papers, not having been designed so as to add up to a coherent whole, are, in the nature of the case, diverse and episodic.

Instead, I will attempt simply to sketch their various approaches, and then to offer some remarks of my own on what, as I see it, is the heart of the problem and on what seem to me to be possible ways forward.

Of the essays which follow, the first two stand apart from the rest as primarily philosophical rather than literary or historical inquiries. Canon (now Professor) Woods, in 'The Evidential Value of Biblical Miracles', asks some of the basic questions about definition. He seeks for 'appropriate criteria for the recognition of the miraculous activity of God in the world of our present experience'. He points out that we cannot now accept it as axiomatic that what seems to be beyond human power must be divine: these are no longer the only alternatives recognized. Neither can we be wholly satisfied with the 'moral criterion', valuable though it may be within its limits. The trouble is that, applying human criteria (and we have no other sort), we can, at most, only succeed in showing that an event is not human, not in proving that it is divine. Professor Woods observes, further, that, when we use analogies (as, again, we are bound to do), we tend to use mechanical ones, and that these, whatever their value when 'prudently' used, have obviously grave limitations. To conclude, he recognizes that the appeal to miracle no longer carries the evidential value it did in a past era; that the difficulty of trying to talk about God in human terms is more clearly recognized by our generation than formerly; and yet, that such an attempt is not useless, provided it goes hand in hand with careful historical research. As far as he goes, Professor Woods seems to give his blessing to the greater part of this book which represents the spade-work of comparative study requisite for any historical approach to the subject.

Miss Hesse examines the concept of the miraculous in the situation created by the discrediting of Newtonian physics in favour of quantum physics. In this situation, the notion of miracle as a 'violation' of a mechanical system no longer has meaning. And yet, it would be a mistake, she goes on to observe, to imagine therefore that no scientific considerations any longer stand in the way of investigating reports of miracles on the merits of whatever historical evidence can be brought forward. For contemporary science continues, despite its relativistic tendencies, to expect a certain stability and uniformity in nature, and to be suspicious still of alleged events which seem to disturb its expected order; and most of the New Testament miracles are of this kind. In the absence, therefore, of quite overwhelming demonstration, the scientific mentality continues to be unconvinced that such things can have happened. But perhaps the miracles can be so interpreted as not to violate this conviction. They would, Miss Hesse claims, lose nothing of their religious depth or effectiveness thereby. Finally, she touches on exactly the problem raised by Professor Woods— namely, how the acts of God can be distinguished at all in 'special and providential events' as distinct from 'the ordinary course of nature and of history'. Thus, 'the fundamental problem is not about miracle, but about transcendence'.

After these opening essays from philosophical angles, there follow two on miracles in the Old Testament and four on miracle in other ancient literature outside the New Testament. Mr. Ross's chief point is that the Hebrew mind of the 'classical' period of the Old Testament did not think, like that of the Greek rationalist, in terms of a closed, self-sufficient system: it did not think in terms of Nature. Spring follows winter in obedience not to a natural system but to a particular command of God: 'when he is asked *why*, the answer that leaps to the Israelite's mind is in terms not of causes in the physical, scientific world, but of God'; 'he sees the world not as a *physical* structure, but as a *power* structure'. The Hebrew believes in regularity as much as the rationalist; but for him it is a moral regularity in God's consistently faithful character, not a merely physical regularity. Furthermore, the Hebrew of the period in question was sure of God, and did not look for proofs of his existence: he only wanted to be sure what God's character was. It was a later, Hellenistic argument that tried to prove the existence of God by miracle. For our part, we may be able, conjecturally, to translate miracle stories into rational terms; but we can still ask: What did God's character look like as a result of what happened?

Fr. Barnabas Lindars offers a valuable comparative study of the Elijah and Elisha cycles of miracle stories and the Gospel stories. He distinguishes between miracle viewed as a direct act of God (shading off into a theological interpretation of a historical event), miracle viewed as an act of God mediated by man, and miracle stories told without any special reference to God, simply to enhance the reputation of holy men. This last is common to hagiography all down the ages. Against this background, he examines the relevant material, freely recognizing the presence, in some of it, of the purely hagiographical, as well as occasions when natural events seem to have been reinterpreted in a theological manner. Each case has to be tested on its own merits, remembering the habits of story-tellers and the circumstances of transmission. But, however impossible it may be to get to the bottom of what happened, there remain the impressions to which the stories testify—in the case of Jesus, an impression of unique authority, only enhanced by the remarkable restraint which his own personality seems to have exercised over the traditions.

Dr. McDonald, invited to read a paper on miracle from the standpoint of a classical scholar and an ancient historian, chose Herodotus as his type, since Herodotus 'seems to represent most faithfully the common Greek conception of the interaction of the human and the divine'. Whereas Thucydides is the ancient historian who approached most closely to the modern tendency to explain what looks incalculable by psychology and sociology, Herodotus, closer to the common mind, is prepared to consider

the divine where he feels the influence of unknowable forces.
If we try (contrary to his own unsystematic method) to deduce
from Herodotus' remarks a systematic statement of his belief,
we might say that he believed in the coherence of a universe
which includes both the divine and the human. This being so,
there is no action that does not lead to a reaction; and, though
man cannot avoid taking action, the free man will act in a way
true to himself, and will learn by the consequences; whereas to
act sinfully is to provoke Nemesis. In this total system, it is the
unseen forces that are represented by the gods, and there is
nothing in human life that is not a part of the divine order and
balance of the world. And although Herodotus was sceptical
about common superstition, he believed that the holy places of
the gods had a sanctity that preserved them from sacrilege.
Dr. McDonald then applies to modern life the lesson of this
kind of ecological interaction.

The late Mr. Mackay's study of Plutarch, written specially for
this collection shortly before his sudden death, shows us the mind
of a cultured and religious pagan, contemporary with early Christianity. Plutarch is prepared to accept what may be styled the
abnormal, when he finds it well-attested, and to relate it to the
purposes of the gods. But it is striking that healing miracles
are virtually absent from the 'abnormalities' in question, which
are found, rather, in dreams, portents, and so forth. Plutarch's
vehement repudiation of the legends of Numa's birth from a
virgin and of Romulus' ascension may, possibly, represent
reactions against Christian stories.

Mr. Sweet, in a most interesting attempt to analyse what was
behind the account of the mechanics of miracle in Wisdom 19,
shows that, although the author of Wisdom uses what, in their
day, passed as quasi-scientific terms, it is against a characteristically Jewish background and with a view to glorifying Israel
that he applies them. The famous attempt, at the end of the
book, to 'explain' miracle, in terms not of derangement but of

rearrangement of what was already there, is a compromise in the interests of maintaining God's regularity. The book is apocalyptic and Jewish as well as Hellenistic and rational.

It is instructive to see how similarly Josephus emerges from an independent investigation. Fr. MacRae's picture of Josephus shows him as influenced by a degree of rationalizing and as the victim of tensions between Judaism and Hellenism: 'as a Jew, Josephus does not balk at accepting the miraculous wherever he encounters it, because what he sees in it are God's *pronoia* (providence) and *dynamis* (power). But as a Hellenist he does not hesitate to offer a pseudo-scientific or pseudo-philosophical explanation as well whenever one comes easily to mind.'

The remaining essays are all concerned with specifically Christian literature. Mr. Glasswell examines Mark's handling of the miraculous. He observes that, in strong contrast with, for instance, the contemporary stories of Apollonius of Tyana, Mark's stories show a certain reticence and that their point does not lie in the mere recounting of wonders: they are told, rather, to illustrate the power of the faith which Jesus calls into being. In Mark, miracles are not called signs; they do not point to faith so much as represent truths about the nature of faith in Jesus; they are certainly not regarded as evidential. Mark must be seen as illustrating the identity of Jesus, not as making a false appeal to history to demonstrate the truth of the Gospel. The proper place of miracles in the church's proclamation is as part of a summons to faith. In other words, the shape of Mark's work reveals his concern with the historical Jesus combined, at the same time, with his realization that he can only be recognized for what he is by faith, not by any compulsive evidence from history. The theme, therefore, of the messianic secret, with which the miracle stories in Mark are so closely concerned, is an inner necessity of Mark's presentation of the development from the historical Jesus to the proclaimed Lord. 'Miracles are what happens when one believes in Jesus and it is faith in Jesus which truly perceives a miracle and by that faith that the miracle becomes a sign.'

Examining the handling of the miraculous in Acts, Professor Lampe, rather similarly, makes a case for distinguishing it from the attempt, common in the apocryphal Gospels and much of the later Christian literature besides, to use miracle as evidence of the divine. Luke is much closer to the Old Testament—especially to Deuteronomy, the Deuteronomic Psalms, and the Prophets—than to the Hellenistic narrator of marvels. The phrase 'signs and wonders', though it sounds like a reference to demonstrative marvels, actually denotes in the Old Testament something internal to God's work of salvation and judgment. Signs and wonders are not conjuring tricks designed to induce belief in God, but, for the most part, focal points at which the continuous activity of God becomes manifest both to his people and to their oppressors. So 'in Luke's understanding of the matter, miracles are part and parcel of the entire mission of witness. The whole is miraculous, in so far as it is a continuous mighty work of God.' In 'his impressionistic and "supernaturalized" account of the progress of the gospel, Luke selects certain particular mighty works as typical. These are also focal points at which the meaning of the mission and its impact are dramatically summed up and illustrated in concrete form.' 'It is reasonable to hold that in all cases alike' (both of past and of contemporary miracle) 'Luke believed that the miracles which he recorded were concrete historical events, but that their parabolic significance was such as to entitle him to arrange them in his story, furnish them as it might be appropriate with explanatory speeches, and write them up in the light of Old Testament parallels and parallels in the ministry of Jesus.'

Dr. Bammel contributes an original and unusual essay in source-criticism. The phrase in John 10. 41 'John [the Baptist] worked no miracle, yet all that John said about this man

[Jesus] was true' is frequently attributed to the attitude (apparent, for instance, in Jn. 3. 22 ff.) which minimizes the Baptist's status over against that of Jesus, and is traced, accordingly, to an alleged rivalry between the Baptist's followers and Christians. Dr. Bammel inclines, rather, to find its setting in the conflict between Jews and Christians. Jewish tradition (until a comparatively late period) had tended to surround the prophets with miracle stories. The fact that there is virtually no trace anywhere of miracle stories associated with the Baptist may mean, not that they have been suppressed by opponents of his movement, but that there never were any. The sentence under consideration will then mean that, even though John lacked the authority of miracle, yet his witness to Jesus was sound. Dr. Bammel further discusses whether this phrase may not originally have stood as a summary at the end of a block of source-material describing miracles worked by Jesus, and he offers some consequent reflexions on the composition of St. John's Gospel.

The last two essays concern the post-New Testament period. In the second of his two contributions, Professor Lampe examines the attitudes to miracles in the early Christian apologists. After acknowledging in the apologists the traditional appeal to miracle as evidential, he shows how, when the apologists had to reply to the charge that Christian miracles were no more wonderful than those ascribed to pagan gods and heroes, they had to begin to appeal to the doctrine, or the character, of its teachers to lend credence to the miracles, rather than vice versa. They appealed to eyewitness, to the moral character of the witness, to the impossibility of hoodwinking large numbers of converts. When objectors took the line that Christ's miracles did indeed take place, but were due to sorcery, the apologists had more difficulty. Origen appeals to Christ's moral teaching, and also argues that the miracles were only symbolical—signs and foreshadowings of the 'greater works' promised by Christ to the disciples—thus spiritualizing the Gospel miracles into the status

of parables. And if non-Christians work miracles, that only
shows that one must ask about the purpose and the moral
consequences, not merely the fact, of a miracle. Eusebius rebuts
the charge of sorcery by asking whence it could have been
derived, why Christ used none of the apparatus of sorcery, and
why demons fled him. As for the appeal by the apologists to
contemporary miracles, this is shown chiefly to relate to exorcism, though exorcism which seems to be subtly different from
that with which Gospel stories are concerned and to be conditioned by the change from Jewish to pagan opposition to
Christianity. In short, the appeal to miracle, though made at
different levels by the apologists, was made, by the more serious
Christians, with more restraint than at a later date; and the
more sophisticated recognized it as a double-edged weapon, to
be used only in a supporting role.

Finally, Mr. Wiles, treating the early church more generally,
from the third century, sketches a shift of approach, occasioned
by difficulties in the historical appeal to miracle as time passed
and the Gospel period receded, considers the more philosophical
type of argument used by certain early Christian writers about
the possibility of miracle, and offers some observations about
the connexion between miracle and the idea of God as creator.
The diminishing force of miracle-stories was met partly by
connecting the Gospel miracles with Old Testament prophecy,
partly by appealing to moral 'miracle' as more noteworthy;
but the Gospel miracles were still affirmed as historical. On
certain levels, indeed, they were affirmed simply in popular
appeal, by writers who, on another level, recognized the need
for more strenuous thought about them. On this latter level,
much thought was given to the resurrection of Christ and, in
him, of others: Origen tended to spiritualize it away; others, to
resort to the idea of sheer divine omnipotence.

So far as they go, the essays that have been thus briefly indicated offer, among other things, a comparative study of various

attitudes to miracle in the ancient world. And out of the three-dimensional perspective which thus begins to form itself, certain interesting conclusions seem to emerge, in spite of the fact that these studies were not designed as a unity. One is that it is not much good asking, in connexion with any miracle-story relating to the remote past: What actually happened? A more profitable question is: What ideas did the narrator intend to convey? This question elicits a significant contrast between the narrator who conveys an impression of arbitrary power in his hero, and the narrator who represents the power as undeviatingly true to morality and mercy. It is to this latter class that most of the biblical narrators belong, especially the Evangelists; and it seems legitimate to draw certain deductions as to the character of the person whom they reflect.

On the other hand, if it is no good, because of the remoteness of the events, asking what *did* happen, we—or, at any rate, I, for one—cannot help going on asking: What *may* have happened? and, also: What *can* still happen? We are still, it would seem, confronted with the necessity to choose between believing in a 'closed' or an 'open' system—either a mechanical, 'Newtonian' system, in which nothing can happen without causes which (potentially) are physically perceptible, or else a system which (like that deduced from Herodotus' remarks in Dr. McDonald's essay) *includes* the 'transcendent' within its regularity and its interlocking order.

In other words, we are still left asking whether Mr. Ross's Hebrew is or is not closer to reality when he looks for consistency in the power of God rather than in an impersonal system of causation. And it seems worth while to take seriously this assumption that the ultimate and the most inclusive field in which consistency is to be sought is the realm of the personal. The most urgent question for the modern inquirer is thus, perhaps, whether such an assumption is compatible with an honest and open-minded attitude to all that science is discovering.

Thus, the question: Where, and within what bounds, do we look for consistency? seems to be the focus of the whole discussion; for another conclusion emerging from these essays— and, indeed, for me, at any rate, from many years of desultory discussion—is that the existence of consistency is an axiom. That somewhere there is regularity and consistency, seems to be generally treated as axiomatic. Indeed, it is obvious that no discussion of any sort is possible unless the validity of logic is allowed; and this itself is an instance of such an axiom of consistency.

This being so, the heart of the problem, the key question, seems to be, as I have said: Within what bounds, and on what level, do we look for our consistency, and how far is that consistency determinative in our judgments?

This question at once divides the debaters into distinguishable groups. For the thoroughgoing materialist, the only area of reality is that of phenomena ultimately, or in principle, perceptible by the senses. Therefore, any event that is claimed to contradict those laws of regularity which have been derived from prolonged observation of the working of such phenomena must, on this showing, be placed in one or other of two categories. Either what contradicts these laws is ultimately explicable in terms of such phenomena—let us, for brevity, call them material phenomena—in which case the formulation of the laws must be revised so as to include it. This conclusion, which involves nothing more than such a reformulation of the laws, is not a widening of the realm of recognized reality. The event, once explained in these terms, ceases to be an exception to the regularity of the material system and there is no question of miracle. Or else, secondly, what is claimed as an event is shown to be actually or probably fictitious, and is simply dismissed accordingly. So long as the only reality recognized is material, there is no alternative to this twofold classification, short of sacrificing the axiomatic conviction of regularity.

On the other hand, anyone who, holding as tenaciously as the materialist to the axiom that somewhere there is regularity, believes, unlike the materialist, that there is reality beyond the 'material' (or that which is, in principle, within the realm of sensory perception), will have correspondingly more room in which to manœuvre. He may adopt one or another of three positions.

He may hold, like the pure materialist, to the consistency and regularity only of a material realm, but, unlike the materialist, may believe in wholly capricious irruptions into it from a different realm outside. One who entertains such a notion is essentially pagan and superstitious. He believes in the reality of the trans-material, but not in its consistency, thereby watering down the only consistency he recognizes—that of the material realm—and placing it at the mercy of inconsistency. This is the seat of that element of insecurity that attaches to all pagan, superstitious, and fatalistic outlooks. From such a viewpoint, 'miracle' means nothing more than the interruption of a normally calculable regularity by incalculable caprice, and there is nothing genuinely religious about the notion.

Or, secondly, he may hold that there are two more or less independent realms of consistency—the material realm and the trans-material realm. The material may be impinged upon by the trans-material in such a way as to interrupt, suspend, or upset its limited regularity, although the trans-material, in thus impinging on the former, will remain consistent with itself. This is the kind of 'model' that seems to be implied by the language of many who, while claiming to be Christians, speak of God 'intervening' or 'suspending the laws of nature', as though the latter somehow had a measure of independence. For such, 'miracle' is an interruption of a normally calculable regularity by a will and purpose consistent with itself but beyond the calculation of men. There are two spheres, each with its own regularity, but there is no common, all-embracing system.

There is, however, a third position which I take to be the only one tenable by a consistent theist. This position refuses to treat the material and the trans-material as separate systems, even though they may be distinguishable. To do so would be to entertain deism rather than theism, and would imply an intolerably mechanical and inorganic relationship between Creator and creature. Rather, whatever consistency or coherence there may be within the material realm is a part of a larger whole, and is derived from and dependent on it, just as the human body seems to be organically one with the entire personality of which it is a part and a manifestation. To isolate the mechanical consistency of the human frame viewed as a material construction from the larger consistency of the total person would be to forget all that we are beginning to learn about a psychosomatic relationship, and to make its movements less predictable, not more. In the same way—the theist holds—the only ultimate regularity is to be looked for not within the material realm by itself but in the character of a personal God. It is of his character that the material realm is a manifestation: and what is possible and probable in it is better measured by what is known of the character of God than by what is observed on the much narrower scale of the purely mechanistic.

If we have reason to believe that the character of God is best seen in Jesus, and that the consistency of sheer moral perfection is the ultimate consistency, then we may have to revise our ideas of what is and is not 'possible'. And if we have reason to find in Jesus a unique degree of unity with the will of God, what is to prevent our believing that, where God is perfectly obeyed, there the mechanics of the material world look different from what they do in a situation dislocated by disobedience? It is not that regularities and consistencies are suspended or over-ridden; it is rather that our idea of how things work is based on too narrow a set of data. If the ultimate *locus* of consistency is in the realm of the personal—in the character of a God who 'cannot deny himself'—then what is (in our present conditions) unusual need not be ultimately an intervention or an irruption or a dislocation or suspension of natural law: it need only be what 'normally' happens—indeed what is bound to happen—on the rare and 'abnormal' occasions when a right relationship is achieved in the family of God.

This formula has the advantage of offering a comprehensive criterion by which to test miracle stories. Why do we universally refuse to believe in the miracles in the Infancy Narratives of Thomas? Surely because they are all out of character with a Jesus who, as we have reason on other grounds to believe, took seriously the meaning of 'sonship'—a Jesus who, in the temptations, repudiated the conjuring-tricks of exhibitionism and the selfish cruelty of power for power's sake. Why do we not think that God held the sun still for Joshua? First, because the evidence points strongly to the conclusion that this narrative is a fragment of ancient poetry, not even an attempt at scientific record; secondly, because it is impossible to conceive of so radical a dislocation of the whole stellar system occurring without leaving some further trace (to put it mildly!) in the history of the world; but, thirdly, because, besides all this, there is no evidence that this is the kind of way in which a personal God helps and trains his children. On the other hand, why should we not allow that it seems consistent with all we know of God if perfect goodness of character 'cannot' be held by death—in other words, that the resurrection of Jesus was inevitable, given his absolute obedience to the will of God? Each alleged 'miracle', inside and outside scripture alike, may be treated along these lines, with the application of all the 'normal' criteria of likelihood, remembering only that 'likelihood' applies to a situation which, for all but the pure materialist, does not exclude but includes the trans-material—a situation in which, on the theistic showing, the trans-material is personal and includes the material; a situation in which, on the Christian showing, the ultimate consistency is in the character of the God and Father of our Lord Jesus Christ.

2

THE EVIDENTIAL VALUE OF THE BIBLICAL MIRACLES

BY

G. F. WOODS

G. F. WOODS

Professor G. F. Woods was a Rustat and Lady Kaye Scholar of Jesus College, Cambridge, where he read History and Theology. On being awarded the Burney Studentship, he studied in Marburg and Heidelberg. After work in a parish and on the staff of a theological college, he served as Director of Ordinands in the Diocese of Bristol from 1938 to 1945. Returning to Cambridge after the war, he became Chaplain and later Fellow and Dean of Chapel of Downing College. During his residence in Cambridge he was a University Lecturer in the Faculty of Divinity. In 1955 he was appointed Stanton Lecturer and he was elected to the Hulsean Lectureship in 1962. His book, *Theological Explanation*, was published in 1958, and he contributed two essays to the volume entitled *Soundings*. He is an Honorary Canon of Bristol Cathedral and one of his special interests is Post-Ordination Training in the Church of England. In 1964, he was appointed Professor of Divinity in the University of London, King's College. In the same year he was appointed an Honorary Fellow of Downing College.

THE EVIDENTIAL VALUE OF THE
BIBLICAL MIRACLES

HISTORICAL STATEMENTS can reach a very high degree of probability. They never attain logical certainty in the sense that they cannot be denied without a logical contradiction. It is not logically possible to deny that a circle is circular, but it is always possible to deny that an alleged historical event took place. The denial may be extremely unreasonable, but it is not logically prohibited. I believe that a high degree of probability may be claimed for many of the accounts of miracles in the New Testament, particularly the claim that Jesus survived his death. But in this essay I am not concerned with the defence of the probability of any of the miracle stories but solely with the use of these as part of the evidences of the truth of Christianity. Moreover, I am omitting any study of the very various ways in which the appeal to the miraculous is used and not used in the New Testament. I am considering what became the classic method of using this type of evidence and I raise the question whether this remains equally valuable in our own age.

All proving is testing. We find those proofs satisfying which satisfy the tests for which we ask no further proof. Evidence is acceptable to us when it appears to be so evident as to require no further evidence. Methods of proof are ways of exhibiting what we can accept as obvious. It follows that the traditional proofs or evidences for some established belief are bound to need revision when significant changes take place in the range and pattern of what is taken to be obvious. This is true of the evidences of Christianity. William Paley, for example, gave a brilliant exposition of the evidences for the truth of the Christian religion. The argument was well suited to the contemporary methods of distinguishing the true from the false. Belief in the biblical miracles, especially the miracles recorded in the

Gospels, formed an essential element in his defence of the truth
of the Christian faith.

In his reliance upon the evidential value of miracles, Paley
was reproducing what had become the classic scheme of Christian evidences. Theology was taken to be a system comprising
both natural and revealed theology. Natural theology was the
knowledge which might be attained in a study of the natural
world by the unassisted human reason. Its main function was
the exposition of the traditional rational proofs for the existence
of God. Revealed theology republished the truths of natural
theology and offered further revealed truths which were not
discoverable by human reason. The evidence for accepting these
truths known only through revelation was distinguished into the
internal and external evidence. The internal character of the
revealed truths was believed to be congruous with reason and
conscience. The external evidence was the biblical account of
the prophecies and miracles associated with Christ. The essential point in appealing to these was that they were taken to prove
the divinity of Christ. The miracles done by him or concerning
him showed him to be divine. They were works beyond the
power of man and recognizable as the works of God. When,
particularly on the basis of this evidence from the miraculous,
Jesus was accepted as divine, it became reasonable to accept as
true what he chose to disclose about the being and acts of God.
The truth of the Christian revelation was not proved directly
by the appeal to miracle and prophecy. These were accepted
as the credentials of Christ as an ambassador of God who was
in the secret counsels of God.

The appeal is made to accounts of miraculous events in the
past. They form part of the historical evidence for the truth of
Christianity. Obviously, this appeal was easier to make when
the biblical narratives were more generally accepted as literally
true. The Canonical Scriptures provided evidence which was
acceptable as evidence without further question. Though, in
fairness to Paley, it must be recalled that he was consciously

commending the truth, for instance of the resurrection of Christ, not simply on the ground that the account occurred in the Holy Scriptures, but on the ground of the inherent probability of the narrative. The advancing progress of biblical criticism has created a new situation. What used to be taken as obvious is now by no means so obvious. It may now reasonably be claimed that informed opinion treats the Scriptures as neither wholly reliable nor wholly unreliable. The Bible is not treated as a single piece of writing which is wholly true or wholly false, but as a vast body of literature which must be distinguished into many parts and many strata, each of which requires patient study. It is now seen to be profitless to discuss whether the miracle stories are all true or all false. They do not form a monolithic unity. It is far more useful to consider what is probably true in each particular report. And it is now generally recognized that in calculating the probability of any particular account, the critical historian is bound to be influenced by the standards of probability which he accepts concerning what is likely to happen in the realms of nature and human nature. Though it is also true that his fundamental presuppositions about what is probable ought not to remain insensitive to the available accounts of what in the past has been taken to be miraculous. But it cannot now be reasonably denied that any appeal to accounts of the miraculous in the biblical writings must be made with a proper respect for the work of responsible biblical criticism.

The first principle of the traditional appeal to the evidence from the miraculous was that a miracle could be identified as a work beyond the power of man. If any unobserved miracles took place, they could have no public evidential value. It was the observed miracles which could be identified as the works of God. It used to be thought that this act of identification offered no great difficulty. But it has become far more exacting as the natural sciences have progressed. It is now no simple matter. Do we know the exact limits of the powers of man? Are we

thinking of his powers as an isolated individual or as a member
of a group of men? Have we in mind his own personal powers
or do we include his power to manipulate the natural order?
Do we really know the full potentialities of the natural world?
Can we be sure that the future will not disclose a series of
natural powers which are at present unknown to us? I do not
see how we can be sure that we know the limits of human
power, or the limits of what we call the natural order. Even so,
as a matter of common sense, we do accept general standards
of natural probability which we trust in the everyday business
of keeping alive. We do not really expect that a steamship will
ever fly. But there is a real distinction between accepting the
general stability of nature as a fact and affirming that we know
precisely the limits of its potentialities. We seem, therefore, to
be driven to the somewhat paradoxical conclusion that we do
not know enough of the limits of the natural order either to deny
the possibility of miracles or to identify one if it takes place.

The second principle in the proof of the Christian revelation
by an appeal to the miraculous was the belief that acts which
were beyond the powers of man were acts of God. What man
could not do must have been done by God. For those who
already accept the truth of Christianity, this is not an unreasonable conclusion, but it is a step which has become increasingly
difficult to take. It is not clear how anyone can identify an act
as an act of God if he has no idea of God prior to observing the
act. If he has no idea of God prior to observing the act, it is
not intelligible how he can attribute the act to God. It seems
more probable that, in observing what he takes to be a miracle,
his belief in God is confirmed and his idea of God is modified.
The miracle provides corroborative evidence of the existence
and character of God. It offers evidence of the existence
and activity of a God whose existence and power to act
were not wholly unknown. Very probably, there is a complex
interplay between observing what are taken to be miracles
and the observer's idea of God. Experience and theology have

a mutual influence upon one another. If this is what happens, we have moved into a new situation in which it is no easy matter to detect the precise part which an accepted account of a Christian miracle plays in our acceptance of the divinity of Christ. Some will believe him to be divine because of the miracle; others will accept the miracle because they believe him to be divine. There is certainly something quite unsatisfactory in using the miracles to prove his divinity and then contending that we can accept the miracles because he is divine.

It was far easier to conclude that an act which appeared to exceed human powers must be an act of God when alternative explanations were fewer. What appears to be a miraculous occurrence may now be attributed to a wide variety of causes other than to the action of God. It may be understood as an instance of a complex natural event. Such a view is confirmed if what has happened is later explained in natural terms. But many of our contemporaries would now be inclined to believe that there must be a natural explanation, even when it is not within sight. The failure to find a natural explanation would not convince them that one would not ultimately be found. Another alternative interpretation is to assume that what is taken to be miraculous is some kind of uncaused event. It took place without being caused. Such an uncaused event is more profoundly causeless than what is called a random or chance event when these happen within some system or series of systems. On this view, the supposedly miraculous event is not simply not due to God. It is due to nothing at all. It is an unexplained and inexplicable fact. I believe that to many minds the notion of uncaused events will be offensive but it is not easy to show why it is justifiable to take offence. Obviously, when an assumed miracle is interpreted as an event without a cause, it has no value as evidence in favour of belief in God or in exemplifying or confirming our idea of the character of God. It is simply not a divine event. The complicated natural event may in a sense

C

be said to be of evidential value. It can be taken as an insight into the complex workings of a natural order which is accepted as the creation of God. A sense of the wonder of nature as the handiwork of God may be prompted and encouraged by observing some natural event which is striking and impressive. An exceptional natural event may open our eyes to what is wonderful in the familiar. The astonishing may check the familiarity which breeds contempt. But I do not think that this kind of impressive natural event is legitimately called miraculous in the more traditional use of the word which includes the claim that the event is in some way genuinely out of the ordinary and attributable to the purposive activity of God.

When it is assumed that a miracle has a cause and that this cause is in some sense above or beyond the normal system of natural causes, we are not confined to the view that this supernatural cause must be the work of God. It may have other origins. It could be an impersonal cause which in some way acts upon the sequence of natural causes. The miracle might then receive some kind of physical explanation, but it could not be understood as the outcome of some purposive activity. It would be a purposeless fact. But it is also possible to think that a miracle is the result of some kind of supernatural personal causes which are other than divine. Miracles can be attributed to good or evil spirits which are subordinate to God. We may also suppose that a miracle is the consequence of a plurality of causes which are superior to natural causes. The unity of the observed miracle may be due to the unanimity of purpose possessed by a plurality of spiritual beings. It may well be that there are good grounds for accepting the Christian claim that the historically probable miracles in the Gospel narratives are most reasonably attributable to the action of God, the Father of our Lord Jesus Christ, but it cannot be said that this is the only explanation of what are taken to be miraculous happenings. In our contemporary situation, we cannot say for certain that any historically established event which is beyond the powers of human nature and of nature must be the work of God.

If we feel somewhat daunted at the difficulty of devising a criterion which will enable us to identify an event in our experience as being plainly beyond all natural powers and plainly due to the greater power of God, we may be attracted by a different type of criterion. Instead of speculating about the limits of natural and supernatural powers, we may say that a miracle done by the God of Christianity will be of a character which is in harmony with the mind and spirit of Christ. This is a moral criterion. The fact that many of the Gospel miracles are miracles of healing will encourage us to think that they are the work of God who wills the health of his creatures. Miracles of goodwill show the subtle harmony of the diverse acts of a will which is good. Though the miraculous acts may be infrequent, they may be seen to be in line with some unchanging purpose which is good. They are not chaotic, though they may be exceptional. Those who are healed are made whole. The miraculous power, like grace, perfects nature. The frustrated purpose of nature is somehow miraculously achieved. The natural order is somehow liberated or released from the constraint of some impeding power. The created order is somehow recreated by the God who originally created it. This is undoubtedly an attractive way of identifying the special acts of God and is more practicable than trying to define precisely the frontier between the powers of man and nature and God. But it is a theory which is not without its difficulties. If remedial miracles take place, the problem still remains why situations arise which require to be remedied. The problem of evil remains. Indeed, if we begin to think that divine miracles may easily be done, the problem of evil is intensified. So often, a tragedy might have been averted by a minute miracle and no miracle has taken place. The infrequency of morally admirable miracles is a problem. It may be replied that the Gospel miracles required the physical presence of

Christ. This may be so, but in that case we still face the problem of the accidental element in his meeting with those whom
he healed. If his itinerary had been different, the distribution
of the miraculous acts of healing would have been different.
Despite these genuine difficulties, the moral criterion has a very
important part to play in identifying what we are willing to
call acts of God.

The basic problem about finding appropriate criteria for
recognizing the miraculous activity of God in the world is that
we are unable to think clearly of the relation of God to the
world. We tend in thinking of this relationship to use terms
which refer primarily to the relationships of people and things
within our present experience. We are always liable to think
too anthropomorphically of God and his acts. We seek to avoid
this error by the use of analogy in language about God. A way
is sought between anthropomorphism and agnosticism. It is
well known that no analogy is perfect. In being perpetually less
than adequate, any analogy is subject to fluctuations in its
popularity. For a period a particular analogy is highly respected,
but as its imperfections become manifest it begins to lose the
respect in which it was once held. Every theological analogy is
either rising or falling in public esteem. Many analogies take
the form of explanatory models. We envisage a situation in
terms of which we may speak analogically of the activity of God.
The models may be impersonal or they may combine personal
and impersonal elements. We may, for example, envisage the
natural and the supernatural worlds as two worlds which stand
one above the other. We imagine a kind of two tier structure.
Such a model is useful but gravely inadequate as a representation of the relationship of God and the world. Our view of the
model would be changed if we no longer stood upright. It is
merely a convention to envisage the two worlds as somehow
standing horizontally one above the other. We could think that
the natural and the supernatural stood side by side or lay
diagonally in contact with one another. We could visualize

them as two concentric spheres in some kind of contact. We could think that there were many grades of world. We might think of a kind of laminated universe. Other problems arise in envisaging the miraculous contact between the two worlds or orders. If the world which makes contact is subject to some overriding power which controls the contact which is made, we find that we are not thinking of two worlds but of one world containing two subordinate worlds which come into contact with one another. If we think that the two worlds are incapable of coming into contact, we are left with a model which completely fails to represent the contacts which are said to be made. The fact is that we cannot construct a model to represent adequately the situation in which a divine miracle may take place.

In making mental models which are designed to represent the operation of divine miraculous power, we naturally have a preference for those which at first sight appear to be most easily understood. We should not choose them as explanatory devices if they did not appear plainer than other models. No one wishes to explain the obscure by the more obscure. It is not surprising that the most popular analogical models of the miraculous should be those which use our simplest experiences of something affecting something else in an unusual or uncommon way. We may think of an external cause entering another causal system. We think of it as intruding or intervening. In thinking of the mode of entry, we are liable to think of the way in which a physical thing may be inserted into a gap between two other physical things, as one might insert a shilling in a slot. It is easier to think of something entering a gap than of its entering a solid surface. This type of analogical thinking leads to the unfortunate assumption that every miraculous act enters some kind of gap or crack in the natural order. When working models are used, there is the same tendency to use as analogies the occasions when the process is affected in ways to which we are accustomed. We can think of an external cause deflecting the course of something which is in motion. The external cause is represented as like the movement of a rudder which affects the direction of a ship through the water. Or we may think that a process is arrested or stopped or suspended by some external cause. The miracle is then understood as an act which somehow interrupts a natural process. All these analogies are insufficient. They become seriously misleading when they are taken to be accurate representations of the relation of God and the world. But they are not valueless. They can be used prudently.

What, then, may be said in reply to the question whether the biblical miracles remain of equal evidential value for the truth of Christianity as in other days? As our knowledge of the natural order is not complete, it is not justifiable to say that miracles cannot take place. It is not logically unthinkable that they may take place. It may be thought highly improbable that they ever take place but no human mind is in a position to say that they cannot take place. For those who accept theism and for those who believe in the incarnation, it remains quite reasonable to approach sympathetically the accounts in the Bible of what are taken to be miracles done by the power of God. But it cannot be denied that the evidential value of the miraculous is closely interwoven with the metaphysical views of those to whom the evidence is offered. Those who reject theism and do not believe in the divinity of Christ have many alternative interpretations of the reported miracles. Theists and atheists, Christians and those who disbelieve Christianity, cannot avoid the intricate task of examining the historical probability of each account of what is said to be a miraculous event. This is an intricate matter because the weighing of historical evidence is affected by the metaphysical presuppositions of those who weigh the evidence. There are no metaphysically neutral scales. And, if the historical account of what is said to have been a miracle is accepted as broadly reliable, the question remains of judging whether the contemporary interpretation of the event as a divine miracle is true. At this point further problems arise. It does not now appear possible to determine the precise position of the frontier between the powers of man and the powers of God. What is thought to be beyond the powers of man need not necessarily be the work of God. It may be due to natural causes. It may have no cause at all. It may be the result of an impersonal supernatural cause or of a personal supernatural cause other than God. It may prove more profitable to study the miracle of divine grace operating in the personalities of sinful men than to attend exclusively to alleged miracles in the more physical order of nature. I think the moral criterion is more useful but it is hardly decisive in identifying a divine miracle. We cannot be quite sure that an unusual event is a divine miracle because it is congruous with a purpose which is morally worthy of approval. And there are moral problems associated with any view which suggests that a miracle can happen whenever the moral need for one is clear. Many of the problems in identifying divine miracles spring from the fundamental fact that the mind of man cannot fully comprehend the being and activity of God. The relation of God both to the natural order and to any miraculous events in the natural order is beyond our full understanding. In thinking and speaking about the being and activity of God, the Christian theologian is always trying to avoid on the one hand an unduly literal use of language about God and on the other hand an unduly sceptical belief that nothing meaningful can be said about God. It is unfortunate if basic problems about the miraculous are overlooked or misrepresented by the analogical models and linguistic devices which happen to be in use at a particular time.

My own tentative conclusion is that the problem of the evidential value of the miraculous in support of the truth of the Christian faith is unlikely to receive a generally accepted solution for a very long time, if ever. In the meantime, it is a matter of balancing probabilities. This may sound a disappointing conclusion, but to accept probable evidence remains sensible where it is the best evidence available on matters where we cannot avoid making an explicit judgment or passing an implicit judgment in the action which we take or omit to take. We can still admire the sober wisdom of Bishop Joseph Butler who said, 'To us, probability is the very guide of life'.[1]

[1] *Works of Joseph Butler.* Ed. W. E. Gladstone. Vol. I, Clarendon Press, 1896, p. 5.

3

MIRACLES AND THE LAWS OF NATURE

BY

MARY HESSE

MARY HESSE

Miss Mary Hesse is a graduate and Ph.D. of London University in applied mathematics. Formerly a Lecturer in Mathematics and in History and Philosophy of Science in the Universities of Leeds and London, she is now a Lecturer in the Philosophy of Science in the University of Cambridge.

Her particular research interests are: the nature of scientific language and the function of models in scientific theories; methodological problems in the history of physics. She has also an amateur interest in the relations of science and theology.

Publications: *Science and the Human Imagination* (*1954*)
Forces and Fields (*1961*)
Models and Analogies in Science (*1963*)
and papers in journals of philosophy and the history and philosophy of science.

MIRACLES AND THE LAWS OF NATURE

THREE DIFFERENT kinds of events are commonly called miracles:

Someone may say: 'His recovery was a miracle', or, 'It was a miracle that a serious accident was avoided'. As these phrases are used nowadays, there would probably not be any implication of a divine or providential act in the events described. What is pointed to by use of the word 'miracle' is the remarkable, unpredictable, coincidental, nature of the events, and also, usually, the fact that the outcome was in some way significant and desirable in the context of human purposes. There need, however, be no suggestion that the events are in any way outside or in conflict with the general course of nature and its laws. In a universe as complicated as ours, however orderly it is, we still expect some fortuitous concourses of events, unpredictable coincidences, and when they happen to fall in with our purposes we call them miracles, but we do so without any of the religious or superstitious overtones of that concept such as belonged to it in former ages. If the word 'miracle' is used in this sense, it would generally be admitted that it is a somewhat illogical and anthropocentric concept, since we do not apply it to coincidences and accidents which are, humanly speaking, disastrous.

Secondly, there are events which, if they in fact occur as reported, seem clearly to violate the accepted order of nature. That a man should walk on water, or revive a three-days-old corpse, or multiply a few small loaves and fishes to satisfy the hunger of a multitude—these are not merely accidental conjunctions of otherwise law-abiding events, they are non-natural, violent disruptions of the stable and predictable order of things. They are also, as were the first kind of miracle, significant and meaningful, for in their context they may be both in themselves

35

desirable for human good, and also significant of the power and authority of their agent.

Thirdly, there are events which may or may not be mythical, which share with the second kind of miracle the characteristic of violating the laws of nature, but not the characteristic of meaningfulness. Such would be isolated, unintelligible, 'queer' happenings, or the pointless demonstrations of a wonder-worker or magician. I shall not say anything more about this category, since it may be assumed that, whatever there is of interest in it, is already included in the other two categories.

Are the miracles which are commonly given religious signifi-cance examples of the first or the second category? It has traditionally been important to religious apologetic to interpret miracles as altogether outside and even contrary to the estab-lished order of nature, so that they may be seen as evidence of the specific acts of God, or as guarantees of claims to divine inspiration or divine status on the part of the miracle-worker. More recent interpretations of the miracles recorded in the New Testament, however, have tended to put the matter the other way round and, regarding the truth of Christianity as given, to see certain events in this context both as what might be expected when God breaks through in a unique fashion into human history, and also as reinforcements and illustrations of the claims of Christ. Seen like this, it may not be necessary to regard miracles as 'violations' of the laws of nature, but rather as miracles of the first category which gain their significance from the context of the Incarnation. Before considering this point, however, it will be as well to try to make the conception of 'violation' of the laws of nature a little more precise.

We can best begin by considering a type of science which, although it is now known to be false, does at least allow the notions both of 'law' and of 'violation' to be precisely defined. This is the mechanist and determinist science often associated with the name of Laplace (1749–1827), who first made explicit the implications of a thoroughgoing application of Newtonian mechanics to nature. According to this view, nature is ultimately composed of mechanical particles, wholly subject to Newton's laws of motion. In that case, as Laplace saw, the state of the universe at any given instant, comprising the positions and momenta of all the particles, determines its state at any future (and past) instant, and hence the whole process of nature is unique and rigidly determined. A 'violation' of the laws of nature, then, has a clear meaning in terms of an event or process which is not in accordance with the laws of motion, and hence breaks this uniquely determined sequence. It is most naturally understood on the analogy of a workman who deliberately interferes with the mechanism of an otherwise determinate clockwork system, and this is the image of God which is associated in this view with the idea of miracle. Undoubtedly a great deal of popular reaction to the notion of miracle is still conditioned by this view.

We may leave aside the unsatisfactory implications of this view for our image of God, because its presuppositions in terms of a philosophy of science are in any case completely unacceptable. Objections to it fall into three main groups:

1. Newtonian mechanics as a universal theory of physical particles has been shown to be false. This is nowadays an often repeated and trite remark, but its full consequences for our problem are not always fully realized. The first and most obvious consequence is that Newtonianism has been replaced in modern physics by a theory, quantum theory, whose laws are not deterministic but statistical, that is, they do not determine occurrences of single events, but only proportions in large classes of events. It is important to notice that according to quantum theory this is not merely a question of *ignorance* of laws which may after all be fundamentally deterministic, but of irreducible indeterminism in the events themselves. Even in Newtonian theory, of course, it is true to say that in practice we would be too ignorant of the precise state of the universe at

any instant actually to make the predictions which according to Laplace are in principle possible, but it is not predictability by a human observer which is in question here, but the actual determinism of the universe. Newtonian theory asserts that the universe is deterministic, whether or not we can actually carry out the predictions; quantum theory asserts that we cannot carry out the predictions because the universe is in essence indeterministic.

Radical as the transformation from Newtonian to quantum physics is, however, it does not have any direct effect on the acceptability of the idea of miracle. At first sight it might be thought that in theory, as far as isolated events are concerned, anything at all would be consistent with the statistical laws of quantum physics, even though perhaps very, very highly improbable. In this case, the notion of 'violation' of quantum laws by single events would lose its meaning. But statistical laws in science are in fact regarded as violated if events occur which according to them are excessively improbable, and in ordinary scientific contexts such violation leads to abandonment of the law, just as in the case of deterministic theories. There is no question that most events regarded as significantly 'miraculous' in religious contexts would, if they violate Newtonian laws, also be excessively improbable on well-established quantum laws, and therefore would be regarded as violations of these also. Thus, if we consider only the currently accepted theories of physics, the credibility of such miracles is no greater than in Newtonian theory.

2. From another point of view, however, there is no doubt that abandonment of the deterministic world-view in physics has made it more difficult to regard the existing state of science as finally legislative of what is and what is not possible in nature. The very fact that what appeared for three centuries to be an absolutely true and universal theory has been shown to be false must cast doubt on all future claims of science to have reached such a universal theory. Science is continually growing and

changing, sometimes quite radically. It is far less easy to see it to-day as a monolithic and cumulative progress towards the whole truth than was the case a hundred years ago. We are by no means sure, even in physics, that existing quantum theories will last many decades. Moreover, we have no guarantee that existing theories will prove adequate in sciences other than physics, and in the sciences of complex systems such as the human psyche and human social groups we have only the bare beginnings of any theories at all. Miracles which are religiously significant must be regarded as social phenomena of great complexity, and in the absence of any clear idea what 'laws of nature' would look like in this domain, it is impossible to know what a 'violation' would look like either.

3. Most fundamental of the attacks upon the idea of a law of nature presupposed by Newtonian science was Hume's interpretation of laws as nothing more than observed uniformities of events disclosing no necessary connexions in nature. It might be thought that this interpretation altogether precludes the idea of 'violation', because an event which does not fit into any set of observed uniformities is, if it occurs, just a fact like any other, and cannot conflict with any other. It merely implies that certain uniformities are not after all universal. Hume himself, however, did not draw this conclusion. He argued rather that laws are what are established by universal experience of uniformities, and they create a high expectation that all other experience will be in conformity with them. A report of a miracle which 'violates' the uniformity can therefore only be believed if the weight of testimony in its favour is much greater than the expectation that the uniformity will be maintained. Hume does not consider that in any case of alleged miracle there has ever been sufficient weight of testimony, and for this reason believes that miracles do not in fact occur, although he cannot consistently rule out their possibility.

From this discussion it is tempting to draw the conclusion that on any view of scientific laws other than the Laplacian, which is in any case discredited, no events can positively be shown to be violations of generally accepted laws. Thus the conception of a miracle as a violation of the laws of nature seems to be an empty one, and it seems that no scientific considerations stand in the way of investigating reports of miracles on the merits of whatever historical evidence can be brought forward. But it would be a mistake to draw this conclusion too quickly. The influence of science is not only felt within those areas where there are workable scientific laws and theories, but also much more generally, in a habit of expecting a certain stability and uniformity in nature, and a suspicion of what appears to be unusual and unexpected. Hume's discussion is perhaps a better analysis of this habit of mind than of scientific laws proper. However 'loose' the concept of scientific law may now have become, and however much it may be admitted that the writ of science does not, or not yet, run in the area of human life and human history, there still remains the strongly entrenched belief that there is a distinction between the surprising and unpredictable event which happens by accident in the ordinary course of nature, and events which disturb more fundamentally its expected order. Most of the New Testament miracles, if taken as literal reports of what occurred, are events of the latter kind, and Hume at least describes the attitude of a scientific age correctly in saying that although such events cannot be ruled out *a priori*, nevertheless we require overwhelming evidence before we are disposed to accept them. In the nature of the case it is rarely possible to obtain such overwhelming evidence for any historical event, and so, for the scientific mentality, the presumption is much stronger that the kinds of things that demonstrably do not happen most of the time, never have happened. It is chiefly in this sense that there can be said to remain a scientific prejudice against the conception of miracle.

But is it necessary or even theologicially desirable that a Christian interpretation of the New Testament miracles should depend on violation of the expected order of nature even in the weak sense that has just been described? Many would hold that it is not desirable, because it seems to reduce the activity of God to the level of wonder-working: such activity would be intrinsically pointless, irrational, impersonal, the kind of cosmic cheating which Christ appears specifically to have repudiated when tempted to throw himself from the pinnacle of the temple. How and whether the records of miracles can be interpreted or discounted so as to eliminate the element of 'violation' is for scholars to decide. But it is certainly the case that, for the scientific mind, the miracle stories would not lose their religious depth or effectiveness by such a process of reinterpretation— rather the reverse, for the real personal and historical meaning of events such as the healings and demonstrations of power and authority might then be allowed to emerge from irrelevances of credulity and superstition.

There is finally, however, a much more difficult question which is related to the problem of miracles, but is more general and less specifically related to the scientific world-view. This is the sense in which the acts of God can be distinguished *at all* in special and providential events as distinct from the ordinary course of nature and of history. We may admit that the natural world as a whole, and specially the domains of personal life and of human history, is only 'loosely' ordered, as a sophisticated view of the laws of nature requires. But there still remain two areas where theology seems committed to laying special stress on the transcendental character of some otherwise 'natural' events rather than on others. The first is the whole area of human free-will; for if this is interpreted in terms of the initiation of natural events by an independent agent in some sense *outside* nature, it may not imply any violation of the order of nature, but it does fit uneasily into the unitary scientific view of man with his hereditary and environmental conditioning. And even more difficult to understand from the scientific point

D

of view is theological talk about the special acts of a transcendent God. The offence of particularity is still with us, whether these special acts violate or conform with the laws of nature. The fundamental problem is not about miracle, but about transcendence.

4

SOME NOTES ON MIRACLE
IN THE OLD TESTAMENT

BY

J. P. ROSS

J. P. ROSS

John Ross went to Oxford in 1948 as scholar of Oriel College. He took Greats in 1952, and after two years in the Education Branch of the Royal Air Force returned to read Theology. He trained for the ministry of the Church of England at Wycliffe Hall, and from 1957 served as curate of Hornchurch. In 1959 he joined the staff of Ridley Hall, Cambridge, where he spent four years as Tutor in Old Testament Studies, and in 1962 he was appointed Assistant Lecturer in Divinity at Cambridge.

SOME NOTES ON MIRACLE
IN THE OLD TESTAMENT[1]

THE HEBREW, writes Koehler, lives 'in a world of continuous miracle. Miracles meet him at every step.'[2] My contention is that, in the classical period of Old Testament literature, what we mean by 'miracle' was unknown. In different ways, Koehler and I are saying much the same thing; it is for you to decide which of us is the less misleading.

The case turns on what you mean by 'miracle'. It is more than a pleasantly surprising event. If, on the one day in the month when you have an ample joint in the oven, friends drop in unexpectedly for dinner, it may be a wonderful coincidence, but it is scarcely a miracle. In ordinary usage, 'miracle' denotes a breach of regularity in the functioning of the world; and more than a breach, a *planned* overruling of some known scientific principle. 'Miraculous' healing is a good example; it is scientifically unaccountable, yet not merely random, because it is purposeful.

I believe you are still thinking in terms of breach of regularity even when you refer to such things as the stability of the natural order, or the growth of a plant, as miraculous. Viewed on their own, as unique phenomena, they may well appear astonishing. But they are miraculous only if they can be seen as exceptional variants of a larger class, whether known or hypothetical. When we speak like this of growth, we are thinking of it as an astonishing exception to the rule of inanimate,

---

[1] This paper was presented as a general statement of a point of view, for discussion. Any full treatment of the subject would of course have to begin with a detailed study of the use of such words as *'oth, mopheth* and the roots *pl', plh.*

My debt to Dr. H. W. Robinson, *Inspiration and Revelation in the Old Testament*, is apparent. I should like also to acknowledge with gratitude the help of Professor D. W. Thomas; but he must not be held responsible for either the contents or the presentation of this paper.   [2] L. Koehler, *Hebrew Man*, p. 134.

mineral existence; if we speak like this of the stability of the natural order, we are contrasting it with all the other systems we make or know, whose common feature is a tendency to degenerate. And in both cases we imply that there is some purpose, some will, behind this irregularity. You would only call an unaccountable earthquake a miracle if it achieved some end.

Israel, on the other hand, could not concern itself about scientific irregularities or breaches of natural law, because it had no interest in science and did not think in terms of Nature. This is not to say that Israelites could not recognize obvious causes and effects. They knew such sequences as seed-sowing— rain—harvest, and the procession of the seasons; but they did not pursue this line of thought. Much less did they give any sort of autonomy to these observations. Spring follows winter, harvest follows rain, not because it is meet and right for it so to do, not in obedience to a law of nature, but in obedience to a particular command of God. Each year it is up to him whether to send a harvest or not.[1]

Cause and Author

This tendency to think in terms of personal will rather than mechanical cause and effect is strikingly illustrated in the third chapter of Amos. Here we get as near as anywhere in the Old Testament to an expression of observed natural laws, with the repeated formula: 'Does X happen, unless Y?' But of the nine or ten examples of cause and effect, only one, or at the most two, are mechanical; three concern animals, where there is an element of volition; and the rest are human, personal situations. When the prophet wanted to speak of what we should call the inexorable regularities of nature, even then he spent most of his time on *human* nature, on the way people act and will.

---

[1] The covenant with Noah (Gen. 8. 22) does not seem in practice to have prevented Israel from praying for a harvest each year. Jahweh might well withhold it, for one reason or another (e.g. 1 Kgs. 17. 1; Am. 4. 6 ff.; Hag. 1. 10 f.).

We, however, cannot nowadays escape an interest in science. We are constantly asking how and why things happen, and unless we are consciously talking theology, we expect an answer in terms of material or psychological cause and effect. For instance, if you seriously ask: 'Why did it rain yesterday?' you expect an answer in terms of barometric pressures and movements of warm or cold air. Or if you ask: 'Why are the steelworkers on strike?' you expect an analysis of the situation in terms such as general human acquisitiveness, and the history of the trade dispute. Whereas to the first question: 'Why did it rain?' an Israelite would give the simple and final answer: 'Because God made it'; to the second, he might give either of two replies: they are on strike, either, quite simply, because they have chosen to; or else, because God has sent a striking spirit upon them. There would be no suggestion that they were involved in a trend, a movement, or in any way swept off their feet by the impetus of events.

The author of the Second Book of Kings gives us a good example of this line of thought in his account of the events leading up to the fall of Samaria. His thesis seems to be the accumulation of guilt until the Lord, long-suffering though he is, could spare Israel no longer. If we were in the writer's position, we might speak of a movement gathering momentum, of a graph getting steeper and steeper, of a trend veering further and further from the straight and right and good. We might be inclined to explain how, to begin with, there was an element of freedom in the choice presented to the first kings, but, as the tradition of error and sin became more firmly established, sin became more and more inevitable, and error became more and more headlong. This, as I say, is the sort of way *we* might present his thesis. But he himself knows nothing of any such cumulative pressure of tradition and precedent, of any such growing chain of cause and effect. He speaks as if each king started absolutely from scratch, and deliberately, freely, without any conditioning, chose evil.

In another type of biblical literature we can see the same outlook. As I understand him, the writer of Ecclesiastes is not a theologian, but rather a popular philosopher, treating of which lines of action conduce to happiness, and which do not. But even here one looks in vain for statements of the causes or reasons which lead to his conclusions. Or rather, there are, I think, three rudimentary types of argument. One is: 'I tried this, and I considered, and behold, it was vanity';[1] another is: 'I do not see why you should not' (e.g. 3. 22: 'I saw that there is nothing better than that a man should enjoy his work, for that is his lot; who can bring him to see what will be after him?'). But if you really press him for an explanation, and are not content with a vague shrug—'such is life' (RSV: 'that is his lot'), he turns to God: 'God has made it so'; 'it is God's gift'; 'God gives wealth. . . . God does not give power to enjoy. . . .'[2]

This *Deus ex machina* is a very shadowy figure—the 'One above' of modern superstition. The writer is not a theologian making statements about God. He is not really thinking about God. He is using a figure of speech, a habit of thought ingrained in Israel. When he is asked *why*, the answer that leaps to the Israelite's mind is in terms of God; the language of physical causation does not occur to him.

Order and Power

Both Israelite and Greek looked for a principle of coherence underlying the shifting varieties of phenomena in the world. The Greek rationalist thinker spoke of *kosmos*—an orderly structure built up from a limited number of elements: earth, air, fire and water, or a shower of atoms, or some such speculation. He tried to relate everything to a handful of principles, by chains of more or less scientific and logical reason. We, too, are constantly lengthening the chains of cause and effect which so fascinate us, and should rather like to think that ultimately

---

[1] See ch. 2. 1–11.   [2] 3. 13 f.; 6. 2.

they all join up in one single complex. To take an illustration: I ask, 'Why did it rain yesterday?' and you tell me, 'Water vapour in the atmosphere was precipitated.' I continue, 'Why was it precipitated?' and you answer, 'Because there was a cold air-stream'. Why a cold air-stream? Because of a depression in the Atlantic. Why a depression in the Atlantic? Because it has moved south-eastwards from Greenland. Why has it come from Greenland? And why did it form there?—and so on, and so on, until we hope to link up, via gravity, the rotation of the earth, and countless scientific processes, with the basic physical and chemical structure of the world.

But even if we cannot get as far as that, we have here quite a substantial chain of cause and effect. If this chain is interrupted—if, for instance, we have our cold air-stream but no rain—we find it astonishing, *incomprehensible*, and therefore disturbing. It casts doubt on an area of our knowledge, and on our ability to understand and cope with the world. Further, if such a chain of cause and effect is interrupted for an overriding reason, which yet appears, apart from this one occasion, scientifically unrelated to the normal sequence of events—I mean, for instance, if the rain which normally attends a cold front were withheld, so as not to interrupt the harvest (a type of motive not normally of meteorological application)—then we might perhaps call it a miracle. But this element of purpose, which converts the anomaly into a miracle, does little if anything to make it less astonishing and disturbing. The simple-minded pious may be encouraged to trust in the loving-kindness of the Almighty, but others, who are accustomed to see in the regularities of nature evidence of God's faithfulness, will have to ask: 'Is he really contradicting himself?' If so, there is no such thing as knowledge and certainty. Or have we overlooked something in his regular ordering of nature? Ought our statements of natural law to be amended—for instance, 'A cold front means rain, except during harvest'? But if so, the event follows the rule: there is no breach of regularity, and so, by definition, no miracle.

The Israelite does not face this difficulty. As he sees it, everything that happens is either act of God, or deed of man, or both. He sees the world not as a *physical* structure, but as a *power* structure. He asks, not 'What was the cause?' but 'Who is responsible?' I visualize this structure as a vast V, tapering from infinity at the top to zero at the bottom. At the top is God, capable of anything; at the bottom are the dead, capable of nothing; and at various levels in between come the more or less living. At death's door lie the dangerously ill; a little above them the aged and infirm. In the middle are the normally fit and active, the 'living'; above them those more than normally alive, the inspired, heroes and prophets; and higher still there is room, if you so wish, for ranks of superior spirits, demons, angels, and the like.

Boiling a kettle is a task within the power of even the elderly; building a house requires fit men; slaying a thousand Philistines single-handed is a job for someone higher up the scale again, a hero. In this last case, obviously there is something more than the merely human at work: God's spirit is co-operating. But even in the more normal, man-sized works, if we ask: 'Who is responsible?' there is an element of theological ambiguity in the answer. Every human act can also properly be regarded as act of God. I have noted half a dozen passages in the Psalms where the same event is described in parallel as human and divine. The wicked is snared in the work of his own hands[1] (he has to drink his own medicine); but this is at the same time the Lord making himself known and executing judgment. Similarly, 'the nations are sunk down in the pit that they made; in the net which they hid is their own foot taken'; and as the previous verse shows, this is the Lord's salvation of Zion.[2] There is a more extended example in the same vein in Psalm 7: in 12 f. we read of God's action against the impenitent, and in 14–16

[1] 9. 16.   [2] 9. 14 f.

we have the fall of the wicked in this-worldly terms. In Psalm
22. 15 *God* has brought the psalmist into the dust of death; in
the next verse, it is the assembly of evil-doers that have inclosed
him, and pierced his hands and his feet.[1] You can find examples
of the same sort of alternation in Proverbs; for instance, 10. 2
gives the down-to-earth statement that 'treasures of wickedness
profit nothing, but righteousness delivereth from death', and is
followed by 3: 'the Lord will not suffer the soul of the righteous
to famish: but he thrusteth away the desire of the wicked'. It is
no great surprise that in Proverbs the emphasis is heavily on
human initiative, in Psalms on the divine. The point is that
throughout the gamut of Israelite literature human activity is
recognized as ambiguous: it can also be correctly described as
God's activity.

But the higher we get up the scale, the less the ambiguity.
Samson's mighty deeds were extraordinary, and the extra was
of God. A prophet possessed by the Spirit spoke under divine
compulsion, and to that extent his human responsibility
receded. And at the top of the scale we come to completely
unambiguous happenings, which are acts of God and of God
alone. Rain, for instance. What has man to do with that? It is
an altogether God-sized act. And the Mighty Works are, if
possible, even more so. They are the star turns in the divine
repertoire: for example, the destruction of Pharaoh's army at
the Red Sea, without a human blow being struck. Things like
this are at the very top of the power scale; manifestly they are
far above all human devising; therefore they are the purest,
least ambiguous, most transparent acts of God.

Regularity and Faithfulness

I have digressed a little from the last point I set out to make,
namely to contrast the two different ways in which the Greek
rationalist and the Israelite simplified down the complexities

---

[1] See also Pss. 109. 6 ff.; 119. 29 ff.; 127. 1 f.; 149. 4, 6 ff.

of phenomena into comprehensible systems: the Greek, by linking things in chains of cause and effect leading back to some defined physical source; the Israelite, by thinking of every object and event in terms of will, or power, and ultimately, of the single will of God. We might now look at the world in a slightly different way, and ask: What lies behind the regularities of nature? Why can we bank on the hands of the clock going steadily round, and on the times of sunrise and sunset?

To us, this consistency inheres in the stuff things are made of. Iron rusts because it is iron; stainless steel resists corrosion because it is stainless steel. Chemists and physicists may trace these properties further back, into the elements of which the materials are composed, but ultimately they rest on the same sort of ground. Molecules behave as they do because they are that sort of molecule, and because the atoms they comprise are the sort of atoms they are. So, once we know *what* a thing is, we may be confident about its behaviour.

But what about the Israelite, and his analysis of the world in terms of power? Does not this make the whole world around him arbitrary and unreliable? He knows what he is doing himself; but how far can he rely on his neighbours? How consistent is human behaviour? And God—God does exactly what he likes with nature: he is under no control, no rules. But in fact God is *faithful*; which means, he is consistent in character, although in changing circumstances he may use various means to achieve his constant ends. And because God is reliable, the world is, by and large, reliable;[1] because God's faithfulness far outweighs the petty faithlessnesses of men, and even, as some saw it, the rather more significant chaotic tendencies of certain superior spirits. In spite of such corruption in high places, and even if all men were liars, God would be true; and so, on the whole, the world is a consistent place to live in. Because God is faithful, I can be confident that this chair will not collapse just yet, and that this room will outlast this paper.

[1] Cf. Jer. 31. 35 f.; 33. 20, 25 f.

In a nutshell, then, the difference is this: in our outlook, the regularity of nature is a mechanical regularity, in principle invariable, and regardless of purpose or effect. An arrow flies where it is shot, whether it hits friend or foe. To the Israelite, it is all purpose; the will of the marksman, shown in his aim, combines with the will of God, shown in the flighting of the arrow, to hit the target.[1] By and large, God's will is constant; but new circumstances call for new acts of God.

Miracles as evidence: light or darkness?

I have presented this contrast in rather unrealistically clearcut terms. But you can see the substance in it if you compare the various reactions to miracle and mighty work. Like us, the Israelite was astonished at such events as the opening of a way through the Red Sea. Ours is the astonishment of incomprehension. Part of our world order has been broken. Something which ought not to have happened, has happened. It is inexplicable, and so it *weakens* our understanding of the world. If we do explain it—if we succeed in integrating it into our scheme of things—it is no longer a miracle: it is simply a natural phenomenon, like an earthquake or typhoon, which happened to be convenient. We find the same sort of difficulty in the New Testament, when, for instance, Peter and John heal the lame man at the gate of the Temple. Why are we so tempted to reduce this lameness, in defiance of the text of Scripture, to either a pretence, or at most a psycho-somatic condition? Because as it stands we feel such a story does not illuminate, but rather obscures, the character of God. As long as it remains miracle, it is evidence for nothing except either the strangeness and irrationality of things (i.e. of God), or to show that our reason, our world view, is not adequate, without giving us any guidance we can use, how to make our philosophy more satisfactory.

---

[1] In 1 Kgs. 22. 34, the will of God, fulfilling prophecy, is the dominant cause of the arrow reaching its mark.

For the Israelite, on the other hand, 'mighty works' fell happily within his scheme of things. What could be more natural than that some of the acts of a mighty God should be mighty? You marvelled at them, not because they were inexplicable, but because they were splendid; and perhaps because they were potentially terrible. It was more like a small child's reaction to fireworks: the amazement and delight as a rocket goes up. He does not know how it works, and does not ask. On the other hand, it contradicts nothing in his experience, deals no blow to his philosophy. It is simply new experience, and spectacular.

Manoah, of course, was a little more sophisticated than this when he saw the angel go up in fire from the rock.[1] He was afraid. But not because he did not understand what was happening; and certainly not because he suspected anything obscure or occult. The opposite: it was quite clear to him, beyond a shadow of doubt, that he had indeed been speaking with an angel, that is, with God; and he knew what a terrible thing it was to get so close to God.

For the Israelite, then, Mighty Works were the clearest and purest evidence of God, because in them there was least risk of human interference. But what sort of evidence? Of God's existence? We inherit this question from the Greeks. Whereas Israel was sure of God, and saw the world as dependent on him, the Greeks were sure of the order of nature, and found it a matter for discussion whether there was a place for God anywhere in or around it. Anything which could not be accounted for in the order of nature posed a problem; and theistic apologists were tempted to exploit this situation. The argument is still familiar; it runs like this: 'That which is not natural must be divine. This well-authenticated event, X, is not natural—it is a miracle—therefore it is divine. Now "divine" means "of God"; so this event X is act of God; therefore God exists.'

---

[1] Jgs. 13. 20 ff.

This line of thought may have been known in Israel from
early times, but it did not come into prominence until the
Hellenistic era. As Fr. MacRae illustrates in his paper, it is
rampant in Josephus, alongside the classic Israelite concept of
Mighty Work; and we may find it in places in the New Testament. It is of course unsatisfactory, on at least two counts. To
begin with, it pushes God out of the natural (known nature)
into the 'gaps'. This still leaves him plenty of room; the further
we extend the boundaries of our knowledge, the longer the
frontier we find we have with the unknown. But, after all, the
realm of our knowledge is at least as much part of God's world
as is the domain of our ignorance. And secondly, this line of
argument aligns God *in principle* with the incomprehensible, and
makes any sort of idea of revelation self-contradictory. God—
by definition, the order which orders the cosmos—is to be
proved by miracle, by the unaccountable, by chaos.

The Israelite never doubted that God exists. What he wanted
evidence of was God's character. Perhaps the nearest we get in
the Old Testament to the use of miracle as a demonstration of
God's existence is in Elijah's battle with the prophets of Baal
on Carmel. Even there, the issue was not strictly ontological. As
I see it, there were two issues: (1) To what name does God
answer in Israel? (2) Who is *persona grata* with him? The miracle
made it clear to the onlookers that Israel was to worship Yahweh
alone; and that Elijah was his prophet.

In the other prophetic mighty works the point is usually to
support the prophet's claim to be a man of God. He does a
God-sized work, God must be with him, and what he says must
be taken seriously. This does not tell us very much about God.
We do not learn for the first time in 2 Kings 20 that he can
interfere with shadows. Any Israelite knew that he could do
this. What he learnt was that God was present and interested
in that particular situation. Either because of this particularity,
or because they were not regarded as very significant, miracles
of this type do not appear to have impressed the Old Testament

writers much. The story is told, and done with. Hezekiah's sundial appears twice, only because of parallel narratives in 2 Kings and Isaiah.

The classic Mighty Works of God, which are referred to repeatedly in the Scriptures, are the creation and preservation of the world and of Israel. The Exodus is specially prominent, as the basis of the Covenant; but even in its most legal contexts it does not cease to show something of the character of God. In the Psalms this aspect is emphasized, and the other Mighty Works are also used to illustrate the greatness of the Lord, and his love for Israel,[1] or his justice;[2] and regularly there is a call to worship—adoration, thanksgiving, rejoicing. Particular miraculous events like the plagues of Egypt fall within this scheme, but they are not singled out for special mention; the great works are the Creation, the Exodus, the Conquest, and, in more recent history, less closely specified victories, military and moral, won for the nation and the individual.[3] The Psalmist does, in fact, invite his hearer to count his blessings, and these, alongside the crossing of the Red Sea and the setting of the stars in their courses, all come under the heading: Wonderful, Mighty, Works of God.

The Mechanics of Mighty Works

My main concern has been to argue that 'Mighty Works' caused no difficulty to an Israelite: they fitted in smoothly to his outlook on life. However, there *is* a mystery: a question Israel did not ask, or at any rate did not stop to hammer out a generally accepted answer. I have spoken of the ambiguity of human acts, that they could also be spoken of as acts of God. But what is the relationship here between God and man? How does God work in the world? In fact, *what* did the Israelite think of God as actually *doing*?

---

[1] Pss. 78, 96, 105.   [2] E.g. Ps. 9.
[3] For personal blessings in the setting of Mighty Works of God, see esp. Pss. 71, 72, 111. For military successes in this context, see Pss. 46, 76, 118. Cf. also Ps. 126.

It was perhaps perverse of me to look for an answer in the Psalms; but, for what they are worth, here are my conclusions. By far the greatest number of references to acts of God, actual or desired, are concerned with adjusting people's places on the scale of power or life. The wicked are to be depressed towards Sheol, the righteous raised from sickness and humiliation to health and honour. This is sometimes expressed in picturesque language, which must surely be treated as metaphor. Or does the Psalmist really want the arms of the wicked broken literally by God,[1] or private thunderstorms of brimstone to pour down upon the head of the ungodly?[2] Often the language is much more general: 'requite my enemies with evil';[3] 'destroy their plans, confuse their tongues';[4] 'send you help from the sanctuary';[5] 'thou hast delivered me from every trouble'.[6] A substantial number of these references are definitely in terms of life, sickness and death. 'Lighten my eyes, lest I sleep the sleep of death.'[7] 'There is no soundness in my flesh, because of thy indignation.'[8] 'Slay them not, lest my people forget.'[9]

This is very much the sort of activity we should expect to see attributed to God the life-giver. And if we take 'life' in its broader sense, of power, fulness, then we can bring into this scheme the verses which speak of victory, happiness, wealth and security as gifts of God. But scarcely ever is there a glimpse at the mechanism, so to speak, by which these good things are provided, any more than the dozen or more references to the Creation tell us by what means the world was created. Now the Creation may be thought of as a strange remote event, about which no questions may be asked; but it is difficult to imagine that even an Israelite could help asking how God was going to set about such mundane things as crippling his enemies and filling his own house with good things.

We can find three partial answers. One is that the overwhelming emphasis is on personal, as distinct from material,

[1] 10. 15.   [2] 11. 6.   [3] 54. 5.   [4] 55. 9.   [5] 20. 2.
[6] 54. 7.   [7] 13. 3.   [8] 38. 3.   [9] 59. 11.

acts of God. They are concerned mostly with health and sickness, morale and confusion, glory and shame, achievement and failure. The picture is of God inspiring and, so to speak, 'uninspiring' *people*.

The second line is that, not having a doctrine of an autonomous world of Nature running according to its own laws, the Israelite had much less difficulty than we have in recognizing God's direct control over the growth and increase of flocks and herds—which is after all a department of God's 'special subject', Life—and even over the success of trading ventures, the quality of manufactured goods, and whether or not a house would collapse upon its owner.

Lastly and leastly, there is just the hint from time to time in the Psalms that God sometimes achieves his aims through the agency of men. A pit is to be prepared for the ungodly to fall into: with impious intent, he digs it himself.[1] The wicked are snared in the work of their own hands.[2] This is really a special case of my first line, God's personal activity, inspiring and confounding men's plans. It is not so much a case of human co-operation, as of God's will overruling human wills—in this particular case, bringing Nemesis upon them. This idea is exploited more freely by the prophets, as they wrestle with the will of God in international affairs.[3]

On the whole, however, the fact remains: Israel did not believe in an autonomous Nature, and consequently did not have to ask how God intervened in it—the modern problem of miracles. This does not mean that we can avoid the question ourselves; but we must try to set it aside while we study what the Old Testament writers intended to convey when they spoke of the Mighty Works of God. And in the New Testament, we must ask ourselves to what extent we are dealing with familiar Hellenistic thought forms, and how far we are involved in the strange traditional outlook of Israel.

[1] 7. 15.   [2] 9. 16.   [3] E.g. Is. 10. 5; 47; and Nah. 2.

Experience, Outlook and the Description of Events

This is no superficial matter. I have been speaking of the Israelite outlook on the world and the way it affects one's assessment of data—what one finds credible and incredible, marvellous and commonplace. It was not left to theologian-historians to interpret Israel's military history as acts of God; that is the way the participants themselves saw it. The most humdrum tactical stroke, the most brilliant strategy, the most astonishing coincidence (and in course of time what appears to the modern mind the most incredible exaggeration), were all acts of God, differing, perhaps, in magnificence, but not in credibility. But one must go further, beyond the assessment of events. One's outlook and experience dictate what one thinks one sees, hears, touches. There is a thud and a tinkle outside my study window. 'How careless camel-loaders are these days', says my Arabian visitor. 'That must have been a big pack falling off.' I, with my knowledge of Cambridge traffic, took it to be an accident. In this case, we can look and see which of us is right. But verification is not always so easy. I see a conjuror cut a piece of string or a lady in two, and then restore them. But my experience, my philosophy, tells me this is impossible; so I say: 'I have seen a very clever trick'. Israel won a battle in a hailstorm. We can see no connexion between the weather and the war, unless one commander or the other had deliberately chosen to fight when a storm was likely. But the Israelites saw, heard and felt God fighting for them with hailstones from heaven. Within their framework of thought, this is not an interpretation, but a perfectly straightforward description of what happened. This is one of the things Kaufmann is getting at when he writes (of the Conquest): 'There never was a "realistic" account of the events. The account of the events was "idealistic", "legendary", right from the start. Every warrior who came from the battle-line to the camp and told his story to the women and children related "legendary" things, "idealistic" history stamped with the idea of the miraculous sign.'[1]

As we consider a miracle story, then, the question before us is not 'What is the original, primitive, factual account?' but 'What should *we* have seen if we had been there? How should *we* have described it?' Where it is convincingly possible, we are justified in seeking and accepting scientific explanations. In thus transferring the event from the category of miracle to that of digestible history, we are not weakening the testimony of Scripture. These things are recorded (with possibly one or two exceptions) not that we should gape in amazement, but that we should be edified, and edified, not by anomalies, but by plain evidence of the character of the God we serve. Usually, however, scientific explanation is not now possible. The Israelite did not share our scientific interests, and it is only rarely that he gives the answers to the sort of questions we should like to ask.

But in either case we can proceed to the further question: 'What did this Mighty Work teach Israel about the character of God?' There may be insights which will open our eyes to eternal truth, even if we cannot fit the event into our own experience of the world. But if we can—if we can say: 'This is what happened; this is how I should have described it if it happened yesterday; and *that* is the way Israel saw it'—then we have as it were a bilingual text, a key to translate more and more of our present experience into Old Testament terms and see what it looks like then. In this way Israel's insights come into the heart and reality of our life. Not that their point of view is the only, or altogether the best, way of looking at things. We are not likely to forget our twentieth-century outlook completely. But we may avoid the temptation to imagine that our own way of thinking is complete and perfect, and that no improvement is possible to the framework within which we appreciate reality.

[1] Y. Kaufmann, *The Biblical Account of the Conquest of Palestine* (Eng. tr. 1953), p. 75.

5

ELIJAH, ELISHA AND THE GOSPEL MIRACLES

BY

BARNABAS LINDARS, S.S.F.

BARNABAS LINDARS, S.S.F.

Frederick Chevallier Lindars won a Hebrew Scholarship at St. John's College, Cambridge, and studied Oriental Languages and Theology there, with a two-year interval in Military Intelligence. After Ordination, he served as a curate in the parish of St. Luke, Pallion, Sunderland, and in 1952 joined the Society of St. Francis, taking the name of Father Barnabas. In 1961 he published *New Testament Apologetic*, for which he was awarded the B.D. degree. He is an Assistant Lecturer in Old Testament Studies in the University of Cambridge.

ELIJAH, ELISHA AND THE
GOSPEL MIRACLES

IN CONSIDERING the miracle-stories of the Gospels, it may be useful to distinguish three aspects which apply to the attitude to miracle throughout the Old and New Testaments.

There is first of all the idea of miracle as an act of God, which may happen without any human agency. The resurrection is an event of this kind. 'God raised Jesus from the dead' is the classic New Testament expression, rather than 'Jesus rose'. This kind of miracle shades off from wonderful events which, to the biblical mind, can only be explained as acts of God, to natural occurrences in which, on reflection, the direct intervention of God is perceived. The Exodus from Egypt, which is the cardinal factor of the faith of Israel, can be spoken of quite simply in such words as 'I brought you out of the land of Egypt' (Exod. 20. 2), which need not imply more than a theological interpretation of an historical event. On the other hand signs and wonders attended the Exodus, which proved to the faithful Israelites that this was indeed an act of God.

The second aspect is the agency of man in performing the acts of God. This has special importance in biblical thought, because Yahweh is pre-eminently personal, and the idea of an impersonal, mechanical divine power is foreign to it. Yahweh speaks through the prophets, wins battles through the judges whom he raises up, and performs wonders through holy men. Occasionally it is actually stated that such deeds are not due to human capacity, but to the power of God acting through men. We find this both in earlier theology (Joseph, in Gen. 41. 16 —E), and in normative Judaism (Daniel, in Dan. 2. 30)—both are concerned with the interpretation of dreams. Yahweh does wonderful things through men according to the measure of his spirit (*ruach*) which rests upon them or is in them. It has often been noted that this is the factor common to both the judges and the great prophets, and it is the justification for the use of the word 'charismatics' for both in recent writing. We should also note the phrase 'man of God' ('*ish ha-'Elohim*), which was current in Judah in the time of the monarchy for the more usual 'prophet' (*nabhi'*). Such men have a special endowment of the spirit, and it is not surprising if they perform wonderful deeds in Yahweh's name. When Luke reports that the people who witnessed Jesus' miracle of raising the son of the widow of Nain 'glorified God, saying, A great prophet is arisen among us' (Lk. 7. 16), he is describing a reaction which is entirely in keeping with biblical ideas.

The third aspect takes this a stage further. Miracles are sometimes ascribed to such holy men without any kind of declaration concerning God and his power and his purposes for men. They simply testify to the peculiar power or virtue which belongs to a man of God, and take the form of incidents common to hagiography all down the ages. There is an excellent example of this sort of thing in the Elisha cycle. In 2 Kings. 13. 20–21, we read how a dead man revived through contact with the bones of Elisha. Christian hagiography is full of comparable stories of the potency of relics. They denote a superstitious attitude devoid of the theological awareness which is so clearly marked in the Bible as a whole. They simply attest the wonder that surrounds a holy man in popular memory, and invite the critic to classify them as folk-lore.

The above distinction in the attitude towards miracle indicates that, although the possibility of miracle is always present in biblical thinking, it is likely to be given a different emphasis in different literary strata. In the Old Testament miracle as a divine act (the first of our three senses) is an essential element of the salvation-history, and occurs in texts dealing with the faith of Israel. We find it, of course, in the Book of Exodus, but this is not because it is primarily an historical writing, but because it is the cult legend, which is solemnly recited in the national festival. So, too, the remarkable deliverances of Israel at times of national crisis are told from the point of view of salvation-history, and consequently show a tendency to emphasize the miraculous character of the events. This is the tradition of the 'holy war', in which Yahweh fights for his people, and is a special characteristic of the Deuteronomic editing of the early traditions of Israel in the Book of Judges. But we find the same attitude in the prophetic literature, where the concepts of the salvation-history have been transferred to the future. Deutero-Isaiah looks towards a repetition of the miracles of the Exodus when the people return from exile. 'I will even make a way in the wilderness, and rivers in the desert' (Is. 43. 19). Such miraculous happenings become more marvellous, not to say fantastic, when the prophet's vision embraces the ultimate future, like the waters that will flow from the restored temple in Ezekiel 47, and the tremendous upheavals described in Zechariah 14. Finally, cosmic disturbances on the grand scale become part of the stock-in-trade of the writers of apocalyptic eschatology. The Book of Revelation is full of them. They also figure in the 'little apocalypse' of Mark 13. If this chapter reports genuine sayings of Jesus, it indicates that he accepted the current eschatological ideas. This is not to say, of course, that he necessarily took them literally, merely that he worked within this frame of ideas in order to convey his own message.

When we turn to the historical books of the Bible, we find that miracle plays only a subordinate part. It is here that we should expect to find examples of our second group, in which holy men are the agents of God's power. Such examples do occur, but it is significant that this is generally in contexts where the early traditions of Israel are handled from the point of view of salvation-history. Moses is the agent of the ten plagues which precede the deliverance of the people from Egypt, and of the miracles of the manna and water from the rock in the wilderness. In the case of the brazen serpent (Num. 21. 9) it is clear that we have to do with the cult legend connected with an object of veneration in the temple (cf. 2 Kgs. 18. 4). The Books of Joshua and Judges contain both aetiological legends (e.g. the story of Gideon and the angel, Jgs. 6. 11–24) and traditions that embellish Yahweh's part in the battles of Israel (e.g. the sun standing still, Jos. 10. 12–14). The same is true to some extent of the early chapters of 1 Samuel. But with the account of the struggle between Saul and David all this is changed. From now on we are in the age when records begin to be kept. The historical narrative attains a high standard of objectivity. This is still true in the case of the Books of Kings, although the work is written from a definite theological stand-point as a sacred history. Only in the section dealing with Elijah and Elisha (1 Kgs. 17–2 Kgs. 13) do we have accounts of miracles comparable to the miracle stories of the Gospels. The section dealing with Isaiah (2 Kgs. 18. 13–20. 21 = Is. 36–39) also has a miraculous element, which need not be taken into account for the purposes of this essay. The post-exilic historical books, Ezra-Nehemiah and 1 Maccabees, continue to be notably free from reports of miracles. The miracles in the story of Tobit and in the early chapters of Daniel do not come into consideration here, as these are tendentious folk-tales rather than historical reporting.

We must therefore confine our attention to the Elijah and Elisha sections of Kings. Literary analysis of 1 and 2 Kings shows that the compiler made use of some kind of official record of the bare facts of each king's reign and his military achieve-ments, which he cites as 'the chronicles of the kings of Israel' and 'the chronicles of the kings of Judah'. For the beginning of his narrative (the reign of Solomon and the subsequent division of the kingdom) he has fairly full information, though his sources are of unequal merit. For the final part (from the fall of Samaria to the fall of Jerusalem) he has better resources, which is only to be expected, seeing that he probably wrote the history shortly afterwards. But for the intervening span of about two centuries he has to fill out the chronistic framework as best he can, using such material as was available to him. If we omit the parts dealing with Elijah and Elisha and with Isaiah, the only section of any consequence is the history of the house of Omri, contained in 1 Kings 16. 17–2 Kings 11. 20. The legends of Elijah and Elisha have been so closely woven into it that its continuity as a separate source is largely obscured. It is a succession-narrative, told from the point of view of the Yahwistic party at Jerusalem. It is thus hardly surprising that the compiler drew on legends of the prophets to give fulness and colour to what would otherwise have been a very bare sketch.

These stories can now be examined on their own merits quite apart from our estimate of the Books of Kings as a whole. The two prophets differ in that Elijah is a lone figure from Gilead on the east side of the Jordan, whereas Elisha seems to have been connected with the Sons of the Prophets, though not necessarily attached to any one community of them (cf. 2 Kgs. 2. 3; 4. 1, 38; 6. 1; 9. 1). This suggests that it is to one of these groups that we owe the collection of these tales. As Elisha was Elijah's assistant and later his successor, we may suppose that the preservation of the Elijah stories is due to his initiative. This may account for the fact that this cycle is largely free from the element of mere hagiography, and is more concerned with the display of Yahweh's power through his prophet. By contrast Elisha had no successor of equivalent stature. The stories about him mostly reflect the wild and credulous Sons of the Prophets, who revered him as their great leader.

Although we can in this way make an immediate distinction between the Elijah and Elisha cycles, and must bear in mind that they probably grew up as separate collections, it is necessary to make another kind of literary distinction which cuts across both. There are, in fact, three types of material involved. In the first place there are traditions which are closely linked to the historical narrative. In the Elijah cycle there are his prophetic work in connexion with the drought in the reign of

Ahab (1 Kgs. 17. 1–3, and the setting of the miracle on Carmel, 18. 1–20, 41–46), his flight from Jezebel after slaying the prophets of Baal (19. 1–8), his denunciation of the affair of Naboth's vineyard (21), and his prophecy against Ahaziah (2 Kgs. 1). Similarly the Elisha cycle contains a tradition of the prophet's part in the Moabite revolt (2 Kgs. 3. 4–27), his instigation of Hazael's coup at Damascus (8. 7–15) and of Jehu's coup in Israel (9. 1–13), and his symbolic prophecy concerning Joash's campaigns (13. 14–19). Secondly there are, in the Elisha cycle only, tales of the prophet's work in the wars between Israel and Syria (2 Kgs. 6. 8–7. 20) and of his intervention at the court on behalf of a widow (8. 1–6). It is clear that these are told regardless of the historical narrative, simply to enhance the picture of the prophet himself. They therefore belong with the third group, which are the miracle stories that preserve the tradition of Elijah and Elisha as great men of God, and cover the rest of the material.

The traditions that belong closely with the historical narrative must first be examined, because here the motive of the reporting is not so much to enhance the memory of the prophet as to explain the course of events in the troubled years of the latter part of the ninth century. If we exclude for the moment the miraculous element in the story of Elijah and the prophets of Baal on Mount Carmel (1 Kgs. 18) and in his prophecy on Ahaziah's sickness (2 Kgs. 1), all the items in this group concern the intervention of prophets in the affairs of the kingdom, comparable to the work of the classical prophets later. Elijah seizes the opportunity presented by the drought to denounce Ahab's religious policy (cf. 1 Kgs. 18. 18), slays the prophets of Baal in vengeance for the slaughter of the prophets of Yahweh (19. 1, cf. 18. 13), denounces the treatment of Naboth—an episode which typifies the popular disgust with Ahab and Jezebel—and prophesies Ahaziah's death as a divine judgment. In the Elisha cycle, the story of the Moabite revolt in 2 Kings 3, which perhaps

comes from an independent tradition, may well imply a strata-
gem rather than a miracle. The other items in this group do not
include miraculous elements. Nevertheless, there are miracles
in two of the Elijah stories. The superb description of Elijah
calling down fire from heaven in 1 Kings 18 can be detached
from its historical setting as a tradition of the transference of a
shrine on Mount Carmel from Phoenician to Israelite control.
Although this view (supported by Alt and Noth) is denied by
some scholars (Eissfeldt and Gray), the story as it stands fails
to be convincing, because it does not allow enough time for the
slaughter of the prophets of Baal before Elijah's flight and the
coming of the rain, so that it remains probable that there has
been some telescoping of events in the transmission of the tradition. This means that we can still suppose that a story of a
miracle, told to give credit to Elijah as a religious hero, has
been welded into the general historical framework of his denunciation of Ahab's policy. The real point of the story of Elijah
and Ahaziah's messengers (2 Kgs. 1) is the prophet's rebuke
and pronouncement of the king's death. It is pressed home by
calling down fire from heaven on successive deputations. The
fact that there are three of these is a sure sign of folk-lore. This
again means that the story has been transmitted to enhance the
memory of the great prophet. It may be regarded as a favourite
example of Elijah's place in the struggle between the Yahweh
enthusiasts and the baals.

We may now look at the rest of the material purely from the
point of view of hagiography. Here are traditions which have
been collected in order to preserve the memory of two outstanding personalities. The Elijah cycle begins with three
miracles connected with the drought in the reign of Ahab.
1 Kings 17. 3–7 describes how Elijah is fed by ravens in the
wilderness. Although the feeding of a hero by animals is a well-
known motif of folk-lore (cf. the legend of Romulus and Remus),
it has been suggested that in this case the word for 'ravens'

should be read as 'Arabs'.[1] That friendly Bedawin tribes should
help Elijah in this way is not impossible, but it runs counter
to the whole tenor of this series of tales. This is an example of
the modern tendency to find naturalistic interpretations of
miracle stories, which we shall come across again as we examine
these stories. But in the temptation narrative in the Gospels we
read that 'angels ministered' to Jesus (Mk. 1. 13, followed by
Mt. 4. 11). In both cases we are dealing with events that lie
outside the range of evidential inquiry, because they depend on
personal (and presumably subjective) telling by the subject
himself, and may be no more than his way of recounting his
experience.

The other two miracles of 1 Kings 17 are concerned with a
woman of Zarephath. Elijah prophesies that her barrel of meal
and jug of oil will not run out so long as the drought continues.
Subsequently the woman's son dies, or almost dies, and Elijah
lays him on his own bed, stretching himself on him three times,
and the boy revives. Naturalistic interpretations have been
suggested for both these miracles. Gray supposes that 'the
generosity of the widow (i.e. in giving hospitality to the prophet)
touched the conscience of her better-provided neighbours', who
presumably maintained her supplies of meal and oil. This is
similar to the 'lunch-basket' theory of the miraculous feedings
in the Gospels. According to this theory the generous action of
a boy in offering his five loaves and two fish (the boy is only
mentioned in Jn. 6. 9) prompted others who had food with
them to share it with those who had none. One can hardly
resist the impression that the theory in each case is merely a
device to save the historicity of the incident without straining
credulity too far. The revival of the boy *could* be due to the fact
that he was not really dead, and the precaution of taking him
up to the more hygienic upper room did the trick. It would
then still be possible for the woman to be convinced that a

[1] Reading '*arabhîm* for '*ôrebhîm*. Although this proposal involves no change in the
consonantal text, it receives no support from the ancient versions.

miracle had happened. But from the point of view of contemporary belief the health of Elijah, who is a man full of God's spirit (*ruach*), is transferred to the boy. The story ends with the woman's confession of faith—faith in the power of the prophet's intercession and in the influence of his abundant endowment of *ruach*.

In the latter story we should also note the threefold action of Elijah in stretching himself on the boy. Folk-lore loves to have things in threes! The suspicion that we have to do with folk-tales rather than precise memories is confirmed by the fact that the very same motifs also occur in the Elisha cycle. In 2 Kings 4. 1–7 Elisha tells a destitute widow to fill as many vessels as she can get from her small supply of oil. Then follows a miracle of revival of a woman's only son. She is a woman of Shunem, and not the same as the widow in the preceding story. The story is superbly told at considerable length. The boy is again put in the prophet's chamber. When Elisha is fetched he stretches himself on the boy twice (not three times). The boy sneezes seven times (this at least is another folk-lore number!) and opens his eyes. The woman's confession of faith is only hinted at. Another folk-lore feature earlier in the story is the fact that the woman and her husband have long been childless before Elisha prophesies the birth of the child. The fact that two such similar stories occur in both cycles causes little surprise. Christian hagiography contains plenty of examples of the transference of traditions from one saint to another. For instance, traditions of the English saint Etheldreda have been filled out from those of the earlier French saint Radegund.

Returning to Elijah, the next miracle is the fire from heaven in the struggle with the prophets of Baal on Mount Carmel (1 Kgs. 18). This has already been referred to above, but it must be added that, in view of the drought, the ordeal seems to be a rain-making ceremony. Baal needs to be wakened from sleep to produce a storm. Similarly Elijah's four pots of water

poured over the sacrifice may be to induce rain, like the water-
pouring at the feast of Tabernacles (see commentaries on Jn.
7. 37). He does this three times. Elijah's prayer—which, like
several details in this story, betrays the interests of the E writer
of the Pentateuch—has very similar motivation to Jesus' prayer
before raising Lazarus, to evoke faith in God (Jn. 11. 42). The
prayer is answered with lightning, which sometimes *precedes*
rain in the Holy Land according to Dalman, and the people
cry out 'Yahweh, he is God!'—a cultic exclamation. Elijah
then crouches at the top of the mountain. T. H. Robinson
suggested that this was to simulate a rain-cloud, but Gray
regards it as an act of concentration. He then sends his messenger seven times to see if the rain is coming. Seen in this light,
the whole episode is a trial of strength between the baal-
worshippers and the Yahweh-worshippers, turning on the success of the rain-making ceremony. It wins popular acceptance
for Yahweh. The naturalistic interpretation is difficult to resist
in this case. It shows Elijah as a most powerful intercessor on a
memorable cultic occasion. It is referred to, as an example of
answer to prayer, in James 5. 17 f.

Our study of the Elijah cycle thus leads to the conclusion
that, whether a natural occurrence lies behind the miracles or
not, the spiritual power of a man of God is the real motive of
these stories. This is the impression that he made on his contemporaries. It was only natural that they should express it in
terms of miracle stories, because the possibility of miracle was
an unquestioned presupposition of their thought. The expression
of great spiritual awareness by means of physical phenomena
appears again in Elijah's solitary experience on Mount Horeb
in 1 Kings 19. On the way, he is miraculously fed by an angel.
This seems to be another version of the motif already examined
in connexion with 17. 3–7, but we should hardly take the angel
to be an Arab! But then we have the wind, earthquake, fire
and still small voice (perhaps the whistling of the wind after
the violence of the storm has passed). Most readers take this to

mean apprehension of God through inner experience, rather than through spectacular phenomena, and this is surely right. The narrative has a poetic quality which forbids literal interpretation. Yet the experience may well have been accompanied —on the large-scale and external level—by a raging storm, so that the story has an ambivalence which shows how easily memories of spiritual power pass over into ideas of the miraculous. There can be no question of accepting the elements of prophecy and spiritual experience in the Elijah cycle and rejecting the miracle-stories just because they contain miracles.

The ascension of Elijah (2 Kgs. 2) really belongs to the Elisha cycle. It concerns the 'double portion' which is given to an eldest son according to the law of inheritance (Deut. 21. 17), and is Elisha's experience of receiving this prophetic endowment as Elijah's official successor. Various explanations are given for the different elements in the story. (a) There is the folk-lore triad—visits to the Sons of the Prophets at Gilgal, Bethel and Jericho. (b) At Jordan Elijah parts the waters with his mantle. This is claimed by Kraus to be 'a rite in the amphictyonic sacrament at Gilgal' commemorating the Exodus, a liturgical act for which the cultic narrative is preserved in Joshua 4. If so the incident can be regarded as symbolic rather than miraculous. (c) The whirlwind and fire are said to be a dust-storm, or at least imagery inspired by one. (d) The chariot is said to be an elaboration from *Elisha's* title 'the chariots of Israel and the horsemen thereof', mentioned in the account of his death (2 Kgs. 13. 14). Whatever may be made of these suggestions, the miraculous elements have a deeper purpose than recording marvels in order to impress the credulous. They express the great significance which was attached to Elisha's position as Elijah's successor in popular thought. This build-up of a highly impressive and symbolical description of what was again primarily a spiritual experience may perhaps have a bearing on our estimate of the account of the Transfiguration of Jesus in the Gospels.

F

The Elisha cycle continues with a series of miracle-stories, which runs without a break from 2 Kings 2. 19 to 8. 6, with the exception of chapter 3, which seems to come from a separate stratum of tradition. Some of them are readily amenable to naturalistic interpretation. In 2. 19–22 the prophet purifies the water of Jericho by throwing in salt. This can be explained as a rite to restore fertility. In 2. 23–25 some rude boys are torn by bears. This might be no more than the superstitious connexion of a natural calamity with a notable event that immediately preceded it (compare the Gadarene swine in the Gospels). The miracles of 2 Kings 4 have been dealt with in conjunction with their parallels in the Elijah cycle above, except 4. 38–41 (Elisha purifies a poisoned pot) and 4. 42–44 (he feeds a hundred men with twenty loaves). In the first case, it is explained that the gourds (*citrullus colocynthus*, according to Dalman) were used to make the mixture potent to work up prophetic frenzy, but unfortunately they have a powerful laxative effect which can be fatal! Casting in meal perhaps reduced the effect. But Gray cites a West Highland tradition of the use of meal (oatcake broken over a person's head) to act as a charm against evil influence, which he thinks could be the explanation of Elisha's somewhat similar action. The second, in which firstfruits are used, could be 'a special sacramental meal' (Gray), which explains the emphasis on the leavings.[1] The meal, though small in quantity, was satisfying as a sacrament. This Elisha-incident may support a naturalistic interpretation of the Gospel feedings, where a very small amount of food is used to point a spiritual lesson. It is noteworthy that the numbers of men and of loaves are restrained, compared with the Gospel feedings. The story of Naaman the leper (2 Kgs. 5) may be left over for the moment, and we continue with 6. 1–7, which tells how Elisha caused an axe-head to float. He does this apparently by poking about in the river with a stick, and perhaps guiding it to the brink where it can be reached by hand. If so, it is not really a miracle at all,

[1] 'Ears of corn' in 5. 42 are probably 'orchard fruits'—see commentaries.

but this impression has been built up because the man of God was so clever. Faith in his sagacity was justified. Passing on to 8. 1–6, we have a story of how a woman recovered her inheritance. It is a not very convincing tale of coincidence, and does not embody any truly miraculous element. Finally, there is the story in 2 Kings 13. 20–21 of how a dead man revived through contact with Elisha's bones some time after his death. Presumably his grave had become a place of pilgrimage, like the sepulchre of the man of God, mentioned in 2 Kings 23. 17. Superstitions tend to collect around such places. The incident is comparable to the stories connected with relics which abound in the history of hagiography.

The fact that naturalistic explanations can be found so readily for these short anecdotes may serve as a reminder of the gulf that separates our modern way of thinking from that of Old Testament times. Whether they have been built up from purely natural happenings or not, they have been remembered and valued because they give vivid expression to the powerful impression which the prophet's personality made on his contemporaries. Sophisticated people would be more likely to try to convey this impression by recounting incidents in which the man's character is the decisive factor. The popular mind seizes on the marvellous and the extraordinary. Half-way between these two kinds of outlook stands the motive which controls the longer narrative-stories in the Elijah cycle (see above, p. 72), and also the Elisha stories of 2 Kings 4, and, finally, the stories of the cleansing of Naaman the leper (5) and of the chariots of fire at Dothan (6. 8–23). It is the presence of a miracle in what is fundamentally a story of prophetic power and insight. The miraculous element is inextricably bound up with the story, but it is not the major purpose of it. The point of the Naaman story is the superiority of Yahweh over other gods (compare Elijah on Mount Carmel). The command to wash seven times is a folk-lore motif. All the other details are designed to enhance Yahweh's superiority—Elisha's standoffish attitude in sending his servant to the distinguished visitor; Naaman's confession of faith that 'there is no God in all the earth, but in Israel'; his request to take back soil to Damascus; and the transference of the disease to Gehazi, because Yahweh takes no payment. The chariots of fire at Dothan (6. 17) must be classed with the story of Elijah at Horeb as a concretized spiritual experience, which in this case is communicated to the prophet's companion. It is part of a longer complex about Syrian raids (6. 8–7. 20), which are notable for their lack of exact historical setting. The story of the relief of Samaria turns on a prophecy by Elisha which seemed impossible of fulfilment (7. 1–2), but the event is a stroke of good luck, which is only miraculous in so far as it is peculiarly timely.

It remains to gather up the impressions gained from studying the two cycles of miracle-stories, and to see what bearing they have on the Gospel miracles. We began with a distinction between miracle as a divine act and miracle as a feature of hagiography. The first implies a theological outlook, which may be summed up in the concept of the salvation-history. It runs into the second, in so far as a holy man may be the agent of God in effecting the work of salvation. In the New Testament St. Paul is the great representative of the theological outlook, and his letters are notably free from mention of miracles in the other sense. St. John shares this approach. When he makes use of traditions of Jesus which embody miracles, he is always careful to make them subordinate to his theological purpose. In the Synoptic Gospels miracle-stories are told more simply, but we would be mistaken to suppose that there is no theological motive at work. From the point of view of the Evangelists, Jesus is the agent and focus of the inauguration of the kingdom of God, to which the whole salvation-history pointed, and his miracles are signs that the kingdom is near. A frequent motif in the miracle-stories is a challenge in order to elicit faith. The story of the Syro-phoenician woman (Mk. 7. 24–30) is a particularly striking example. It is notable that Matthew has made the faith-motif even more explicit in his handling of the anecdote (Mt. 15. 21–28).

Prior to the Gospels, and to any written sources that the Evangelists may have used, there was the oral tradition of the sayings and deeds of Jesus, which many different people remembered. It cannot be expected that all this material should be of equal worth. Memory is fickle. Although the use of much of the tradition in the missionary and catechetical work of the church (*kerygma* and *didaché*), and no doubt in liturgy too, ensured that the theological interpretation remained central, some of it at any rate can have had little more than hagiographical interest. Just as in the case of Elijah and Elisha, the miracle-stories are the form in which people expressed the great impression that Jesus made upon them. We have to recognize that the nature of the precise event which lies behind a tradition often eludes us. In some cases a naturalistic interpretation may be possible (e.g. the Gadarene swine, cf. p. 74 above). In other cases attempts to find explanations of this kind should be resisted. This applies particularly to the Temptations and the Transfiguration, which belong to the class of concretized spiritual experiences. Both accounts include typological enrichments, which make it impossible to disentangle the facts from the interpretation.[1] A symbolical (sacramental) interpretation of the Feeding miracles is more satisfactory than a naturalistic one (cf. pp. 70 and 74 above). Occasionally a miracle may have been applied to Jesus from the stock of folk-lore, like the doublets in the Elijah and Elisha traditions.[2] Many of the healing miracles would hardly be regarded as miracles if they had been seen by modern observers, whose presuppositions are so different from those of first-century Galilee, and could be

---

[1] The influence of typology has also been discerned in the Elijah stories. It is possible to regard his retreat to Horeb, and other details, as indications of an attempt to present him as a new Moses. But I think this is doubtful.

[2] E.g. the coin in the fish's mouth, Mt. 17. 24–27, for which there are parallels in both Greek and rabbinic literature.

credited to other healers and exorcists of the time equally well.
The fact that they are mostly set in Galilee is not without
importance. The people of Galilee were of mixed stock, though
they had been largely Judaized under John Hyrcanus (135–
105 B.C.). In New Testament times they were noted for their
credulousness and their enthusiasms. After the fall of Jerusalem
(A.D. 70) the rabbis tend to discountenance emphasis on miracles,
classing Christians with Galileans in this respect.[1] The Gospel
passages in which numerous miracles are summarized (Mk. 3.
7–12, etc.) are typical of the sort of exaggeration to which these
people were prone.

This may seem a very negative conclusion, but in fact it has
positive value. Because of the circumstances in which the oral
tradition was formed we cannot expect to get to the bottom of
all the miracle-stories. This does not nullify the unique impression to which they testify, that Jesus was a prophet, and more
than a prophet—the one in whom God's redemptive work was
concentrated. In spite of all the temptations to enhance the
miraculous, the authority of his own personality exercised a
restraining influence on the tradition. In the Acts of the
Apostles we have traces of miracle-stories connected with the
apostles which show less restraint. The traditions about Peter's
miracles no doubt belong to a milieu where he was revered as
'our founder', i.e. the Joppa area, and show a tendency to
collect such stories for their own sake. It is not surprising that
such stories proliferate in the Apocryphal Gospels and Acts.
The distinction is similar to that which we observed between
the Elijah and Elisha collections. There is, in fact, evidence
within the Gospels themselves that Jesus had no wish to be
famed as a worker of miracles. Paul and John are undoubtedly
right in turning attention to the theological meaning of Jesus.
Although it is true that apologists for Christianity have pointed
to the miracles as evidence of Christ's divinity since the early

---

[1] See the references in W. D. Davies, *The Setting of the Sermon on the Mount* (1964),
pp. 284 f., 299 f., 450 f.

days of the church, the solid structure of christology and of the theology of redemption has never been allowed to rest upon such flimsy supports alone. The miraculous element in the Gospel tradition need not be denied outright, but it has certainly been exaggerated, and needs to be treated with agnostic reserve. What we must look for is the Jesus whose life so deeply impressed his contemporaries, and seek to grasp the meaning of his message and the significance of his person for the salvation of the world.

6

HERODOTUS ON THE MIRACULOUS

BY

A. H. McDONALD

A. H. McDONALD

Dr. A. H. McDonald is a Fellow of Clare College, Cambridge, and a University Lecturer in Ancient History in the University of Cambridge: previously Professor of Ancient World History in the University of Sydney, Australia.

His special interest lies in historiography, Greek and Roman, but in the general context of historical interpretation. He sees the place of human symbolism against the feeling of man's place in nature, whether this is held in simple faith or with modern scientific knowledge. He tries to show that Greek anthropomorphism did not ignore a wider view of the world. He learned to think in these terms when he studied the attitudes and beliefs in East Asia during the war.

HERODOTUS ON THE MIRACULOUS

ONE MAY well ask why this paper, which discusses the pagan thought of a Greek historian on his own terms, should appear in the present work. And why Herodotus? First let me say that it is not an attempt to prove Greek influence upon the Christian view of miracles. Then let me stress, on the other hand, that if we are to consider our own attitudes in the light of general human experience, the Greeks have something to add to our understanding. And Herodotus, writing with deceptive artistry about men and circumstances, seems to represent most faithfully the common Greek conception of the interaction of the human and the divine. He was not trying to define a pattern but to describe the signs and wonders, with the tolerance of a man who had learnt of such things elsewhere as well. He is a universal historian treating a wide field and going back in depth, and his respect for the complexities of human experience enhances his value.

Herodotus stayed too close to popular thought? Perhaps so— but preserve us from the rationalizing historian who trims and cuts his material so that we are at the mercy of his opinions. Herodotus permits us to make our own judgments. And was Greek popular thought so negligible? Greek mythology has almost an inspired gift of symbolizing experience—from Prometheus and Sisyphus to Oedipus himself. It helps to clarify conceptions in human terms.

Herodotus flourished in the heyday of Greek freedom during the fifth century B.C., after the triumphant repulse of Persian power. He had grown up at Halicarnassus in western Asia Minor and seen life in the Aegean. He had travelled as far as Scythia in the north and Egypt to the south, and he could draw on knowledge of Persian affairs in the Middle East. He was at Athens under Pericles—Athens the brilliant city but the proud ruler of the Aegean. He went out to Thurii in the Greek West, which was no less distinguished than the Greek homeland. Then, he saw the free Greek world divide in a civil war—the Peloponnesian War, which would destroy most of what had been gained in the struggle against Persia. Meanwhile he had collected material for a history of the field of Greek and Persian relations in their widest perspective, and he brought it into focus on the Persian Wars. This is the work in which we have to study his religious thought.

Surely the subject was large enough to be interpreted in the light of the observable evidence which Herodotus sets out so copiously? This depends upon the historian's view of the world. Even the rationalist Polybius, who had similar scope in describing the expansion of Rome, called in the factor of unpredictable 'fortune', however conventionally. Herodotus did not believe that human affairs could be judged entirely in their own terms. One must not despise this opinion. Why do the best laid plans go awry? Perhaps they have taken too little account of external forces which break in from the outside. Or why in the regular conduct of political and personal matters does irrationality so often take charge? Perhaps our calculations have forgotten the demoniac element in human behaviour. The modern method is to enlarge the field of political, social and economic inquiry and to intensify the study of psychology and sociology, but even then the subtle interaction of factors may defy analysis. The ancient historian who approached most closely to this method was Thucydides: the pathology of civil war brings the deepest human passions most clearly to the surface. Herodotus had a wider, more complex historical field. Though he accepted the limits of interpretation too readily, he fulfils the prime function of the historian, that is, to plot the whole variety of the evidence he has gathered; after which he may attempt to explain what he thinks he understands, and indicate what he regards as inexplicable. Herodotus shows the balance of his subject, but he does not impose a strict pattern. He comments freely as he goes along, and where he feels the influence of unknowable forces he is prepared to consider the divine.

The appreciation of mythology is never simple, once the cultural context of the original insight has changed. The more vivid the anthropomorphic imagery, the more tempting to see the divine figures in individual isolation: we set up statues and forget their background. The Greeks were almost too successful artistically. The Homeric deities make a human impression, as one would expect in heroic saga. The Attic tragedians struggled with the problems of human life as they saw it lived under divine pressure. Aeschylus tried to extend the conception of Zeus, in the light of the traditions; Sophocles could more effectively show that man was not the master of his fate; and Euripides attacked the iniquities of the conventional mythology. Yet dramatic representation is essentially personal, and we are at the mercy of our own attitudes in conceiving the background. Professional scholarship in its study of the Greek cults—properly enough for its purpose—tends to concentrate upon the details of ritual. But all the time the Greeks felt the natural coherence of the universe in which they lived, with its unseen forces that seemed to have such drastic effect. They could sense it more directly than we do as they watched their mythology enacted on the stage. We may discern it behind the remarkable speculations of their early philosophers, and appreciate the work of the Sophists, the Hippocratic school, and Thucydides in defining the human problems in closer human terms. But for the evidence for Greek beliefs, and for free contemporary comment, sharpened by wide observation, we should consult Herodotus.

It is an error of method to expect a working historian to write like a theologian or philosopher. One has to look not for the definition of his terms but for their implications in regard to his general attitude. Herodotus comments upon events as they arise, each in its own light. He is sometimes pious, sometimes sceptical, often apparently casual and unsystematic, yet his words do seem to reflect a single, flexible view of the world:

he had a standpoint from which he could consider freely the
obscurities of human experience and look for the signs of divine
power. Let us now try to appreciate the mode of his thought.
The following account may appear too systematic: in that sense
it is contrary to Herodotus' own method; and no-one can be
sure about the weaving of implications. It should be read not
as a strict definition but as an impression of the workings of his
mind.

Herodotus speaks naturally about 'the gods', as any Greek
would speak in general terms, but he does not show them inter-
fering in men's affairs with the individual directness that we
find in Homer and the Attic drama. Indeed, he seems to make
little of their identities and names. The ancient Pelasgians, he
remarks (II. 52), at first worshipped the gods for their influence
without reference to names; they learnt the gods' names from
Egypt and accepted them only after consulting an oracle. The
Greeks, he adds (II. 53), did not know the origins, forms and
functions of the separate gods until Homer and Hesiod composed
their genealogies and described them specifically—a comparatively recent thing. We find here a certain historical perspective
with regard to the details of mythology; Herodotus did not
deny the gods but conceived them as manifestations of divine
power, differently described in different lands: they had their
place in the universe, they should be worshipped for the part
they played, but one did not have to base one's belief upon
detailed mythology. Where he feels there was divine intervention, he does not treat it in anthropomorphic terms.

It is the coherence of the universe, containing both the divine
and the human, that Herodotus keeps in mind. What is
coherent, however it may change its inner relationships, is
predictable by those who have the gift of prophecy. Hence the
pervading importance of oracles in his history: the oracles
inform and warn men who are wise enough to consult them.
That is why Apollo and Delphi have a central place: Apollo

acted through the Pythian priestess at Delphi to disclose the forces at work rather than to determine them. Though the oracle might lapse into worldliness, it served cosmic forces that allowed prophecy (cf. VIII. 77).

Herodotus accepted the implications of historical conditions, whether he was in a position to judge them for himself or whether he had to rely on report or tradition; in the latter case he regularly indicates his reservations. He did not despise the lessons of mythology. Like his fellow Greeks—as we find, for instance, in Pindar—he felt the continuity of experience from the early heroic times, at least sufficiently to cite its evidence in commenting on the deeper play of events (cf. I. 1–5). From mythical times onwards the Greek traditions taught the mutability of human fortune. Assuming that events happen in a coherent context of the divine and the human, their pattern suggests that there is a sensitive balance of action and reaction. It points to a basic justice in the natural order, which continually adjusts itself in compensation (δίκη καὶ τίσις); for—in the terms of Greek philosophy—the universe has a 'harmony of strung tension' (παλίντονος ἁρμονία). If one acts, one disturbs the balance, however slightly, and so provokes a reaction; the swing need not be serious, but the stronger the action, the stronger the reaction. One does not necessarily have to sin to cause this effect. Any great success involves a man in danger, as Solon pointed out to Croesus, in Herodotus' words (I. 30–33). The envy of the gods? It is one way of attributing the phenomenon to a universal order in which the gods represent the unseen forces. This belief presumably lay behind the Greek emphasis upon moderation, i.e. μηδὲν ἄγαν. It does not mean that men should not act: the free man will be true to himself, which is his ἀρετή, his 'virtue' as a man, but he must realize his danger. He may be caught in a web of circumstance, like Oedipus, when whatever he does entangles him deeper. Or he may be faced, like Agamemnon, with a choice of evils, so that whichever he chooses will react upon him. Then let him act, as he must do, but he must expect to be acted upon, to suffer, in return; this is the lesson of experience, as Croesus said to Cyrus (I. 207). It may be regarded as a natural principle: 'if you act, you must suffer' (δράσαντι παθεῖν), then 'learning is by suffering' (πάθει μάθος) (cf. Aeschylus, *Agam.* 177). Men are guided to moderation by their religious and social code.

If the laws and conventions of society reflect the procedure which tradition has evolved to achieve as stable a balance as possible, then to commit a sin against the rules of gods and men is to disturb the balance seriously and incur the penalty: 'no man can sin and not pay the penalty' (οὐδεὶς ἀνθρώπων ἀδικῶν τίσιν οὐκ ἀποτίσει) (V. 56). To act thus in conscious wilfulness is sinful pride: it is *hubris*, which provokes Nemesis. The most telling example in Greek eyes was the failure of Xerxes, a failure which they could appreciate in vivid contemporary terms. The Great King had abused his power: his sin was symbolized in the fettering of the sea, an affront to nature (VIII. 109); and Greek valour, serving the laws of the universe, had made him pay the penalty. Aeschylus in the *Persae* and Herodotus have no doubt of the cosmic significance of the result.

Herodotus shows in the concrete detail of the events how it came to pass. His account is set in human terms; yet his conception reflects his belief that there was nothing of significance in human life that was not part of the divine order and balance of the world. Was the defeat of Xerxes a miracle? It was not, for it could be explained intelligibly in the light of human experience, as the Greeks saw it.

What, then, of occurrences that seemed so exceptional as to be miraculous? We have covered a large field before approaching this point, because the single event must be viewed in context. From what standpoint does one assume a miracle? We should hardly consider our local position as necessarily the central place of judgment, in a universe that contains so many places of relative observation with reference to immediate events, however timely they may be to us. Herodotus knew the shifting balance of things as well as the different attitudes in different places, and he was cautious about accepting both the reports and their interpretation.

The Persian fleet—like the Spanish Armada—suffered heavy losses in a storm that arose just when the Greeks needed it. 'It is said', Herodotus notes (VII. 189), 'that the Athenians, on account of an oracle, had called upon the north wind Boreas as their son-in-law to help them, since they believed he had married an Attic woman, Orithya'; he then comments: 'I cannot say whether it was because of this that Boreas fell upon the Persians', but 'the Athenians still address Poseidon as saviour' (VII. 192). When a Persian division approached Delphi, Herodotus tells us (VIII. 36–39), the Delphians consulted the oracle, and Apollo replied that 'he was capable of protecting his own'; a thunderstorm and a fall of rocks from Parnassus put the Persians to flight. Herodotus comments that the rocks could still be seen; he only treats as a report that the Persians had seen two superhuman warriors pursuing them. At the battle of Plataea the Persians were defeated, and Herodotus (IX. 64) recalls that this fulfilled an oracle (cf. VIII. 114); he goes on to discuss how in the battle no Persian died on the sacred soil of the precinct of Demeter, so as to pollute it (IX. 65): 'I imagine', he says, 'if one may do so about divine affairs, that the goddess kept them out, since they had burnt her shrine at Eleusis'; but the goddess had not appeared. We may conclude that, while Herodotus was sceptical about common superstition, he believed that the holy places of the gods had a sanctity that preserved them from sacrilege, not by personal appearance of the gods but through natural conditions which were influenced by their divine power. Thus we return to what seems to have been his belief in an order that combined the divine and the human in the processes of nature.

G

What have we to learn from the Greek experience? It is a long time since Herodotus set it out in historical terms. Since then we have had the Christian revelation, and science has probed the mysteries of nature, whether in biological detail or in the increasing immensity of the universe. Yet, since as men we still have to judge in terms of human experience, and the Greeks were sensitive, we may well study their reactions. Those who live close to nature will readily believe that she maintains a balance, though urban dwellers lose touch with these things, until a natural catastrophe or the fresh onset of an epidemic breaks into their comfortable way of life. When we abuse our natural resources we pay the penalty of dustbowls and depleted seas. If we transfer animals, insects or plants into a fresh environment, we may lose control of them. By reducing the death rate medical science leaves politics and applied science with the task of maintaining the increased population. There is no act affecting natural life which does not call for complementary action, unless nature is to redress the balance in her own brutal way. Man has gained such a degree of mastery over nature that he must fulfil his responsibility by skill and forethought, lest he suffer for the disturbance he can cause, that is, for his sins against the natural order in which he lives. In this sense we have to respect the Greek conception, despite its simpler assumptions.

What of man himself in his complex modern circumstances? How far does he suffer the reaction of what he has done, powerfully, foolishly or sinfully, in his external relations or in violence to his inner feelings, laying himself open to the impact of outside pressure or of personal neurosis? We are better equipped than the Greeks to understand the conditions affecting ourselves. For, if we have lost the intimate contact with nature, we have a technique of science from which we may learn about the universe in which we live and our relationship with it. If we still feel, in the face of the mystery of life and death, that there is a divine power affecting things from the motion of a star to the fall of a sparrow we can purge our religion of misleading forms of common superstition. As for miracles—if we are at least as wise as Herodotus—we shall not stand upon a narrow viewpoint but examine the evidence in its setting, and then judge the event in the whole context of our knowledge of the universe of God and man.

7

PLUTARCH AND THE MIRACULOUS

BY

B. S. MACKAY

B. S. MACKAY

After a First in Classics at Trinity College, Cambridge, and a war job which involved the learning of Japanese, Barry Mackay spent six years as a schoolmaster. He then studied for ordination at Ridley Hall, and became a curate on a new housing estate at Farnborough, Hampshire, returning in 1956 to the Staff of Ridley Hall to teach New Testament. In 1962 he became a Fellow and Precentor of Selwyn College, and in 1964 was appointed a University Assistant Lecturer in New Testament. On January 3, 1965, after a sudden and very short illness, he died at the age of 42. The obituary notice in *The Times* on January 6th remarked that 'of his scholarship only occasional articles survive'. It is good to be able to offer here one more of these, finished only very shortly before his death.

PLUTARCH AND THE MIRACULOUS

THE PARTICULAR importance of Plutarch for our purpose is threefold. It lies in the man and his views, in the subjects and scope of his writings, and in the date at which he lived. The first part of this paper deals briefly with these three topics. There follows a more detailed consideration of some of the things Plutarch says about miraculous events. In conclusion, some observations are offered on points of contact between Plutarch and the New Testament.

I

1. Plutarch has been described by Bishop Stephen Neill as 'this charming man . . . his writings reveal a great deal of the old-world piety of the Greek village, and an intense ethical concern'.[1] His charm, though it is not a matter for discussion here, makes the reading of his works a pleasure, and helps to account for their great popularity in Europe from the early Renaissance until the decline of classical learning in this century. It is one of the reasons why Emerson was probably right in his judgment that 'Plutarch will be perpetually re-discovered from time to time as long as books last'.[2] His ethical concern, another powerful reason for his popularity among thinking people, is evident throughout his writings, and is discussed more fully below. But the mainspring of both is his piety, to which Neill's *obiter dictum* does less than justice. It is true that Chaeroneia, where Plutarch was born and where he lived for much of his life, was a small town in the rather unimportant district of Boeotia. It is true that for the last twenty-five years of his life he was a priest of the Delphian

[1] *The Interpretation of the New Testament* 1861–1961, p. 260.
[2] Preface to W. W. Goodwin's revision of the 'Several Hands' translation of Plutarch's *Moralia*, 1870.

Apollo. It is also true that his discussion of religious topics is often couched in traditional terms, and that by a careful selection of quotations the impression could be given that his religion consisted of no more than the acceptance of traditional beliefs about the gods and of the value of religious practices, coupled with belief in the basic rationality of the universe, in fate, and in *nemesis* following *hubris*. At this level, there is nothing distinctive about Plutarch's religion; but there are two respects in which he goes deeper. In the first place, his is no unsophisticated countryman's faith, but the reasoned, mature conviction of a man of experience, who had travelled widely, read extensively, and thought for himself. He is prepared to discuss and to defend the religious view of life to which he subscribes. 'We should', he said once, 'borrow Reason from philosophy, and make her our Mystagogue.'[1] He followed his own precept. In the second place, there is something genuinely personal about his religion; it is never merely formal. One senses, for example—despite his acceptance of conventional religious language—a feeling towards monotheism. In general discussions of divine activity he uses ὁ θεός as often as τὸ θεῖον. In considering how divine guidance operates, he argues that God (ὁ θεός) puts into a man's mind thoughts which stimulate the will to action, and strengthens him with courage and hope.[2] The important treatise 'On the Delay of the Divine Vengeance' is expressed in monotheistic terms throughout. But at times Plutarch not only accepts, but categorically asserts, the independent existence of the traditional gods. Elsewhere he distinguishes between those gods who are men who have attained to godhead because of their virtue, like Heracles or Dionysus, and those who, like Apollo, have always been immortal.[3] But if he is not consistent on the question of monotheism or polytheism, on other matters he is firm. He is convinced that Deity is eternal, powerful, able to communicate with and to influence mankind, and, above all, good.

[1] *De Iside et Osiride*, 68.　　[2] *Coriolanus*, xxxii, 6.　　[3] *Pelopidas*, xvi, 5.

Again and again he comes back to this theme: god is a lover of men (φιλάνθρωπος), the gods are good. Stories to the contrary are false. The first major point in his 'How the Young should be Taught Poetry' is that they should be warned not to believe even the most respectable of poets when they say anything unfitting or distressing (ἄτοπόν τι καὶ δυσχερές) about gods, or demi-gods, or virtue.[1] On the basis of this conviction he attacks Stoics, Epicureans, and, most trenchantly, superstition (δεισι-δαιμονία)—that crippling, negative kind of religion in which proper reverence for the gods is replaced by irrational terror of them. This belief in the goodness of God is fundamental to all his religious thinking.

2. The range of Plutarch's interests is extraordinarily wide. The subjects of his essays and dialogues range from the 'Up-bringing of Children' (*De Liberis Educandis*) to the 'Man in the Moon' (*De Facie Quae in Orbe Lunae Apparet*). In addition to theological treatises, they include a number of philosophical works, as well as works on Natural History, the Theory of Government, History, and the Arts. The titles of many of them show quite clearly the 'intense ethical concern' to which Neill refers: 'How a Man Can Observe his own Progress in Virtue', 'Advice to Married Couples', 'How to Keep out of Debt', 'Is a Quiet Life Really the Best?', 'How to Tell a Friend from a Flatterer', are a few examples. But this ethical interest is, in fact, hardly ever absent from his writings. In particular, the 'Lives' are full of it. These brief biographies of Greek and Roman statesmen, grouped mostly in pairs on the basis of similarities between the men Plutarch is writing about or the situations in which they found themselves, were written with the avowed purpose of providing examples of virtues to be copied or vices to be avoided. This ethically based concern with the whole of life, built on a strong religious foundation, invites us to make comparisons between Plutarch's writings and the New Testament, and, in particular, between the 'Lives'

---

[1] *Quomodo Adolescens Poetas Audire Debeat*, 16, D.

and the gospels. There are, of course, many superficial resemblances which are either misleading or valueless. But there is one respect, I believe, in which a true comparison may be made. Plutarch was convinced of the overruling activity of Deity, not only in the lives of individuals, but in the rise and fall of communities, and in the general course of human history. In other words, there is a sense in which his 'Lives' are concerned, not just with the actions of men, but with the activity of God. Because of this, it is relevant to a study of Miracle in the New Testament to see how a contemporary writer treats the theme of divine guidance and intervention in the lives of the men he writes about.

3. For Plutarch is in fact an exact contemporary of many of the writers of the New Testament. Though it is indeed ironic that no reliable biography survives of this great biographer, enough is known from sound tradition and from internal evidence to place the date of his birth at about A.D. 50, and that of his death at about 120. He was therefore writing during the very years when (except probably for St. Mark's gospel) those books of the New Testament which tell of miracles were brought to their final form.

2

The universe, for Plutarch, is rational, and Deity acts rationally within it. There is therefore no such thing for him as Miracle in the popular sense. That is to say, he has no conception of a god who has made 'laws which never shall be broken' for the guidance of the universe, and who then, from time to time, steps in and breaks them. There is not even the concept used by some Christian apologists of a God who from time to time brings into play higher laws not yet known to men in certain cases which appear to transgress the laws that men know about already. What Plutarch gives us is a large number of particular events, some of them of unusual character, in which Deity is present in power to an exceptional degree.

Plutarch, of course, is as much aware as anybody of the difference between normal and abnormal events, between probable and improbable stories. As a writer whose purpose was, in part, to entertain his readers, he often includes a good story even when he is doubtful about its truth, saving his veracity by prefixing it with a λέγεται, 'it is said', or μυθολογοῦσι, 'the story is told'. He insists on the importance of striking the due mean between too much credulity, which leads to superstition, and too much scepticism, which leads to unbelief.[1] Yet he feels that in cases of real uncertainty the benefit of the doubt ought to be given to faith, for God's ways are not our ways, neither are his thoughts our thoughts.[2] He is himself inclined to be credulous even when no theological question is at stake. The tallest story he tells is perhaps one that comes in the life of Sulla, and can be exactly dated to the year 83 B.C. He relates how a Satyr, 'such as painters and sculptors portray', was captured whilst asleep in a sacred grove near Dyrrhachium. It was brought to Sulla, who spent a long time interrogating it through interpreters. It kept silent at first, but at length it uttered a throaty cry something between the neigh of a horse and the bleat of a goat, which so appalled Sulla that he had the Satyr sent away at once.[3] Though this story is prefixed by 'they say' (φασι), the absence of any further qualification suggests that Plutarch inclined to accept it as true. It is not, therefore, surprising that his writings include a fairly large number of unusual happenings that have theological significance. But in addition there are numerous events of a normal character in which Deity is present to an exceptional degree. For the sake of clarity the material will be discussed under the five headings of oracles, divination, portents, dreams, and other manifestations.

Oracles. In view of his connexion with Delphi, it is no surprise that Plutarch fully accepted that Deity spoke through oracles. Quotations of oracles in the 'Lives' are not in fact as

[1] *Camillus* vi, 4; *De Superstitione*, 171, F.   [2] *Coriolanus*, xxxviii, 4.   [3] *Sulla*, xxvii, 2.

frequent as one might expect. Those that there are are mostly both recent and clear,[1] though there are examples of ancient oracles that are said to be fulfilled in recent events,[2] and of oracles that are hard to interpret.[3] There is an interesting defence of oracular obscurity in the *De Pythiae Oraculis*, in which Plutarch, whilst admitting that clarity is an advantage nowadays when people mostly consult oracles on private business, says that in the olden days it was a good thing that some oracles were obscure, because ambitious men, if given unequivocal oracular support, might have become even more tyrannical than they actually did.[4] This essay is one of several that Plutarch wrote on the subject of oracles; it is clear that they were under criticism in his time. Among the attacks on them that he meets are these:

Many oracular shrines have ceased to function, so how can they have been divine in the first place? (Answer: this is due to the declining population of Greece, in view of which the gods recognize that fewer oracular shrines are now needed.)[5]

Oracles nowadays are often in prose, though they always used to be in verse. Does not this mean that inspiration is failing? (Answer: (*a*) fashions change; (*b*) anyway, some oracles used to be in prose; (*c*) and some are still in verse; (*d*) the aptitude for writing verses was more common altogether in ancient times.)[6]

Oracles at Delphi are often in very poor verse, yet Apollo is supposed to be the god of poetry. How, then, can they be divine? (Answer: the priestess, though inspired, is not necessarily educated. The verses are hers, but the message is the god's.)[7]

---

[1] E.g. *Lysander*, xxix, 5; *Phocion*, viii, 3.   [2] E.g. *Lysander*, xxix, 7.
[3] E.g. *Lysander*, xxii, 5.   [4] *De Pythiae Oraculis*, 607, D, E.
[5] *De Defectu Oraculorum*, 413–14.   [6] *De Pythiae Oraculis*, 402–4.
[7] *De Pythiae Oraculis*, 397.

The so-called 'fulfilment' of oracles could be merely the result of coincidence. (Answer: oracles are often far too detailed for this argument to be convincing.)[1]

Some similar arguments are still used by Christians when challenged on the subject of prayer or the inspiration of Scripture.

Divination. Like everything else in Plutarch's universe, the art of divination worked logically. The prophet (μάντις) has his rules, and if he is skilled at his work he can interpret the signs given by the flight of birds or the appearance of sacrificial animals in terms of divine approval or disapproval of a proposed course of action. Plutarch approves of those who give proper attention to diviners, for this shows due reverence for the gods. But his approval is confined to what may be called 'orthodox' diviners. There are others, freelance men, who are described not as prophets (μάντεις) but as mountebanks (ἀγύρται), of whose pretensions Plutarch is scornful. He describes them as 'rogues, cheats, false prophets'.[2] He twice refers sadly to the fact that a grandson of Aristides was so poor as to be reduced to earning a living as a mountebank (ἀγύρτης) by means of a 'sort of dream-interpreting tablet'.[3] In Plutarch's eyes this made him no better than a beggar. But even orthodox divination was no use to the man who approached it in the wrong spirit. Nicias, encamped before the walls of Syracuse, was a prey to superstition (δεισιδαιμονία). There had been an eclipse of the moon which had frightened him, and his usual diviner Stilbides, who could have set him free from such unreasonable fear, was dead. So the multitude of sacrifices and divinations that he undertook after the eclipse was unavailing.[4] Compare, too, the contrast Plutarch

---

[1] *De Pythiae Oraculis*, 399.   [2] *De Pythiae Oraculis*, 407, C.
[3] Comparison of Aristides and Cato Major, iii, 6.   [4] *Nicias*, xxiii, 5; xxiv.

draws between Perseus and Aemilius Paulus. Here is Sir Thomas North's graphic rendering:

> Perseus the king of Macedon, as Polybius writeth, so soon as the battell was begonne, withdrewe him self, and got into the cittie of Pydne, under pretence to goe to doe sacrifice unto Hercules; who doth not accept the fainte sacrifice of cowards, neither doth receyve their prayers, bicause they be unreasonable. For it is no reason, that he that shooteth not, should hyt the white: nor that he should winne the victorie, that bideth not the battell: neither that he should have any good, that doeth nothing towards it: nor that a naughty man should be fortunate, and prosper. The goddes dyd favour Aemylius prayers, bicause he prayed for victorie with his sworde in his hande, and fighting dyd call to them for ayde.

It is only fair to add that Plutarch goes on to quote Posidonius' account of the matter, which is far less discreditable to King Perseus.[1]

Plutarch is well aware of the rationalist argument against divination, and knows how to meet it. He tells the story of the ram with one horn that had been brought to Pericles from the country. The diviner Lampon had interpreted this as a sign of Pericles' future supremacy in Athens. Anaxagoras, however, had the ram's head cut open, and demonstrated that there was a physiological cause for the growth of one horn instead of the usual two. But Plutarch goes on to say that in his opinion they were both right. Anaxagoras had shown the cause ($a\grave{\iota}\tau\acute{\iota}a$) of the phenomenon, the predetermining reason why it was as it was; Lampon had interpreted its $\tau\acute{\epsilon}\lambda os$, the purpose for which it was as it was, and what it signified. 'Those who assert', Plutarch continues, 'that the discovery of the antecedent cause removes the possibility of significance, fail to observe that in doing away with religious symbols they are abolishing man-made ones as well: for this argument against divination applies equally to gongs, fire-signals and sundials, all of which have a significance that is distinct from their antecedent cause.'[2]

---

[1] *Aemilius Paulus*, xix, 2, 3.   [2] *Pericles* v, i, 2–4.

Portents. The diviner habitually deals with certain particular classes of unsought phenomena like the flight of birds, or with phenomena that are deliberately sought, like the appearance of the entrails of a sacrificial animal. Portents differ from these two classes of phenomena in that they are unclassified and unsought. Unusual phenomena of any kind can be portentous. Thus, Cimon noticed an eagle pecking and scratching at a certain mound on the island of Scyros. 'His thoughts in tune with some divine fortune' (θεία τινὶ τύχῃ συμφρονήσας), he began to dig, and soon discovered the grave of Theseus.[1] A litter of pigs born without ears foreshadows the rebellion of the Syracusans against the rule of Dionysius.[2] But the majority of the portents narrated by Plutarch have to do with sacred sites or sacred objects. Thus, the chaplet that fell on the head of Timoleon when he came to consult the oracle at Delphi was no ordinary wreath, but was one of the votive offerings at the shrine, and was embroidered with crowns and figures of Victory. This was, of course, a very favourable portent.[3] There are also degrees of portentousness even among portents. Flaming spears and shields seen in the sky over part of Italy are exceptional, being contrasted with others which 'were of an ordinary character' (χαρακτῆρα κοινὸν εἶχεν).[4] When the severed heads of the oxen sacrificed by Pyrrhus were seen to put out their tongues and start licking up their own blood, this is described, not surprisingly, as a 'great sign' (σημεῖον μέγα)—a bad sign, presumably, though Plutarch does not explain why.[5] Perhaps if Pyrrhus had been victorious this portent would have been found to be susceptible of a favourable interpretation. More than once Plutarch relates stories of statues of gods that have been seen to weep or to sweat, or that have been heard to utter sounds. In this connexion there is an interesting piece of demythologizing in the life of Coriolanus. Statues of wood or stone, says Plutarch,

[1] *Theseus*, xxxvi, 2.   [2] *Dion*, xxiv, 4, 5.   [3] *Timoleon*, viii, 2.
[4] *Marius*, xvii, 4.   [5] *Pyrrhus*, xxxi, 3.

often develop a mould that is productive of moisture, whilst a
break or split in the material, especially if it occurs deep inside
a figure, may make a moaning or a groaning noise. Such
phenomena may well be used by Deity as signs. On the other
hand, it is quite impossible that any object not endowed with
vocal organs could actually utter words, and in well authenti-
cated cases of people who have heard statues speak, it is best to
interpret the experience as a subjective one similar to a dream.
Yet, when all is said and done, the man of faith will recollect
how much greater god is than man, and will hesitate to set any
limit to what god can do.[1]

Dreams. Plutarch shared the widespread belief that dreams
can give information or warning about the future. There are
many examples of such dreams in the 'Lives'. Sometimes they
are described in theistic terms: a god appears in the dream and
gives some instructions. Thus Themistocles was warned by
Cybele of a plot against his life,[2] and Cicero dreamt that Jupiter
pointed out to him a certain young man as the one who was
destined to rule Rome in peace. Next day he saw some young
men coming away from exercise in the Campus Martius, and
among them he recognized the one he had seen in his dream.
It was Octavian.[3] (A different version of Cicero's dream is
narrated by Dio Cassius and by Suetonius.) At other times
there is no reference to Deity; the dream is about that which is
fated (πέπρωται), or simply about what is going to happen. Thus,
Sulla dreams of victory over Marius;[4] Gaius Gracchus dreams
of his dead brother Tiberius, who tells him that there is no
escape from fate.[5] Occasionally dreams can refer to the past.
Latinus' threefold dream about the 'bad dancer who had led
Jupiter's procession' revealed the god's displeasure at an act of
cruelty that had taken place some days previously. The procession was repeated, and the god's anger was assuaged.[6]

[1] *Coriolanus,* xxxviii.   [2] *Themistocles,* xxx.   [3] *Cicero,* xliv.
[4] *Sulla,* xxviii, 4.   [5] *C. Gracchus,* i, 6.   [6] *Coriolanus,* xxiv.

In the life of Numa there is a discussion as to whether there can be friendship and intercourse between men and gods. Plutarch enumerates several alleged examples, including Sophocles' friendship with Aesculapius, which he describes as 'a story . . . which, to the present day, is still supported by much evidence' (λόγος...πολλὰ μέχρι δεῦρο διασώζων τεκμήρια). He admits that inasmuch as the gods are lovers of mankind, it is reasonable to think that some of them might wish for the company of men of outstanding virtue. But there may nevertheless be something in the alternative theory, that men like Numa and Lycurgus, who had the task of governing and civilizing large populations of people who were both headstrong and uncouth, may have pretended to have converse with the gods in order to provide divine sanction for their actions.[1] In short, if a god appears for certain to anyone in Plutarch, he appears in a dream.

There are two examples, however, of a quasi-divine visitation taking place outside a dream. The story used by Shakespeare in *Julius Caesar* comes in Plutarch's life of Caesar as well as in his life of Brutus. Shortly before his death, Brutus on two occasions saw an apparition which described itself as his 'evil genius' (δαίμων κακός). It is described as looking something like a man, but very large and fearful.[2] Again Dion, whose life is paired with Brutus', saw, shortly before his murder, a vision of a huge figure like a tragic Fury sweeping the house with a broom.[3] These stories raise for Plutarch the problem of evil (which, curiously, does not usually worry him much). He is inclined to think that if the stories cannot be explained away, such apparitions will have to be attributed to the jealousy of evil spirits (φαῦλα δαιμόνια) trying to undermine the virtue of good men, so as to prevent them from gaining in the next world a position superior to that occupied by the spirits. But he does not like this doctrine, and postpones further discussion.[4]

---

[1] *Numa*, iv, 8.   [2] *Brutus*, xxxvi, 3, 4.   [3] *Dion*, lv.   [4] *Dion*, ii.

H

Other manifestations. There is one miraculous phenomenon that does not come under any of the above categories: that of the arrival of good news with preternatural speed. The news of Paulus' victory at Pydna was known in Rome on the fourth day after the battle, though no messenger could possibly have covered the distance so quickly. Plutarch subjoins several other examples of the same kind, concluding with one from his own time concerning the revolt of Antonius against Domitian in A.D. 91. In this instance, the news of Antonius' defeat was somehow known in Rome on the very day it occurred in Germany. Plutarch accepts this story, saying that it lends the colour of probability to the others. He regards the phenomenon as a mark of divine favour, but attempts no explanation.[1]

It might be expected that heroes of the kind Plutarch writes about would themselves sometimes show divine qualities of wisdom or insight, or would possess powers of prophecy or of healing. One of the interesting things about the 'Lives' is the extreme rarity of anything of this sort. Alexander, indeed, is said to have been keen on the theory and practice of medicine, but this was due to Aristotle, not to the gods.[2] When the Propylaea was being built, the best of Pericles' workmen slipped and fell, being very seriously injured. Athene appeared in a dream to Pericles and prescribed a course of treatment which proved entirely successful. We are not told, however, that the treatment was anything but orthodox.[3] The only subject of the 'Lives' with a charismatic gift of healing was Pyrrhus. Sufferers from disorders of the spleen would come to him and, after the sacrifice of a white cock, he would press gently with his right foot against the patient's spleen as the patient lay on his back. Plutarch says that Pyrrhus never refused this service even to the poorest or humblest of sufferers, and that he himself used to be delighted if the sacrificed cock was offered to him as a personal gift. After his death his body was cremated, but the

[1] *Aemilius Paulus*, xxiv, xxv.   [2] *Alexander*, viii.   [3] *Pericles*, xiii.

big toe of his right foot remained unharmed by the flames, having a divine power ($\delta \acute{v} \nu a \mu \iota \nu \; \theta \epsilon \acute{\iota} a \nu$). With the exception of this single adjective, Plutarch does not mention divinity in connexion with Pyrrhus' healing gift at all. Though the gift of the white cock suggests that some of the king's patients were putting him on a level with Aesculapius, Plutarch himself is quite matter-of-fact about the whole story.[1] In this, his attitude contrasts with what Tacitus says about Vespasian's healing at Alexandria of a blind man and a man with a withered hand. The Emperor's success on this occasion showed 'the favour of heaven, and a bias towards Vespasian on the part of the deities' (caelestis favor et quaedam in Vespasianum inclinatio numinum).[2] Plainly there is no expectation whatever in Plutarch's mind that a hero ought to display supernatural gifts of healing or of any other kind.

This prompts a further reflection, which is that divine interventions in Plutarch are almost always moral rather than practical in their effects. Divine power is there all the time operating benignly but unobserved in the world, and in some sense controlling events, though it works always in accordance with fate. It is available to be drawn upon through the ordinary machinery of religion—sacrifice, divination and oracle—at any time, though naturally people use this machinery chiefly at times of crisis, or when in doubt about some course of action. The knowledge of divine favour procured in this way gives the confidence by which the action is carried through successfully. Deity itself sometimes takes the initiative in giving guidance or making known its will, through dreams or portents, or occasionally in other ways. Here, too, there is almost always some connexion with great climactic events in the lives of individuals or of communities, and here, too, the effect is almost entirely moral. The gods do not intervene by striking the enemy army with blindness, or making it hear a noise of chariots and horses, but

---

[1] Pyrrhus, iii, 4.   [2] Tacitus, Histories, IV, 81.

by convincing the man who is fated to win that he is bound to
do so, whilst they show the man who is to lose, by means of
unfavourable portents, that whatever he does he cannot hope
to win.

3

In this final section two questions are posed: How would
Plutarch have reacted to the miracle-stories of the New Testament? And—Are there any definite points of contact between
his works and the New Testament scriptures?

1. There are certain miraculous events in the New Testament
that Plutarch would have accepted without question: the
dreams in the first two chapters of St. Matthew, and elsewhere;
the voice from heaven and the dove at Jesus' Baptism; the
voice from heaven like thunder at John 12. 28; the darkness
and the rending of the veil at the Crucifixion; Paul's deliverance
from the viper at Acts 28. 3–6. Others he would have accepted
with some discussion as to whether they were to be interpreted
subjectively or objectively: the Transfiguration, the conversion
of St. Paul, and all the visionary experiences and appearances
of angels. The stories of Ananias and Sapphira, of Simon Magus,
and of Elymas would have appealed to him as examples of
Nemesis.

He would have understood and approved of exorcism,
especially that of the slave girl in Acts 16. He would have
accepted ordinary healing miracles, though, convinced as he
was that illnesses of the mind are far more serious than those
of the body,[1] he might have wondered at the stress laid on
bodily healing in the gospels. But one can hear him asking
questions about the restoration of sight to a man born blind; he
could have echoed the sentiment: 'Since the world began was
it not heard that any man opened the eyes of one that was born
blind.'[2] As to nature miracles, he would probably have been

---

[1] *Animine an Corporis Affectiones Sint Peiores, passim.*   [2] Cf. Jn. 9. 32.

inclined to accept the stilling of the storm, to tell the story of
Jesus' walking on the water with the prefix 'the story is told'
(μυθολογοῦσι), and to question severely the possibility of the
multiplication of bread and fish, the turning of water into wine,
or the raising of the dead to life. Like his Athenian contemporaries, he would have found the Resurrection of Jesus incredible,
though he would have been far too well-mannered to mock.[1]

Hardest of all for Plutarch to accept would have been the
idea of the Incarnation, with its corollary of the uniqueness of
Jesus. To a man of so eclectic an outlook the particularity of
the Christian message would have been the greatest scandal
of all.

2. Editors normally deny that there is any visible trace of
Christianity in the works of Plutarch, and comment on the
strangeness of this phenomenon. Surely, it is said, a man of such
wide range, who mentions Judaism more than once, must have
come upon Christianity somewhere or other and taken notice
of it? Whatever explanation may be offered, it is undoubtedly
the case that no undisputed echoes of Christianity have been
found in Plutarch's works. But I believe that there are at least
two passages which are at any rate worth looking at with a
view to seeing whether such an echo is a possibility.

The first passage occurs in the course of the discussion referred
to above on the possibility of friendly converse between gods
and men. It reads:

> Yet the Egyptians make a distinction which might seem con-
> vincing, asserting that, whilst it is not impossible for a divine
> spirit to associate with a woman so that she conceives, for a man
> there is no such thing as sexual intercourse or bodily contact with
> a divine being. But they ignore the fact that in sexual intercourse
> both parties experience a similar, reciprocal communion.[2]

Perhaps it is not altogether insignificant that Plutarch takes
some trouble to refute the theory that 'it is not impossible for
a divine spirit (πνεῦμα...θεοῦ) to associate with a woman'. For on

---

[1] Cf. Acts 17. 32.   [2] *Numa*, iv, 4.

another occasion he mentions a woman who claimed to be
pregnant by Apollo—a story which he dismisses—using merely
the simple phrase 'to be pregnant by Apollo' (κύειν ἐξ
'Απόλλωνος).[1]

The other passage which might be significant is his long
refutation of the story that Romulus was taken up into heaven
and deified, so that his body disappeared without trace. He
spends two long chapters telling the story, produces parallels
which either suggest a rational explanation or are obviously
legendary, and ends:

> Many such stories are told by writers who improbably deify the
> mortal part of human nature along with the divine. To refuse to
> acknowledge the divinity of virtue would be both impious and
> ignoble; but to confuse earth with heaven is silly. Let us take the
> safe course, and allow that Pindar was telling the truth when he
> said:
>
> > 'Every man's body must follow the way of mighty Death,
> > But yet there remains that which lives,
> > A mere shadow of the life that was;
> > It is this alone that comes from the gods.'
>
> From heaven it came, to heaven it returns, not with the body,
> but only when it is utterly separated and set free from the body,
> and becomes altogether pure, and free from flesh, and undefiled.
> . . . We must not, therefore, send good men's bodies to heaven with
> their souls, for this is against nature. Rather, we must hold to the
> belief that it is in accordance with nature and divine justice that
> good men's souls become heroes, heroes become demi-gods
> (δαίμονες), and that demi-gods . . . become gods, receiving this
> most fair and blessed consummation as their due.[2]

The doctrine supported here is typical of Plutarch, and there
is nothing very unusual about the language. Yet the vigour of
this usually most tolerant man's refutation suggests that he may
be arguing against something more immediately relevant than
the ancient legend about Romulus. Perhaps it is germane to
note that only one New Testament writer describes the Ascension; that this same writer tells at length of the Virgin Birth;

---

[1] *Lysander*, xxvi, 1.   [2] *Romulus*, xxviii, 6–8.

that he wrote avowedly for the interested outsider; that we have
noticed in his writings a number of miracle-stories that would
commend themselves to Plutarch; and that there is an ancient
tradition that he lived to a great age in Boeotia. Perhaps, then,
it is not altogether impossible that some whisper had reached
Plutarch's ears of the things most surely believed by St. Luke.
This cannot be proved. But in any case Plutarch stands before
us as a fair example of the kind of person whom Luke was trying
to convince.

8

THE THEORY OF MIRACLES IN THE WISDOM OF SOLOMON

BY

J. P. M. SWEET

J. P. M. SWEET

John Sweet was born in India in 1927. He read Greats
and Theology at New College, Oxford; spent a year at
Yale Divinity School on a Commonwealth Fellowship;
and was trained for the Anglican Ministry at Westcott
House, Cambridge. He served as an assistant curate in
Mansfield, Nottinghamshire, 1955–8. In 1958 he was
appointed Fellow and Chaplain of Selwyn College,
Cambridge. In 1960 he became an Assistant Lecturer,
and in 1964 a Lecturer, in New Testament in the University of Cambridge. He married in 1961, and has a
son and a daughter.

THE THEORY OF MIRACLES
IN THE WISDOM OF SOLOMON

THE LAST chapter of the *Wisdom of Solomon* contains a theory of miracles phrased in the scientific terms of the day which, though paralleled in Philo and based on a Hellenistic commonplace, is unique in the biblical literature. It is briefly that miracles are 'not a derangement but a rearrangement of the harmony of the universe',[1] after the Greek idea of the mutual interchange of the four elements: earth, water, air, fire;[2] and that these rearrangements take place in accordance with, and to reveal, the moral principles on which the world is built. After referring to the crossing of the Red Sea, the author continues: 'For the whole creation in its nature was fashioned anew, complying with thy commands, that thy children might be kept unharmed' (19. 6);[3] and at the climax of the chapter and of the whole book: 'For the elements changed places with one another, as on a harp the notes vary the nature of the rhythm, while each note remains the same' (19. 18). The marginal note in the RSV admits that 'the meaning of this verse is uncertain', but the general drift is clear enough: just as musical notes always have the same sound but in a melody can be longer or shorter in rhythm, so the elements remain in essence what they are, but strengthen or weaken their effect according to the place given them by God in the rhythm of his wonderful activity.[4] 'For land animals were transformed into water creatures, and creatures that swim moved over to the land [sc. the crossing of the Red

---

[1] A. T. S. Goodrick in the *Oxford Church Bible Commentary* (London, 1917), on 11. 20.   [2] See e.g. Epictetus Fragment 8; Philo, *Vit. Mos.* I. 17. 96–8.

[3] All quotations are from the RSV.

[4] Cf. 16. 24: 'For the creation, serving thee who hast made it, *exerts itself* to punish the unrighteous, and in kindness *relaxes* on behalf of those who trust in thee'—another musical metaphor, concealed by the RSV: the tightening or slackening of strings varies the sound they make.

Sea by the Israelites and their cattle, and the plague of frogs].
Fire even in water retained its normal power, and water forgot
its fire-quenching nature [sc. the thunderbolts in the middle of
the hail, Exod. 9. 24]. Flames, on the contrary, failed to consume
the flesh of perishable creatures that walked among them [sc.
the plague of flies, etc., which are assumed to have been still
present when the thunderbolts arrived, cf. 16. 16–19], nor did
they melt the crystalline, easily melted kind of heavenly food
[sc. the manna which could be cooked yet was melted by the
sun, cf. 16. 20–27].' Then the book ends somewhat abruptly:
'For in everything, O Lord, thou hast exalted and glorified thy
people; and thou hast not neglected to help them at all times
and in all places' (19. 22).

Here is an attempt to hold together the biblical doctrine of
Creation—God's constant physical and moral control of the
world which he called into being out of nothing—and the
assumptions of Greek philosophy, that the world was shaped by
God out of pre-existing matter and runs according to the
immutable laws then implanted.[1] In neither tradition was the
world regarded as wholly impersonal or its laws as merely
physical. Thus the miracles recorded in the Old Testament, so
far from being breaches of natural law, could be held to reveal
the (moral) laws on which the world is built. Discussing the
Egyptian Plagues the author writes: 'In return for their foolish
and wicked thoughts, which led them astray to worship irrational serpents and worthless animals, thou didst send upon
them a multitude of irrational creatures to punish them, that
they might learn that one is punished by the very things by
which he sins. For thy all-powerful hand, which created the
world out of formless matter, did not lack the means to send
upon them a multitude of bears or bold lions, or newly created
unknown beasts . . .'—or even blow them away with a single
breath—'but thou hast arranged all things by measure and
number and weight' (11. 15–20). In other words, natural law

---

[1] See e.g. Plato's *Timaeus* 27D–57C.

is the personal will of God, who made the earth by his power and established the world by his wisdom, but in deference to the Greek assumption of uniformity the author makes it clear that though God *could* have done anything he chose, he has in fact 'arranged all things by measure and number and weight', and the philosophical phrase 'out of formless matter' strengthens the impression of rationality.

Opinions differ on the degree to which the writer took seriously the philosophical phraseology he used (as for example at 9. 15), but it seems clear that to call him *anima naturaliter Platonica*, or, for that matter, *Stoica*, is a mistake. Certainly he thinks of immortality of the soul, not resurrection of the body. But 'wisdom', so highly personified in 6–10, is far from being equivalent to the Stoic *anima mundi*; in the rest of the book it is merely parallel with 'word' and 'hand', a poetic, Old Testament way of talking of God's action in the world. The author is essentially a man of the Bible, and the Bible is equally concerned to deny inconsistency in God and his world—witness the promises in Genesis 8 and 9, echoed in Jeremiah 31 and 33.[1] 'Measure and number and weight' (11. 20) is biblical phraseology—cf. Job 28. 25 and Isaiah 40. 12, 26, a passage alluded to in the following verses of chapter 11. Furthermore, it is part of the stock-in-trade of the apocryphal apocalyptic literature, in which 'historical events are not depicted according to the manifold variety of life, but are methodically arranged under artificial categories of measure, number, weight'.[2] There is a great deal more in *Wisdom* which in thought or phraseology

---

[1] Note the Midrashic theory mentioned by H. A. Wolfson in his article 'Philo on Free Will' in the *Harvard Theological Review* 35 (1942), p. 142, note 58: 'all the miracles recorded in Scripture were created during the six days of creation by the decree of God in agreement with every natural object at the time He brought it into existence (Gen. Rabbah V. 5)'—this from 'a desire to reconcile the possibility of miracles with God's expressed promise to observe the laws which He has established in the universe (cf. Ex. Rabbah XXI. 6)'.

[2] R. H. Charles, *Enoch*, p. 132, quoted by Gregg in the *Cambridge Bible*, p. 112; cf. 4 Esd. 4. 36 f.

is apocalyptic— J. Fichtner calls it *ein apokalyptisches Weisheits-buch*, or more cautiously *apokalyptisierendes*[1]—and it is against the background of apocalyptic that its theory of miracles is best considered.

Though there can be no certainty about the book's date, place of origin, or purpose, there is fairly general agreement that it was written in Alexandria in the first century B.C.,[2] and that its aim was to encourage faithful Jews under persecution, and warn apostates and potential persecutors, by showing how everything works according to God's plan and what the fate of wicked and righteous is within that plan. Further, it sought to improve the Jewish image (and convert their neighbours?) by showing the superiority of their religion and the benevolence of their God in terms of the divine wisdom whose workings were evident in their history. But the main aim of encouragement and warning is one that it shares with apocalyptic; and in addition to the determinist phraseology already discussed we may note the use of a past worthy as mouthpiece, the avoidance of proper names, the frequent references to *wrath* (especially 19. 1, 4), the description of the final *Parousia* (5. 17 ff.), the use of the Sodomites (unnamed) as an example, and above all the preoccupation with the plagues of Egypt (again unnamed). Yet in outlook it is poles apart from all other apocalyptic works except in some respects the New Testament. Dangerous though it is to speak as if 'apocalyptic' were homogeneous, the difference may be crudely expressed thus: that *Wisdom* is this-worldly where apocalyptic is other-worldly, and vice versa. Apocalyptic sees this world as under the control of the Evil One, doomed and without hope, and the end as breaking in from the outside in pure catastrophe; yet it still sees the future in this-worldly terms: resurrection of the body, a renewed heaven and earth. *Wisdom*, on the other hand, sees the future in other-worldly

---

[1] *Die Stellung der Sapientia Solomonis, Z.N.T.W.* 36 (1937), p. 124.
[2] The apparent lack of acquaintance with Philo (*c.* 20 B.C.–A.D. 50) tells against the date A.D. 38–40 held by Goodrick and others.

terms of immortality of the soul and spiritual rewards and punishments after death, but all on the basis of what has happened and is happening in this world—there is not going to be anything *new*; the eschatology is as much realized, or in process of realization, as that of the New Testament.

This distinction must not be exaggerated. It is difficult to talk of life after the Judgment without using this-worldly terms, and *Wisdom* does so too—3. 8, for example, suggests some sort of millenial reign of the righteous—but the main drift is clearly one of fellowship with God and heavenly reward, or the opposite, *without* concrete specifications.[1] Again, *Wisdom's* eschatology is no more completely realized than that of the New Testament. There is clear expectation of some sort of *Parousia*, apart from the description in 5. 17 ff., in the references to 'visitation',[2] 'day of decision'[3] etc., and G. Kuhn[4] has drawn attention to a striking structural parallel between the later chapters of *Wisdom* and the *Revelation of St. John*. But it is doubtful whether every apocalyptic motif is to be taken as primarily a veiled reference to the future. The emphasis of the book is on the past and present—without leaving the future implications out of sight. Certainly there will be a reckoning, but, as in the parable of the Sheep and the Goats, it is on the principles of sifting that the spotlight falls—the scenario is taken over from tradition, and there is no elaboration of the subsequent fate of righteous and wicked.

The matter is important for the interpretation of one of the texts in which the theory of miracles is set out. Kuhn claims, on the grounds of the structural parallel with Revelation 21, that the 'fashioned anew' of 19. 6 refers to Isaiah 65. 17, and that the

---

[1] Cf. the reference to manna in 19. 21 which, at first sight an anti-climax, may be more pointed than it seems: manna is 'angels' food' (16. 20), a symbol of the heavenly rest where men neither marry nor are given in marriage but are as the angels of God.

[2] 2. 20; 3. 7, 9, 13; 4. 15; 14. 11; 19. 15.   [3] 3. 18.

[4] *Beiträge zur Erklärung des Buches der Weisheit*, *Z.N.T.W.* 28 (1929), 334 ff. Cf. J. Fichtner, *Weisheit Salomos* (H.A.T., 1938), p. 43.

author's key concept is the refashioning of the whole universe
as the type of God's future New Creation. It is indeed characteristic of apocalyptic to paint the future in the colours of the
past—*Endzeit wird Urzeit*—and to put an account of past history
into the mouth of the pseudonymous author in the guise of a
prediction. But the emphasis is always explicitly on the future;
at some point the historical retrospect passes over into genuine
prediction. In *Wisdom*, on the other hand, the emphasis is
straightforwardly on the past; it is not narrated under the guise
of prophecy. There is a stylized account of the final showdown
in 5, but it culminates in what is as much a general statement
as a prediction: 'Lawlessness will lay waste the whole earth,
and evil-doing will overturn the thrones of rulers' (5. 23), and
so it goes on in 6, which warns kings to seek wisdom. The
book's appeal is based on the nature of things *as they are* and
their inevitable consequences, as revealed in the past, especially
in the Exodus, rather than on a future external intervention.
So far from expecting something *new*, the author thinks of
continuous renewal and refashioning of the universe by God,
or by Wisdom who represents God's immanent control of the
world. 'While *remaining* in herself she renews all things' (7. 27;
cf. 19. 18: 'The notes vary the nature of the rhythm while each
note *remains* the same'). All of significance has happened in
Creation; the *Parousia* is not something new in the apocalyptic
sense but a seeing of things as they really are.[1]

In the apocalyptic tradition, then, miracles express God's
transcendence over a rebellious world, and are essentially predictive—foreshadowings of the final showdown when 'this evil
age' and its rulers will be destroyed, and 'that age' of God's
kingly rule will have come. Breaches of the natural order—
eclipses, meteorites, earthquakes, famines, especially the marvels
recorded in sacred history—are taken as the pattern of God's
final dealing with this world. In projecting its total destruction

---

[1] 4. 17 f.; cf. 1 Jn. 3. 2.

and the complete newness of what follows, the tendency is to step up the extraordinary. The sun is darkened, the moon turned to blood, the stars fall (cf. the plagues and disasters in the Revelation), while in the new earth one vine has a thousand branches, each branch yields a thousand clusters, each cluster a thousand grapes.[1] The New Testament differs in that a new series of miracles, answering to the prophecies of the Messianic times, is taken to show that the Age to Come has already broken in; the element of the fantastic and irrational is under the control of what actually happened. Miracles are now parabolic rather than predictive, and there is a deprecation of the merely miraculous which stems from Jesus himself, though the final showdown is for the most part still visualized in the catastrophic terms of apocalyptic.

In *Wisdom* too miracles are parabolic—but they are the miracles of the past. They disclose the general principles on which the world is based rather than indicate the presence of the world to come or foreshadow its breaking in. They do not threaten the structure of the world but reveal it.[2] The world is not in need of redemption from outside: 'the generative forces of the world are wholesome, and there is no destructive poison in them' (1. 14). Evil lies in human choice: 'But ungodly men by their words and deeds summoned death' (1. 16)—apart from the one reference in 2. 24: 'through the devil's envy death entered the world, and those who belong to his party experience it.' There is no need of redemption from outside because the immanent wisdom of God has from the beginning been saving those who will be saved;[3] the godless are tolerated for a time in the hope that they may repent.[4] There will be a final con-

---

[1] Apoc. Baruch 29. 5; cf. Enoch 10. 19.

[2] This is not to deny all truth in Kuhn's contention; the author was not averse to having his cake and eating it. The contrast with the N.T. is conspicuous at 10. 21, where a Messianic prophecy from Isaiah 35 of the dumb speaking is applied backwards to the Exodus, to the hymn of praise after the crossing of the Red Sea.

[3] E.g. 7. 27; 8. 1; 10. 1 ff.   [4] 11. 23–12. 2; 12. 19 f.

I

frontation and sifting, but God's judgment has already been revealed in the past.[1] There is thus a genuine evangelistic appeal to outsiders, based as in Christianity on the nature of God as revealed in history, as opposed to the threats of apocalyptic which serve merely to hearten the suffering insiders with the prospect of the reversal of fortunes.

Consequently, though *Wisdom's* embroidery of the miraculous element of the tradition is as bizarre in its way as anything in main-stream apocalyptic, it is all rational and didactic.[2] The whole of creation serves God's purposes (5. 17, 20; 16. 24 f.; 19. 6, 18), both the living agents,[3] the insects and animals of various sorts, and the inanimate elements which on occasion are rearranged by the Creator, like notes by a composer, in order to make his purposes clearer. The water from the rock is given not simply to satisfy thirst or show God's power, but to provide a parallel with the water turned into blood and illustrate the balance of beneficence and chastisement built into God's world. 'Water was given them out of flinty rock, and slaking of thirst from hard stone. For through the very things by which their enemies were punished, they themselves received benefit in their need' (11. 4 f.; cf. 16. 24). Fichtner points out the similar contrasts in *Daniel*: fire, which did not harm the righteous who were thrown into it, slew those who merely threw them in (3. 21 f.); the lions, which did not touch Daniel who had spent all night among them, made mincemeat of his accusers before they reached the bottom of the den (6. 23 f.). But the author of

---

[1] 18. 14–19.

[2] The use of the vocabulary of miracle is significant. 8. 8 shows a scientific interest in σημεῖα καὶ τέρατα, like that of Sir Thomas Browne. Otherwise the words σημεῖον, τέρας, θαυμάζω and θαυμαστός, παράδοξος, ξένος are used almost entirely with regard to the special disclosure situation of the Exodus (10. 16 f.; 11. 14; 16. 2, 3, 16 f.; 19. 5, 8).

[3] Men are in a special position. They are created to share God's rule (9. 2 f.; cf. Gen. 1. 26; Ps. 8. 7)), as his servants (ὑπηρέται, 6. 4; cf. 16. 24 f.; 19. 6), but capable of ignoring him. Over against Platonism human free will is a breach in the uniformity of nature analogous to miracle. Cf. H. A. Wolfson, *H.T.R.*, 1942, p. 146.

Wisdom goes one better. Fire not merely did not harm the righteous, it brought them the positive benefit of a moral lesson (16. 22–28). Whereas the Egyptians were killed by beasts normally harmless, the Israelites were saved though bitten by beasts normally deadly (16. 5–12), and the biting was disciplinary and prophylactic, to remind them of the law, with the antidote ready provided.[1]

God does not resort to the knock-down marvels of popular superstition: the insignificance of some of the means he employs is a mark not of weakness but of purposefulness—the right tools for the job (11. 17 ff.; cf. 12. 9). A second principle is laid down: 'one is punished by the very things by which he sins'— as the Egyptians who worshipped vermin were punished by vermin. It is not simply that a man reaps as he sows: the manner of the harvest is such as to teach him this. God does nothing merely out of love or anger—he always has a lesson in mind. There is much of this in the Old Testament, of course, especially in the Deuteronomistic books, but it is heightened in *Wisdom*. For example, the manna yields the traditional lesson in 16. 26 (cf. Deut. 8. 3), but the author continues: 'for what was not destroyed by fire was melted when simply warmed by a fleeting ray of the sun, to make it known that one must rise before the sun to give thee thanks, and must pray to thee at the dawning of the light' (16. 27 f.).

Finally, intertwined with all this is God's purpose to glorify Israel, summed up in the final verse: 'For in everything, O

---

[1] The author is careful to explain that the brazen serpent did not work by magic: 'For he who turned towards it was saved, not by what he saw, but by thee, the Saviour of all' (16. 7; cf. 16. 12). How it worked is not absolutely clear. 'They received a token of deliverance to remind them of thy law's command' (16. 6 RSV) is probably a mistranslation—in view of 16. 11, 'remind' must refer back to 'they were troubled'—but it still represents the general sense of the passage: the symbol is instructive, not sacramental, and functions by turning them to God; cf. 18. 25, reading ἐφοβήθησαν: 'To these the destroyer yielded, and these *the people* feared' 'these' are Aaron's high priestly garments, which reminded them of God in their forgetfulness. According to 'the theory', plague should be explained as due to the elements working to this effect, and desisting, at God's command. But the author embroiders the Numbers story in traditional Jewish manner.

Lord, thou hast exalted and glorified thy people, and thou hast
not neglected to help them at all times and in all places' (19.
22).[1] The judgment of G. Bertram[2] on Philo holds also for
Wisdom: that he uses the concept of the wonderful not with
regard to the *mysterium tremendum* of the divine rule but against
the background of a rational explanation of the world, not for
the honour of God but for the glorification of the Jewish religion
and its exponents.

What, then, is the value of *Wisdom's* theory? According to
Fichtner,[3] the peculiar charm of the Jewish-Alexandrian literature lies in its tragic destiny, in that it has no continuation or
after-life. Has the theory any future in a scientific age? Goodrick speaks of the author's 'not unscientific explanation of
miracles' (p. 374), and Gregg makes this comment on 19. 6:
'As in 16. 21, 25 nothing new came into being when a miracle
occurred: there was only a transmutation of elements, in some
ways comparable to that which is now suggested by physicists
between radium and helium.'[4] But is this 'not unscientific' or
pseudo-scientific? Do the scientific facts adduced provide more
than a literary analogy? In the *Timaeus*, although it is true that
the world is seen as a living organism, nevertheless the laws
implanted at creation are regarded as immutable; constant
musicianly control by God is an alien conception. The difference here is theological rather than scientific in the modern
sense, but ancient science was theological, and the author was
no more a genuine Platonist than most religious apologists
to-day are scientists, though equally ready to appropriate
phraseology which seemed to support his ideas. He is firmly
rooted in the biblical certainty that the stars in their courses
fought against Sisera,[5] from which the philosophical doctrine
of the mutual interchange of elements is as different as chalk

---

[1] Cf. 3 Macc. 7. 21–23, an Alexandrian work with many similarities.
[2] Kittel, *T.W.N.T.*, III, p. 35, *s.v.* θαῦμα.   [3] *Z.N.T.W.*, 36 (1937), p. 132.
[4] This was in 1909. To-day one might cite the changes of particles described by
Feynmann in the *Listener*, 13 August 1964.   [5] Jgs. 5. 20.

from cheese. Goodrick justly remarks at 5. 17: 'That "Wisdom" had any idea of the philosophical truth that nature does avenge the violation of God's laws is of course out of the question, though common experience might have taught it him.' The flavour of the work is wholly literary and *a priori*. The author is at home not in the real world but that of the traditions of the past, highly embroidered—a fantasy world as much as that of the apocalyptists.

But over against the attitude of apocalyptic, that lying behind *Wisdom's* theory of miracle has considerable value in that it holds together belief both in the uniformity of the world as understood by educated men of the time, and in God's control of the world. Too often these beliefs are held in water-tight compartments, or one at the expense of the other. In particular the religious attitude which expresses itself in apocalyptic is content to jettison this world as godless, and the knowledge of it attained by the science of the day as 'fleshly', part of the rebellion against God which holds the world in thrall. On the other hand, *Wisdom,* in its theory of miracle, holds confidently to the doctrine of Creation—to the goodness of the world, against all appearances, as created by God, to the principle *gratia non tollit naturam sed perficit*, to the immanence as well as the transcendence of God. Certainly the author does not solve, or even face, the problem of the existence of evil in a morally good world, or hold together immanence and transcendence to the satisfaction of the demands of either. But truly biblical religion requires that this doctrine of Creation should be held, and that it should be given imaginative expression. In his determination to see miracle as rational (which of course is quite different from 'rationalizing miracles') he has achieved an impressive literary composition. His fatal weakness is to be living in a make-believe world, not (like the New Testament writers) under the control of fact. His uninhibited exploitation of the traditional Jewish embellishments of their history and his detection of built-in moral lessons in every episode undermines the rationality he intends to establish. Here at least, in allegori-cal exegesis of the Bible, his work has 'continuation and after-life'—*damnosa hereditas*. His main concern is not philosophy but religious propaganda, and the danger of propaganda is that it may spoil a good case.

9

MIRACLE IN *THE ANTIQUITIES* OF JOSEPHUS

BY

G. MacRae, S.J.

G. MacRae, S.J.

The Reverend George MacRae was born in Lynn, Massachusetts, U.S.A., on 27 July, 1928. He studied classics at Boston College (B.A.), philosophy at the Facultés Saint-Albert, Louvain, Belgium (PH.L.), Semitic Languages at the Johns Hopkins University, Baltimore (M.A.), and theology at Weston College, Weston, Mass. (S.T.L.). He has taught languages at a secondary school in Connecticut for two years. In 1960 he was ordained to the Roman Catholic priesthood in the Society of Jesus (New England Province). He belongs to the staff of Weston College and at present is pursuing doctoral research at Cambridge (Christ's College) on Late Judaism and the problem of the origins of Gnosticism. He has contributed articles and reviews on biblical and patristic subjects to a number of journals and to the forthcoming *New Catholic Encyclopedia*. He served for several years as an editor of the bibliographical journal *New Testament Abstracts*. He is a member of the Society of Biblical Literature and Exegesis and of the Catholic Biblical Societies of America and of England.

MIRACLE IN *THE ANTIQUITIES* OF JOSEPHUS

IT WOULD undoubtedly be an easier task to set forth Josephus' attitude towards the miraculous if we possessed the work 'On Customs and Causes' which he projected after completing his *Jewish Antiquities* and to which he alludes so frequently in that work.[1] He constantly defers the philosophical discussion of reasons why to this forthcoming work which, as is clear from the last reference to it,[2] had already been partially worked out in his mind and very likely also in his notes. Nevertheless, we may be able to suggest what was Josephus' understanding of miracles by examining the way he presents them and by recalling the occasional remarks he makes about them in the *Antiquities*. For the most part we shall confine our observations to this work. There is little relevant material in the *Life* or the *Against Apion*, and the series of portents recorded in the *Jewish War* seems to belong to a special category of the miraculous which will not come under discussion here.[3] The *Antiquities* give us Josephus at the height of his intellectual career and freed from the political and other tensions of the immediate post-war period, though certainly not free from a number of other tendentious motives.

Did Josephus believe in the miracles he relates? R. M. Grant has remarked that the problem of credibility in regard to miracles is one that faces primarily 'those who live under the

---

[1] E.g. *Ant.* 1. 25, 29, 192; 3. 94, 143, 223, 230, 257, 259; 4. 198, 302.

[2] *Ant.* 20. 268: 'I also intend to put in writing, in four books, our Jewish opinions about God and his essence and about the laws...'. In this article the text and translation of *Ant.* Books 1–17 are those of H. St. J. Thackeray—R. Marcus—A. Wikgren in the Loeb edition; for Books 18–20 the text of B. Niese is used and the translation is by the writer.

[3] Cf. S. V. McCasland, 'Portents in Josephus and the Gospels', *Journal of Biblical Literature*, 51 (1932), pp. 323–35.

influence of more than one world-view'.[1] This might be thought
a very obvious consideration, but it suggests that to understand
a conflict about belief in miracles in any age or culture we have
first to identify the conflicting world-views present there. There
certainly was such a conflict in Hellenistic Judaism, and in
regard to miracles among other things, Josephus was not entirely
successful in resolving it.

The Prologue to the *Antiquities*, in which Josephus sets forth
his literary project, already reflects this conflict of views. On
the one hand, he wishes simply to make known the history and
institutions of Judaism to the Hellenistic-Roman world (1. 5 ff.),
to vindicate his people in the critical eyes of Rome. The principal lesson to be learned, he says, is 'that men who conform to
the will of God, and do not venture to transgress laws that have
been excellently laid down, prosper in all things beyond belief,
and for their reward are offered by God felicity; whereas, in
proportion as they depart from the strict observance of these
laws, things (else) practicable become impracticable, and whatever imaginary good thing they strive to do ends in irretrievable
disasters' (1. 14).

Josephus' witness to this moralizing history is to be Moses
and the rest of the Scriptures which he sets out to narrate,
'neither adding nor omitting anything' (1. 17). This is a
promise that he does not keep strictly, however, for he adds
numerous details of a fantastic (e.g. the episode of Moses'
Ethiopian wife, 2. 238–53) or a boastful nature (e.g. Abraham
introducing the sciences to Egypt, 1. 166–8), and omits a number of biblical incidents, usually of an embarrassing kind (e.g.
the worship of the golden calf, 3. 95 ff.).[2] There is a polemic
note as well, and it is revealing for our purposes, for Josephus
invites the reader 'to test whether our lawgiver has had a

---

[1] *Miracle and Natural Law in Graeco-Roman and Early Christian Thought* (Amsterdam
1952), p. 182.

[2] A sample list of such omissions is given by S. Rappaport, *Agada und Exegese bei
Flavius Josephus* (Frankfurt a. M. 1930), p. xxviii.

worthy conception of his [God's] nature and has always assigned
to him such actions as befit his power, keeping his words concerning him pure of that unseemly mythology current among
others; albeit that, in dealing with ages so long and so remote,
he would have had ample licence to invent fictions' (1. 15–16).
Not only is there no mythology in the Scriptures, but if the
readers of the *Antiquities* adopt the reasonable and moral point
of view in which Moses wrote, 'nothing will appear to them
unreasonable, nothing incongruous with the majesty of God and
his love for man; everything, indeed, is here set forth in keeping
with the nature of the universe'.[1]

Here Josephus reveals the second component of the conflict
of world-views that characterizes Hellenistic Judaism—the
acceptance of some level of philosophical thinking and the
consequent desire to reconcile the biblical account with it.
Moses wrote in three different ways: 'Some things the lawgiver
shrewdly veils in enigmas, others he sets forth in solemn allegory; but wherever straightforward speech was expedient, there
he makes his meaning absolutely plain' (1. 24). Josephus postpones the philosophical inquiry that might be made and will
confine himself to the narrative of events, professedly forsaking
the allegorical solution as a means of explaining what does not
seem at first sight congruous with the nature of the universe.

If we have dwelt at length upon the Prologue to the *Antiquities*, it was to show that there is a certain ambiguity already
present in Josephus' literary plan because his attitude toward
Scripture is ambivalent, both Jewish and Greco-Roman. The
divine origin of Scripture forbids tampering with it, forbids
even revealing parts of it indiscriminately.[2] But the apologist
must be conscious of his doubting readers as well as of his fellow
believers, and Josephus will not refrain from adding, deleting,

----

[1] τῇ τῶν ὅλων φύσει σύμφωνον, 1. 24; Thackeray compares Philo, *De opif. mundi* 3.
[2] Cf. *Ant.* 3. 90: the Decalogue must not be revealed to pagans; further, cf. *Ap.*
1. 42–3.

even offering rational explanations of some things.[1] Thus we
are led in advance to expect that there will be an ambiguity
also in Josephus' attitude towards miracles.

Providence, Prophecy and Miracle

'Josephus shares with a great number of his contemporaries
of the Hellenistic-Roman world the almost unbroken belief in
prophecies and omens.'[2] The author of this statement, G. Delling, cites many examples in Josephus of prophecy, dreams,
omens, apparitions of the dead, and the like, experienced by
pagans as well as by Jews, which are intended to reveal the
future to men. Significantly, these examples are not confined to
the Bible alone, but some of them are from post-biblical times
and others are interpolations in the biblical narrative. They are
not regarded as miracles, although clearly it is God who thus
makes his will known to men, but rather as part of the normal
processes by which God governs the world. In one of his typical
moralizing reflections on the sacred history, Josephus details
the fulfilment of Elijah's prophecies about Ahab and concludes
that we 'should realize that nothing is more beneficial than
prophecy and the foreknowledge which it gives, for in this way
God enables us to know what to guard against'.[3] Perhaps
Josephus is here reflecting on his own experience as the prophet
of Vespasian's ascent to the imperial throne and of other matters
pertaining to the Jewish War.[4] In any case this experience
suggests strongly that he accepted the prophetic phenomena
as normal.

---

[1] E.g. the longevity of the patriarchs, 1. 104–8. On this question cf. A. Schlatter,
Die Theologie des Judentums nach dem Bericht des Josephus (Gütersloh 1932), pp. 67–9.

[2] G. Delling, 'Josephus und das Wunderbare', *Novum Testamentum* 2 (1958),
pp. 291–309. The present remarks are greatly indebted to this study, which is the
best and most complete treatment of Josephus' attitude towards miracles.

[3] *Ant.* 8. 418; the passage cited is followed by reflections on the superior power of
fate (χρεών), against which not even foreknowledge prevails.

[4] Cf. *War* 3. 351–4, 400–2, etc.

A few examples of prophecy in the *Antiquities* will add some significant details. Josephus inserts into the account of the birth of Moses a prediction by an Egyptian priest that 'there would be born to the Israelites at that time one who would abase the sovereignty of the Egyptians and exalt the Israelites, were he reared to manhood, and would surpass all men in virtue and win everlasting renown'.[1] This prophecy is introduced to give some reasonable grounds for the abrupt command of Pharaoh to exterminate the male children of the Hebrews, but it undoubtedly formed a part of popular Jewish tradition. That this was a revelation of the will of God is clear, for Josephus explains the survival of Moses with the warning that 'no man can defeat the will of God' (2. 209). Another revelation of the future of Moses is given by God himself to Moses' father Amram in a dream, into which Josephus does not hesitate to introduce an apologetic note: Moses shall 'be remembered, so long as the universe shall endure, not by Hebrews alone but even by alien nations'.[2]

The Jewish historian's explanation of the mysterious Urim in the high priest's vestments provides another example of the manifestation of God's will and an open warning that disbelief is but an excess of philosophizing. The precious stone fastened to the priest's right shoulder would light up when God was present at the ceremonies. 'That alone should be marvel enough for such as have not cultivated a superior wisdom to disparage all religious things.'[3] But there is more still: the twelve stones on the breastplate would also light up to announce a forthcoming victory in battle.

Among post-biblical examples, a series of prophecies and omens occur in secular and sacred contexts alike. One of the most vivid of these is the prediction by the German prisoner of

---

[1] *Ant.* 2. 205; for a rabbinic parallel cf. Rappaport, op. cit., pp. 25, 113 f.

[2] *Ant.* 2. 212–16; cf. Rappaport, op. cit., pp. 26, 114.

[3] *Ant.* 3. 216; Rappaport, op. cit., pp. 35–6, has no parallel for this strange explanation.

Tiberius that his fellow-prisoner Agrippa would be freed and
would rise to lofty estate (18. 195–201). This prophecy is
accompanied by an omen, an owl perched on a nearby tree,
which will only reappear as a harbinger of the end of Agrippa's
days; for it is God who has used the bird as a sign for Agrippa
(18. 201). Glaphyra, the remarried widow of Alexander, son
of Herod, was warned of her approaching death in a dream-
vision of her first husband (17. 350–3). This account follows a
dream story about Archelaus, and Josephus concludes the
section with an interesting observation: 'I do not consider such
stories extraneous to my history, since they concern these royal
persons and, in addition, they provide instances of something
bearing on the immortality of the soul and of the way in which
God's providence embraces the affairs of man; therefore I have
thought it well to speak of this. Anyone to whom such things
seem incredible is welcome to his own opinion but should not
interfere with one who adds them to the evidence for virtue.'[1]
The last statement here is a politely defensive reaction to sceptical readers; Josephus seems in the first instance to accept the
dream-prophecies as real events and indeed as valid proofs for
the existence of divine providence.

Thus prophecy and omens are an accepted indication of the
divine will, and in a further series of passages Josephus indicates
that miracles serve primarily as an authentication of the prophet
himself.[2] God shows Moses a foretaste of the wonders he will
perform, exhorting him 'to be assured that his mighty aid
would be ever with him, and to use miracles ($\sigma\eta\mu\epsilon\acute{\iota}o\iota\varsigma$) to
convince all men (said he) "that thou art sent by me and doest
all at my command" '.[3] Samuel proves that his protests against
the election of a king are a manifestation of God's displeasure

---

[1] *Ant.* 17. 354; Josephus' reflections on the miracles are absent from the parallel
passage *War* 2. 116, and this fact may be significant for his general attitude in the
Antiquities, to be explained below.

[2] Cf. Schlatter, op. cit., p. 69; Delling, art. cit., pp. 296–8.

[3] *Ant.* 2. 274; cf. 275–6, 280, etc.; Exod. 4. 1–9.

by prevailing upon God to cause a storm in midsummer.[1]
Elijah prays that fire come down and consume the soldiers sent
to arrest him, in order 'to prove whether he was a true prophet'
(9. 23). The ailing Hezekiah asked Isaiah 'to perform some
sign or miracle in order that he might believe in him when he
said these things, as in one who came from God. For, he said,
things that are beyond belief and surpass our hopes are made
credible by acts of a like nature.'[2] This last passage is the
clearest statement of the use Josephus makes of miracles, and
it is in its entirety his own elaboration of the simple question
asked by Hezekiah in the Bible, 'What shall be the sign . . .?'
Finally, even false prophets are aware that they must be able
to invoke 'wonders and signs to be accomplished by the providence of God'.[3]

The encounter between Moses and the Egyptian magician-
priests (2. 284–7) differs from the biblical account in that it is
even more patently a struggle between human trickery and the
divine δύναμις, and it is not Aaron's rod that performs the feat,
but rather that of Moses himself, as a personal authentication
of the prophet's supernatural provenience. In the *Antiquities*, the
priests, at Pharaoh's behest, are the first to perform, and Moses
then clearly announces his intentions: 'Indeed, O king, I too
disdain not the cunning of the Egyptians, but I assert that the
deeds wrought by me so far surpass their magic and their art
as things divine are remote from what is human. And I will
show that it is from no witchcraft or deception of true judgment,
but from God's providence and power (πρόνοιαν καὶ δύναμιν)
that my miracles proceed' (2. 286). Moses' staff then devours
the Egyptians' staves which, Josephus carefully notes, only
'looked like' serpents.

---

[1] *Ant.* 6. 91–4; cf. 1 Sam. 12. 16–18.

[2] τὰ γὰρ παράλογα καὶ μείζω τῆς ἐλπίδος τοῖς ὁμοίοις πιστοῦται πράγμασιν, *Ant.*
10. 28; cf. 2 Kgs. 20. 8.

[3] τέρατα καὶ σημεῖα κατὰ τὴν τοῦ θεοῦ πρόνοιαν γινόμενα, *Ant.* 20. 168. The parallel
War 2. 259 mentions 'signs of deliverance'. Thackeray points to the New Testament
parallel in Mt. 24. 24 ff.

The Egyptians are charlatans and their deeds deception, because they are merely human; true miracles come only from the πρόνοια and δύναμις of God. And here Josephus writes as a Jew, not a Greek, for as Delling has pointed out,[1] in all miracles in Josephus it is God who is at work, even if he often works through a human agent. In the pagan Hellenistic world wonders are often the work of the men who perform them. We shall see confirmation of this remark below in examining the language of miracle in Josephus. The Jewish historian has indeed accepted the Hellenistic concept of 'nature' and the laws of nature, but he does not regard miracle expressly in relation to these; his Hellenization is not that thorough. Miracles are primarily not so much παράδοξα as σημεῖα τῆς τοῦ θεοῦ προνοίας in which the δύναμις θεοῦ alone is active.[2] In the miracle accounts we have just cited there is no evidence that Josephus himself did not accept them at face value as real historical events.[3]

The Rationalist Formulas

But there are other accounts where it is less easy to determine the writer's own attitude because he incorporates in them what appear to be purely rationalistic formulas. An example of the process may be seen in that prototype of all Jewish miracles, the crossing of the Red Sea, which presents a pattern typical of more than one miracle story in the *Antiquities*.[4] Josephus' account begins with a prayer of Moses explaining the Hebrews' plight, making it clear that only a miracle can save them, and suggesting to God various possible ways to accomplish this: 'Thou thyself knowest full well that escape from our present

---

[1] Art. cit., p. 308.

[2] Cf. *Ant.* 3. 84–8, Moses' speech before revealing the Decalogue. On God's use of signs to show men the way of salvation, see also *War* 6. 310.

[3] Other evidence for Josephus' attitude can be gathered from his readiness to believe in general and from that of his age; cf. Grant, op. cit., pp. 182–3.

[4] *Ant.* 2. 334–48; cf. the discussion of this example in Delling, art. cit., pp. 298–301.

plight passes alike the might and the wit of man; . . . if aught be forthcoming from thy providence (προνοίας) of might (δυνάμενον) to snatch us from the wrath of the Egyptians, we look to thee . . . thine is the sea, thine the mountain that encompasseth us: this then can open at thy command, or the deep become dry land, or we might e'en find escape through the air . . .' (2. 335-7). Moses smites the sea with his staff; it recoils; he then, 'beholding this clear manifestation of God',[1] leads the people across, 'giving thanks to God for the salvation thus miraculously brought by him to light'.

After further description, in which Josephus augments the Exodus details with a thunderstorm (as in Ps. 77. 16-20), he concludes with an explanatory paragraph containing three rationalistic statements which he uses elsewhere in similar contexts. 'For my part, I have recounted each detail here told just as I found it in the sacred books. Nor let anyone marvel at the astonishing nature (τὸ παράδοξον) of the narrative or doubt that it was given to men of old, innocent of crime, to find a road of salvation through the sea itself, whether by the will of God or maybe by accident (κατὰ ταὐτόματον), seeing that the hosts of Alexander king of Macedon, men born but the other day, beheld the Pamphylian Sea retire before them and, when other road there was none, offer a passage through itself, what time it pleased God to overthrow the Persian empire; and on that all are agreed who have recorded Alexander's exploits. However, on these matters everyone is welcome to his own opinion' (2. 347-8).

There is a distinct note of scepticism here in: (1) the appeal to the sacred text, (2) the possibility of κατὰ ταὐτόματον, and (3) the final verbal shrug of the shoulders. These have led Thackeray, for example, to write of Josephus: 'For miraculous events in the O.T. narrative he constantly suggests rationalistic explanations; he is here accommodating himself to incredulous

---

[1] τὴν ἐπιφάνειαν τοῦ θεοῦ, 2. 339; the meaning of ἐπιφάνεια here will be discussed below.

K

heathen readers and to a contemporary canon of historical
writing on the treatment of "myth", but seems quite ready to
accept such explanations himself'.[1] R. M. Grant rejects this last
statement and holds that we simply cannot determine Josephus'
own attitude because he uses the techniques of Hellenistic
romance.[2] Schlatter thinks that Josephus did not reject miracle,
but in such extreme examples as the Red Sea story, he had not
the courage to accept the biblical account at face value when
addressing his pagan audience.[3] Finally, Delling defends
Josephus' faith in miracles even in the present context.[4] If we
are not to reject all the other evidence for Josephus' acceptance
of the miraculous, we must examine these rationalistic statements individually and seek out the motives for them.

(1) Josephus also states that he is merely repeating what he
finds in Scripture in his accounts of the miracles of Elisha (9. 46),
twice in the Jonah story (9. 208, 214), and twice in the history
of Daniel (10. 218, 281). These appeals to the Bible are not
merely an effort to shrug off responsibility for the seemingly
incredible facts, though some trace of this may be present in the
Jonah story. Instead, Josephus seems to have recourse to the
Scriptures precisely to give added authority to his words: 'If
you think I am exaggerating, I have only been faithful to the
Scriptures'. Josephus' reverence for the Bible is clear; it was
mentioned in the Prologue, and one of the passages now in
question (on Daniel 10. 218) explicitly refers to that context.
The *Against Apion* vigorously defends the sanctity of Scripture
and expresses Josephus' belief in divine inspiration.[5] In the
story of Daniel in the lions' den, far from minimizing the sensa-
tional aspects of the miracle, Josephus heightens them by the
addition of details not found in the Bible (Dan. 6. 16–24). To

---

[1] *Josephus, the Man and the Historian* (New York 1929), p. 98.
[2] Op. cit., p. 183.   [3] Op. cit., p. 69.
[4] Art. cit., pp. 299 ff.; we are following Delling's analysis here to a considerable
extent.
[5] *Ap.* 1. 42–3; 2. 218–19; cf. Schlatter, op. cit., p. 59.

prove that Daniel had not been spared simply because the lions were not hungry, Josephus has them fed to satiety immediately before they devour Daniel's enemies in rage (10. 260–1). This heightening of the story does not suggest scepticism of the scriptural version.[1] The important thing, in Josephus' view, is that the biblical accounts make it clear that God was present and at work in the wondrous events related there.

(2) Josephus seems to leave open the question whether or not the Red Sea crossing took place κατὰ βούλησιν θεοῦ or κατὰ ταὐτόματον, and this is certainly astonishing in view of his consistent emphasis on the πρόνοια θεοῦ as the *raison d'être* of miracles. Other passages leave no doubt, however, that the choice of alternatives is not a matter of indifference to him. In a long prayer for judgment upon Dathan—one which follows the model of the prayer quoted in the Red Sea incident—Moses says the following: 'Prove now once again that all is directed by thy providence (προνοίᾳ), that nothing befalls fortuitously (αὐτομάτως), but that it is thy will that overrules and brings everything to its end' (4. 47). Here the opposition between chance and providence is clear-cut; it is expressed in the same language we have found above; and it is resolved unequivocally in favour of providence. It is true that the sentiments are those of Moses, but Josephus regularly makes Moses' views his own. In another passage he attacks the concept of αὐτομάτως directly as a false doctrine of the Epicureans. The fulfilment of Daniel's prophecies has taught us 'how mistaken are the Epicureans, who exclude Providence (πρόνοιαν) from human life and refuse to believe that God governs its affairs or that the universe is directed by a blessed and immortal Being to the end that the whole of it may endure, but say that the world runs by its own movement (αὐτομάτως) without knowing a guide or another's care. If it were leaderless in this fashion, it would be shattered

---

[1] Cf. Grant, op. cit., p. 183. Josephus' moralizing explanation in 10. 262 also supports his taking the account seriously. For the rabbinic parallel to his addition here, cf. Rappaport, op. cit., p. 67 (Midrash Psalms 64, no. 1).

through taking a blind course and so end in destruction . . .'
(10. 277–80).

In view of Josephus' clear attitude to the αὐτομάτως theory,
the statement in the Red Sea story does not express indifference
but invites the reader to reach a reasonable decision on the
matter, especially in the light of the similar phenomenon
reported of Alexander, which Josephus indicates was but a step
in God's plan for the overthrow of the Persian empire. The
comparison is intended to rule out the κατὰ ταὐτόματον alternative.

(3) Finally, there is the frequently repeated refrain: 'However, on these matters everyone is welcome to his own opinion'.
We first meet this formula concluding Josephus' explanation of
the ages of the patriarchs, in the form: περὶ μὲν τούτων, ὡς ἂν
ἑκάστοις ᾖ φίλον, οὕτω σκοπείτωσαν (1. 108); and it recurs often
in the *Antiquities* with a variety of slight modifications, most
often in miracle stories and often also in conjunction with the
first of these three statements considered above. Other examples
of the use with miracles and the like are the giving of the Law
on Sinai (3. 81), the story of Balaam (4. 158), the Daniel cycle
(10. 281), the dream of Glaphyra (17. 354). In other contexts,
it is used with Josephus' refutation of the fable of Moses and the
lepers (3. 268), some examples of the authority of Moses and the
Law (3. 322), the sack of Jerusalem by Shishak (8. 262),
certain circumstances of the death of Caligula (19. 108), and
once in the *Jewish War* referring to the responsibility of the
Jewish factions for their own defeat (5. 257). Since the saying
is not used exclusively in contexts of miracles but rather, in
general, where Josephus makes one interpretation of facts
among several possible ones, it cannot be taken to indicate
scepticism on the author's part. Delling finds particularly clear
proof of this in the use of it in 3. 81 where, if it were an expression of doubt, it would cast doubt on the fact that God was the
author of the Law, and thus Josephus would be guilty of gross
self-contradiction. Instead, it must be regarded as a superficial

gesture of courtesy to the pagan readers who cannot accept the interpretation of the author, an expression of the tolerance of Diaspora Judaism for the religious or philosophical convictions of others.[1]

Thackeray has shown beyond doubt that the formula in question originates in a literary convention of contemporary historiography.[2] Josephus consciously modelled his *Jewish Antiquities* on the *Roman Antiquities* of Dionysius of Halicarnassus, written a century earlier, and in the latter work a very similar formula occurs repeatedly in parallel contexts.[3] It is clear that in the use of this formula Josephus is merely following the convention used by his model and not expressing personal scepticism.

If these apparently rationalistic formulas do not indicate scepticism on Josephus' part, that is not to say that he was entirely free from the rationalistic tendencies of the Hellenistic world. In fact there is evidence enough that he sometimes did choose to explain away the wondrous with some of the ingenuity characteristic of rationalism. We have already mentioned his efforts to account for the longevity of the patriarchs (1. 104–8): among other things their diet was more conducive to long life! Some of the desert miracles of the Exodus receive a rational as well as a supernatural explanation. After obtaining from God the favour of purifying the bitter water, Moses casts a stick into it and bids the people draw off the evil water: 'So they set to work, and the water, belaboured and purified by these incessant blows, at length became good to drink' (3. 8). In the miracle

---

[1] Cf. Delling, art. cit., pp. 300, 306.

[2] *Josephus, the Man and the Historian*, pp. 56–8.

[3] κρινέτω δὲ ὡς ἕκαστος τῶν ἀκουόντων βούλεται, 1. 48. 1, 4; 2. 40. 3; 2. 74. 5; 3. 36. 5. Delling, art. cit., p. 305, draws attention to a Latin parallel in Pliny, *Hist. nat.* 9. 18: *de his opinetur ut cuique libitum erit.* Thackeray also cites the explanation of the literary device by Lucian in his *How to Write History*, 60: 'Again, if a myth comes along you must tell it but not believe it entirely; no, make it known for your audience to make of it what they will—you run no risk and lean to neither side' (trans. K. Kilburn, Loeb ed., vol. 6, p. 71). Josephus uses the device but does not remain impartial to the veracity of what he reports.

of the quails we read: 'A flock of quails—a species of bird abundant, above all others, in the Arabian gulf—came flying over this stretch of sea, and, alike wearied by their flight and withal accustomed more than other birds to skim the ground, settled in the Hebrews' camp. And they, collecting them as the food devised for them by God, assuaged their hunger' (3. 25). Similarly the story of the manna (3. 26–32), but in the incident of the water from the rock there is no hint of explanation (3. 33–8) and the people are 'amazed at this marvellous prodigy'. Again, the miraculous hailstones of Joshua 10. 11 are all but explained away in the *Antiquities*, 5. 205–6.

It is thus certain that Josephus was influenced by a degree of rationalizing, but from the examples given so far it is clear that this was not the dominant tendency of his attitude towards miracles.[1] He was, as we said in the beginning, the victim of tensions between Judaism and Hellenism. He could not have been aware of what seems to us an inconsistency, however, for all the events of the history of his people he regarded as manifestations of God's providence, God working in and through the world, sometimes by-passing it completely to guide his people in a spectacular manner. But in both natural and preternatural phenomena it is the same God who directs his people and for the same reasons. As a Jew, Josephus does not balk at accepting the miraculous wherever he encounters it because what he sees in it are God's πρόνοια and δύναμις. But as a Hellenist, he does not hesitate to offer a pseudo-scientific or pseudo-philosophical explanation as well wherever one comes easily to mind.

The Vocabulary of Miracle in Josephus

A brief survey of some of the words used by Josephus for the miraculous will conclude this study and to some extent reinforce its findings. No pretence is made here of being exhaustive, as there

---

[1] On Josephus' tendency to 'hellenize the Scriptures' see Rappaport, op. cit., p. XXV. One cannot, however, accept Rappaport's generalization about 'die Rationalisierung der meisten biblischen Wunder' in the *Antiquities* (p. XXVIII).

is no adequate lexicon to Josephus available (the Thackeray-Marcus project remaining incomplete). It will be seen that in one place or another Josephus uses many of the usual words for miracle, with some notable preferences.

It seems significant, first of all, that he makes only very sparing use of the word παράδοξον (more usually plural in the sense of miracles), which was a common term in Hellenistic Judaism and, at least in origin if not in ordinary usage, also represented a somewhat philosophical view of the nature of miracles. The word occurs only once in this sense in the New Testament in Luke 5. 26, rarely in the earliest Christian litera-ture, being used with some frequency by Origen. Josephus uses it, for example, of the manna in the desert (3.30), of the water from the rock (3. 38), and of the wondrous activities of Elisha (9.60, to which we shall return presently). But in these citations we do not find the word used as a plural substantive for miracles.[1] Occasionally the adverbial form is found: for example, Daniel's relatives, cast into the fire, are said to escape death miraculously (παραδόξως; 10. 214).

By far the more common word for the miraculous in Josephus is σημεῖον,[2] and this preference is in keeping with his understand-ing of God's providence and power as the agent of the wondrous signified to man. We have already cited several relevant examples (e.g. 2. 274 ff.; 6. 91).

The combination of σημεῖον with τέρας is familiar from the Septuagint and the New Testament; Josephus uses it of the promise of the false prophets in the procuratorship of Felix (20. 168).[3] Hezekiah asked Isaiah to perform σημεῖόν τι καὶ τεράστιον (10. 28). We find τεράστιον again linked with θαυμάσιον to describe the vision at Belshazzar's feast (10. 233). The form θαυμαστόν occurs occasionally, for example to describe the illuminated gems on the high priest's costume (3. 216) or

---

[1] In *War* 4. 238 the word παράδοξα does not seem to refer to miracles.
[2] Cf. Schlatter, op. cit., p. 69.
[3] In the *Jewish War* τέρας is often used for 'portent'.

the dream of Nebuchadnezzar (10. 195). All of these words are rather rare occurrences in Josephus, however.

Although, as we have seen, δύναμις is used frequently in a context of miracles and is along with πρόνοια a key to understanding them,[1] nevertheless we have not encountered any passage where δυνάμεις is used for miracles, as so often in the Synoptic Gospels. *Antiquities*, 9. 60, about to be cited, is a special case.

The most interesting term for miracle in the *Antiquities*—and the one that best fits Josephus' understanding of it—is ἐπιφάνεια (or ἐμφάνεια). First some examples. We have already mentioned the passage in the Red Sea account where we find the following: 'Moses, beholding τὴν ἐπιφάνειαν τοῦ θεοῦ and the sea withdrawn from its own bed to give them place . . .' (2. 339). Referring to the wondrous way in which he has found Rebecca to ask for her to marry Isaac, the servant of Abraham speaks of a 'marriage blest by a divine ἐπιφάνεια' (1. 255). Again, Josephus describes the fire that came down to consume Solomon's sacrifices on the altar as an ἐπιφάνεια (8. 119). In another passage already briefly referred to we find three words used in parallel, παράδοξον, ἐπιφάνεια and δύναμις: on hearing what things Elisha had accomplished, Ben Hadad wondered at τὸ παράδοξον καὶ τὴν τοῦ θεοῦ τῶν Ἰσραηλιτῶν ἐπιφάνειαν καὶ δύναμιν (9. 60).

Such 'epiphanies' are not confined to the remote past of biblical times, for Josephus uses the expression for the miraculous rain that fell when Petronius, governor of Syria, agreed to intercede with Caligula on behalf of the Jews (18. 286). This passage stresses the evidential value of an 'epiphany': Petronius was astonished to see how God watched over the Jews and πολλὴν ἀποσημαίνοντα τὴν ἐπιφάνειαν 'in such fashion that those who were really inclined to think the contrary had not the power left to contradict'.

---

[1] Cf. *Ap*. 2. 167: Moses represented God as 'made known to us by his power, although the nature of his real being passes knowledge'.

On rare occasions also we find the word ἐμφάνεια used in this way. 'And it is said that during the time when the temple was being built no rain fell during the day, but only at night, so that there was no interruption of the work. And this story, which our fathers have handed down to us, is not at all incredible if, that is, one considers the other manifestations of power given by God' (ἐμφανείας τοῦ θεοῦ; 15. 425; cf. 15. 136).

There are a number of passages in which verbal forms of the same root and its cognates are used in the same general sense. Two examples will suffice. For biblical expressions in which the word of the Lord comes to individuals, Josephus sometimes says simply ἐπιφανεὶς ὁ θεός.[1] Secondly, at the dedication of the temple Solomon 'turned to address the multitude and made clear to them the power and providence of God (ἐμφανίζων τοῦ θεοῦ τὴν δύναμιν αὐτοῖς καὶ τὴν πρόνοιαν) in that most of the future events which he had revealed to David, his father, had actually come to pass . . .' (8. 109). This example is not strictly parallel to the others, but it is an important example of the collocation of the key motifs of δύναμις and πρόνοια with the verb ἐμφαίνω. What is revealed in an 'epiphany' of this sort is precisely the providential power of God; in none of the examples adduced does God himself appear.

A few remarks about the development of the word ἐπιφάνεια may be useful in order to situate Josephus' use of it, especially since the word has recently been the subject of some thorough research.[2] As a religious term ἐπιφάνεια is of pagan origin and very ancient. Originally it was meant to signify a personal apparition of a god to a man, but by Hellenistic times it was most often used, in religious contexts, for some miraculous intervention of a god on behalf of man, in short as a synonym

---

[1] *Ant.* 8. 268 referring to 1 Kgs. 14. 4; see also 8. 240; 1. 223; 8. 22.

[2] E.g. Ch. Mohrmann, *Études sur le latin des chrétiens* (Rome 1958), pp. 245–75; E. Pax, *ΕΠΙΦΑΝΕΙΑ. Ein religionsgeschichtlicher Beitrag zur biblischen Theologie* (Munich 1955). The article on the word by A. J. Vermeulen in *Graecitas et Latinitas Christianorum Primaeva, Supplementa* I (Nijmegen 1964) was not available to me.

for miracle.[1] There are many examples of this usage, of which
we may mention one very clear one from Dionysius of Halicarnassus: he refers to a miraculous restoration of the sacred fire
by Vesta, to save the lives of the innocent virgins, as an 'epiphany' and goes on vigorously to defend belief in such 'epiphanies'.[2] Since Josephus deliberately modelled his work on that of
his Roman predecessor in other respects, it is not improbable
that he chose this Hellenistic-pagan term—one which very aptly
conveys his understanding of miracle—in conscious imitation
of Dionysius.

In any case, the language of Hellenistic Judaism did not
commonly use the word in the sense Josephus did. In the
Septuagint such a usage is extremely rare except in 2 and 3
Maccabees. There is an occurrence in 2 Kings 7. 23 to describe
the wondrous deeds done by the Lord on behalf of his people.
In 2 Maccabees 3. 24, for example, with regard to the apparition
that punished Heliodorus, it is said that God 'caused a great
epiphany'; in 3 Maccabees 5. 8, 51 the word is used to indicate
the miraculous character of the fantastic elephant incident.[3]
That the Septuagint might have been the source of Josephus'
usage seems unlikely, however, since it is not generally held
that Josephus knew 2–3 Maccabees.[4] Moreover, most of the
occurrences in these books refer specifically to apparitions, not
of God but caused by him. In Josephus ἐπιφάνεια is more nearly
synonymous with miracle in general. The form ἐμφάνεια does
not occur in the Septuagint.

It is interesting to note, finally, that ἐπιφάνεια in this sense
does not occur in the New Testament or in the earliest Christian
literature; it is revived in this meaning only by Origen, who
defends the miracles (παράδοξα) of Jesus against Celsus with a

[1] Cf. Mohrmann, op. cit., pp. 247–8.
[2] *Ant. Rom.* 2. 68. 1–2; cf. 2. 69. 3. One should compare in particular Dionysius'
defence in 2. 68. 2 with Josephus' argument in *Ant.* 15. 425 cited above.
[3] See also 2 Macc. 2. 21; 5. 4; 12. 22; 14. 15; 15. 27.
[4] Cf. Schlatter, op. cit., p. 54.

reference to 'healings and other epiphanies'.[1] From the New Testament to the application of the word to the Christian feast there is a very interesting semantic history, but it is probably independent of the pagan religious sense which Josephus adopted to describe some of the miraculous acts of God in the history of his people.

[1] *Contra Celsum* 3. 28 (GCS ed., vol. 1, p. 225, line 14). On the Christian usage in general see the works mentioned above in note 2, p. 145.

10

THE USE OF MIRACLES
IN THE MARKAN GOSPEL

BY

M. E. GLASSWELL

M. E. GLASSWELL

Mark Errol Glasswell was born in 1938 and was educated
at the Queen Elizabeth Grammar School, Darlington,
and St. Chad's College in the University of Durham,
where he took a B.A. (Honours Theology) in 1960. He
did research from 1960–3 at Durham under C. K. Barrett
and spent time also at both Tübingen and Göttingen. He
has just completed a PH.D. thesis on the messianic secret
in the Synoptic Gospels. Meanwhile he has spent some
time at Ridley Hall, Cambridge, and St. Deiniol's
Library, Hawarden, and holds a temporary Lectureship
in the Department of Theology, Fourah Bay College,
University College of Sierra Leone. He is considering
the question of ordination.

THE USE OF MIRACLES
IN THE MARKAN GOSPEL

WITH THE decline in emphasis on miracles in the presentation of religious belief has gone a similar decline in emphasis on the gospel miracles in studies of Jesus. The nineteenth-century liberals attempted to explain miracles away either in psychological terms or by similar rationalizations of the miracle-stories. But in so doing they failed to take account of the place of miracles in the tradition and of the religious meaning which was attached to them. This was in part because they attached most importance to that historical development of Jesus' life which the gospels were supposed to reflect. There is still probably a strong preference in some quarters for retaining the miracle-stories in some form or other as direct historical testimony to Jesus rather than first seeing what function they perform in the gospel tradition. Such an approach in fact lays the gospel miracles open to being reduced to the level of 'miracles' such as the one we read of in one of the inscriptions at the sanctuary of Asclepius in Epidaurus which tells of a lame man named Nicanor. When a boy stole his crutch from him he leaped up and chased the thief, though previously he had been unable to walk without it.[1] The gospel miracle-stories were originally intended to tell us more than general truths about sickness, the relationship between mind and body, the tricks of the human senses or those of professional cheats. Though such information has its value the intention of the evangelists was clearly not to provide us with that kind of data.

Form-criticism has told us something of the kind of material used by the evangelists. It has shown us that the gospel material can be separated out into short and independent narratives with their own self-contained form and purpose. We can

[1] See Dibelius, *Jesus* (1963), p. 76.

differentiate simple miracle-stories from other *pericopae* which, whilst telling of miracles, have their interest in some teaching or saying. These latter are called 'pronouncement-stories', apophthegmata or paradigms. But this in itself does not tell us what purpose the creation, use and preservation of such *peri-copae* served nor the significance attached to miracle as such. It may help, however, towards a better understanding of the structure of the gospels themselves. From there it should be possible to see the point of the individual narratives and their contents, at least for the evangelists, who are after all our sole authorities for the use of the individual narratives.

Here we are back at the task which Wrede set himself with regard to the gospel of Mark at the beginning of this century.[1] Since then Bultmann has reiterated, in stronger and more general terms, Wrede's scepticism about discovering an outline of the life of Jesus in the structure of the gospels. If we are willing to learn nothing else from Bultmann, we might learn not to indulge in historicizing interpretations of the gospel accounts before we have first investigated the literary and theological structure of the gospels themselves. This is certainly applicable to the miracle-stories. It is also the conviction of a number of scholars to-day who belong to the generation after Bultmann, some of whom have been his pupils, that in this way we shall also really be confronted with the historical Jesus. If we read the gospels as they were written we shall see the identity of the historical Jesus with the Lord in whom we put our faith and trust. This should be as true of the miracle-stories as of the rest.

The miracle-stories have indeed a very strong place in the gospel tradition. We must find out from the individual gospels what their significance is if we are properly to evaluate the importance of miracle in the tradition. Of course we may have a quite different approach to the possibility and nature of

[1] See his book on the messianic secret, not yet translated into English, *Das Messiasgeheimnis in den Evangelien* (1901, new edition 1963).

miracles from the evangelists and yet come to the same conclusions about Jesus. Thus the way the evangelists present the miracles in the gospels is important. Since miracles fit more easily into a first-century view of the world than into that of our own day, the assertion that Jesus performed miracles may have had in itself the same status for his near-contemporaries as a psychological explanation of Jesus' effect on individual sufferers may have for us. It would be clearly unsatisfactory to leave the matter on that level. The story of Apollonius of Tyana is an example of stories of miracles in the same age as that in which our gospels were produced. It is clear that the evangelists were not thinking of the miracles of Jesus on the same level as that. In comparison with that we can discern a certain reticence in the gospel accounts. The point of the miracle-stories in the gospels does not lie in the mere recounting of wonders and marvels and is above the level of what may be possible given a certain understanding of the world.

In considering the attitude of the evangelists to Jesus' miracles, the work of Mark is of particular interest since the vast majority of the synoptic miracle-stories are based on Mark. Including general healings and exorcisms, there are about twenty-one separate references to miracles in Mark's gospel out of about thirty in the whole synoptic tradition, discounting obvious parallels and the birth and resurrection narratives. The independent references in Matthew (only about two) are explicable as Markan in origin, which leaves us with only one independent healing in 'Q' and six in Luke, including the healing of the ear in Gethsemane. Thus the core of the synoptic miracle-material, as well as formally the most primitive and in general probably the most authentic, is to be found in Mark. The connexions between narratives in Mark is notoriously bald but yet they are built more closely into their context, at least thematically, and according to type and appropriateness, than in Luke, where the special material is fitted mainly into the context of the journey to Jerusalem. Indeed, much of the so-called Markan outline is

L

built around the miracle-stories, except in the latter half of the
gospel where they tend to disappear. The material itself has
more of a narrative style, descriptive and even discursive, than
it has in the more compressed and literary versions of Matthew
and Luke. Yet Mark's interest in the miracles themselves is
ambiguous. The miracles are not appealed to directly as
obvious proof of the claims made for Jesus in the work as a
whole. They are part of a larger picture of the relation between
history and kerygma in the Gospel of Jesus Christ which Mark
is concerned to present. Mark is not concerned simply to record
miracles as such but to relate them to what the Gospel says of
Jesus to show how in the historical tradition we can recognize
and identify the one in whom we believe. As Willi Marxsen
says: 'the healing narratives are not (simply) narratives of
healing but are told to illustrate the power of the faith which
Jesus calls into being'.[1] The healings are not themselves objects
of faith but pointers to faith. The miracles are to be no more
for us than it is so often asserted that they were for Jesus, signs
not portents. They are no more meant to lead to faith in Jesus
as a wonder-worker than they ought to be regarded as, in
Jesus' lifetime, part of an eschatological programme to ensure
good health in the kingdom of God.

Mark is concerned primarily with the Gospel and not simply
with history. His use of the tradition, with its context in the
church's kerygma, serves that concern. His account is not meant
to take the place of the Gospel but to show its origin, basis and
presupposition. The miracles are closely connected with the
Markan secrecy theme in that gospel which shows that they,
like the history, in itself, should not be allowed to take the place
of faith in the reception of the Gospel. The miracles are therefore not even referred to as signs. They seem rather to have the
quality of symbols. They do not point to faith so much as
represent truths about the nature of faith in Jesus. The demands
of that faith remain the same for us as for Jesus' contemporaries

[1] *Anfangsprobleme der Christologie* (1960), p. 42.

though they are now, after the resurrection, clearly articulated in the Gospel in terms of his person. An historical account cannot take the place of that Gospel any more than merely being with Jesus in history was sufficient without the Gospel which followed. Thus in Mark signs are refused to 'this genera-tion'. It is seen as a temptation when the Pharisees demand a sign (8. 11 f.). The ensuing dialogue between Jesus and his disciples about bread, coming as it does after the two feeding miracles, suggests however that there is more to the issue than merely Jesus' refusal of a sign to his contemporaries among the Pharisees. Signs have, after all, to be perceived. No one seems to doubt in the gospel that Jesus performed what we commonly call miracles. That Jesus performed 'mighty works' (*dunameis*) is admitted by Herod (6. 14) and by the unbelievers of Jesus' home-land (6. 2)—though the number there was limited (6. 5). Signs can apparently have apocalyptic force (13. 4). But it is in fact false Christs and false prophets who provide signs and wonders to deceive (13. 22). There is clearly a limit to the extent to which Jesus' miracles are to be regarded as signs, if at all, for Mark. They are certainly not to be regarded as eviden-tial and ought not to be recounted as such. Stress is laid on keeping the healing-miracles a secret, even when historically this can hardly have been possible—see the famous case at 8. 26 where the man is sent home but told not to enter the village. The demon's cries are silenced even after they have been uttered, implying that their present content was not heard or understood by the bystanders at the time as well as that it was not meant to be. Mark is concerned with accounts of Jesus' life as pointers to the origin of the Gospel (see 1. 1), but is clearly concerned that they should not take the place of that Gospel, and that their proper place in the Church's kerygma as part of a summons to faith should be remembered. An account of Jesus' words and actions is for Mark of importance to illustrate the significance of his person in the Gospel, which has Jesus' historicity as its basic presupposition. In this way Jesus is shown

to be both subject and object of the Gospel and in a real sense
its author. This seems to be the point of 1. 15 in relation to the
heading of the gospel at 1. 1. The accounts of the miracles fall
into place as part of this scheme.

The first group of miracles in the gospel belong to a part of
the gospel concerned with the christological question of Jesus'
authority (*exousia*)—1. 22, 27. Decision about the nature of
Jesus' authority seems to be what is demanded of us by the
exorcisms (3. 20 ff.). The source of Jesus' authority is clearly the
Holy Spirit and this is what makes one's judgment so crucial.
This same authority is later said to be given to the disciples in
the context of proclaiming the Gospel (13. 10 f.). The authority
of Jesus is what is at question in the group of controversy-stories
beginning at chapter 2. This is the point of the combination of
miracle-story and conflict-story in 2. 1 ff., where Jesus' healing
of the paralytic is linked with the authority of the Son of Man
to forgive sins on earth. What is to be proved is the authority
to forgive sins and it is this which the miracle is used to support
though it is really anterior to the question of the ability to
forgive sins both in quality and in time. This is clear from the
literary analysis of the construction of this pericope. The miracles
are questionable (3. 1 ff.) and without any independent force
until brought into relation with the Gospel proclamation of
Jesus' authority and then they become kerygmatic. They are
in themselves part of the offence of Jesus' historicity and the
offensiveness of Jesus in history, as these debates show. Yet this
historicity is part of the necessary basis of the Gospel, if confidence is not put in the miracles—or the history—themselves.
The healing of the leper in 1. 40 ff. shows the indirect witness
of Jesus' healings in that the miracle should not (1. 44) and in
fact does not take the place of the Gospel, but the cultus itself
would bear witness to the significance of Jesus who had cleansed
the leper (*v.* 44, cf. Jn. 5. 45). But Jesus' action apart from the
cultus would be condemned historically by the Law. In the
same way Jesus' healing on the sabbath (3. 1 ff.) is condemned,

but it supports the Church's assertion about Jesus the Son of Man (2. 28). The Jewish law can be seen as condemning Jesus or witnessing to his authority. There remains a choice for the hearers of the Gospel from which neither history nor miracle absolves us. The accounts with which Mark presents us illustrate that choice and show us the historical identity of the one in whom we are asked to believe. His identity for faith remains a matter for personal decision. The challenge of Jesus to his contemporaries is renewed in the kerygma and the nature of that challenge is proclaimed in the Gospel. The theme of the messianic secret stands over against false approaches to history or miracle which would preclude the choice of faith and forget that this is based on the Gospel and not on anything to do with the history itself.

The nature and necessity of faith is the point of the next group of miracles beginning at 4. 35. For 'those without' (i.e. outside a faith relationship with Jesus in acceptance of the word of the Gospel) everything is a riddle (cf. 4. 11). The clue to this is found only in the identity of Jesus, who is the one who calls faith into being and answers it. This was not recognized historically by the disciples (4. 35 ff.). In 5. 21 ff. we have two parables of faith, but it is not belief in the miracles that is required. The effect on Jesus' fellow-countrymen of news of his mighty works is one of offence (6. 2 f.). A purely historical knowledge of Jesus is shown to be insufficient. Faith is required, even for the proper perception of a miracle (see 6. 5 f.). Mighty works depend on faith and can have no meaning apart from faith. Thus again the miracles are not to be spread abroad (5. 43 —historically, of course, this command is impossible). Once more, we see that Mark's treatment of the miracles is in line with his understanding of the relation between the historical tradition and the Gospel. Mark is not concerned with Jesus' historical identification as the Christ, nor with the miracles as evidence for this, but with Jesus' identification as the Christ for faith, as he is proclaimed in the Gospel, and with the miracle-stories as illustrations of this. This is the point of the passage which closes this collection of miracle-stories in Mark (6. 5 f.). It is not meant as a purely historical remark on that level as an explanation of why there were few miracles, as Matthew understands it (Mt. 13. 58). Throughout Mark's gospel we reckon with Jesus' historicity as the necessary precondition for the Gospel, with the questionable character of that historicity in itself, and with the articulation of the significance of Jesus for faith which is provided by the kerygma in terms of the Gospel. It is this alone which will provide a proper answer about Jesus' identity and authority when accepted in faith, and not his mighty works (see 6. 14 f.).

At 8. 27 ff. we are given an answer to the question about Jesus' identity and authority only to have it denied prior to the passion. Who and what Jesus is can only be proclaimed after the Resurrection of the Son of Man (9. 9). Meanwhile the passion puts the supreme question mark against the historical Jesus which only the post-Resurrection Gospel can explain but not remove. This section is prepared for by an intermediate section which highlights the difficulty of passing from Jesus' mighty works to awareness of his identity and belief in his person. Mark has developed this section around two parallel feeding miracles (6. 35 ff.; 8. 1 ff.). These are then brought together in their theological significance in a composite passage at the end (8. 11 ff.). The significance of the section is indicated by the two parallel healing miracles in 7. 32 ff. and 8. 22 ff., and the point of the section is illustrated in the incident in 6. 47 ff. 6. 52 provides a link with 8. 11 ff. Its association with the preceding pericope shows that its point, as well as the point of 8. 11 ff., is the disciples' inability to grasp the significance of Jesus whom on any other level they know very well. The relation of the feeding miracles (though they are never called *dunameis*) to the question of signs now becomes clear, though they are associated with it in 8. 11 ff. in an obviously secondary manner by means of the obscure and independent saying found at 8. 15. The disciples' failure to understand the saying is connected directly with their failure to perceive the meaning of the feeding miracles. The Pharisees' request for a sign provides us with the point of this discussion. The feeding miracles are not to be explained naturally or eschatologically, but christologically. They may have had eschatological significance for Jesus, but for Mark the point is that the real sign, the presence of Jesus, was not perceived. Jesus as the dispenser of bread was to be seen as the one who answered man's need (cf. also 7. 27–30). He would also open blind eyes and deaf ears and call forth faith in his person. But it is clear that the historical situation was not the context in which this could be done. Only later would it be possible to look back and recognize in Jesus the Lord and the Christ.

The remainder of the gospel develops further the theme of the relation between history and the Gospel and points forward to the Gospel beyond the history through the passion. In this part there is much less interest in miracles and there are only three, each of which reminds one of the requirements of faith (9. 19, 22–24; 10. 52; 11. 22–24). The last miracle would seem also to have a parabolic meaning concerned with Jesus' authority because of its close connexion in Mark with the cleansing of the temple, the question about Jesus' authority, and the parable of the vineyard. Each of the stories is concerned, however, with the significance of Jesus' person.

Mark is clearly not so much concerned about the historical status of miracles, whether they actually happened—though he would seem to have no difficulty in stating that they did—as with the question of faith in Jesus as he is proclaimed in the Gospel. He uses accounts of miracles to show the nature of that faith. They clearly cannot be used to make the decision of faith unnecessary. Jesus himself clearly did not perform them merely as external phenomena or as the proof of the truth of his message. They can be recounted, like the healing of the paralytic, to illustrate something about Jesus' authority which the

Church believes. The most that can be said is that they indicate the historical identity of the one in whom one is asked to believe. But in themselves they do not demand a particular conclusion about Jesus, nor do they dispel the offence of his person in history. They do not make faith easy. It is not forbidden to speak of them because they would demand faith rather than leave it as a free decision. The commands not to speak of the miracles are there to prevent any false reliance on historical or miraculous proof for the Church's faith in Jesus.[1] This is shown by the fact that in the gospel the miracles can occur in a context of offence and be accompanied by lack of belief and understanding.

The fact that the so-called messianic secret is closely connected with the miracles, either in the shape of commands to silence or lack of understanding, is significant. This is to be connected with the assertion that the miracles are not compelling signs.[2] The activity of Jesus and the *dunamis* he displayed is seen, however, as implying questions about his *exousia*, the authority lying behind his acts of power (see Mk. 1. 22, 27; 11. 27 ff.; 6. 14). The answer to the source of Jesus' power is to be found in the work of the Holy Spirit (see Mk. 3. 29). The exorcisms demonstrate what was proclaimed at the Baptism and repeated at the Transfiguration that Jesus is the Son of God. But the evidence is ambiguous. As Barrett says (op. cit., p. 92): 'to the eye-witnesses (i.e. the disciples) the miracles are not revelation'. On p. 157, Barrett makes reference too to the unreliability of an appeal to a miracle-worker in the ancient world and on p. 158 he adduces the rabbinic background for distrust of the evidence of miracles. It is clear that for Mark the miracles did not compel belief in Jesus and ought not now be used as if they might. The element of secrecy belongs to more than the circumstances of Jesus' life, i.e. more than Jesus' own

---

[1] Cf. E. Schweizer, 'Mark's contribution to the quest of the historical Jesus', *J.N.T.S* 10. 4 (1964), p. 423.

[2] Cf. C. K. Barrett, *The Holy Spirit and the Gospel Tradition* (1947, 1954), p. 159.

intention or the needs of an eschatologically-orientated messianic secret. What is involved is the whole issue of belief in Jesus as Messiah, Son of God, Son of Man, as proclaimed by the post-Resurrection Gospel (see 9. 9), set against history and Jesus' own eschatological preaching and activity, which history has put in question. The miracles which may then have had significance as eschatological signs now have their significance in relation to the person of the miracle-worker himself. The eschatological emphasis of Jesus' preaching and activity has become christological in the service of the Gospel. This is what has happened in the preaching of the Church. Thus Mark's work, in its apparent reflection back on Jesus' life, making use of the Church's kerygmatic tradition, must illustrate the identity of the one proclaimed but not make a false appeal to history to demonstrate the truth of the Gospel. A real relation, however, is shown between the historical Jesus, whose historicity is a necessary precondition of the Gospel, and the Gospel itself. Mark's use of the miracle-stories reflects this concern and illustrates the proper relation between history and the Gospel.

Thus the shape of Mark's work reveals his concern with the historical Jesus, but it is clear that he is aware that it is not the historical Jesus as such which the Gospel proclaims. The relation between the two is more complex. The Church's christology answers the questions raised by Jesus' life and his own relationship with his message and its expression in word and act. But the answer does not come directly from Jesus' life itself. The signs of the kingdom have become signs for faith in Jesus. The theme of the messianic secret is an inner necessity of Mark's presentation of this development in terms of an account of the historical Jesus, if it is not a necessary part of the history itself. Jesus himself is the sole sign of the Gospel as well as of the kingdom of God (cf. Dibelius, op. cit., p. 81),[1] and an

---

[1] It is in this sense, in reflection back on Jesus' life and message, that we accept the truth of the words of Kümmel (*Promise and Fulfilment* (1957), p. 155). Jesus is the sign of the kingdom he proclaimed and its guarantee—but that is the mystery of the kingdom proclaimed by the Gospel.

account of his words and deeds cannot take his place, or be the equivalent of the preaching of the Gospel and its reception in faith. Of this Mark seems well aware, and in accordance with this he looks back to the *arche* (origin) of the Gospel in Jesus of Nazareth. Mark's gospel is in this sense the gospel of the signs of Jesus.[1] The miracle-stories belong to the earliest tradition but cannot take the place of the one to whom they witness. We are not to ask for a miracle or a sign apart from Jesus himself, grasped and met by faith. Even the Resurrection does not appear in Mark as a well-attested miracle in history. The sole sign of the Resurrection is the risen Jesus seen once more in Galilee—not the empty tomb. That the tomb was empty only has meaning if one meets the risen Jesus in faith. Miracles are what happens when one believes in Jesus, and it is faith in Jesus which truly perceives a miracle and by that faith that the miracle becomes a sign.

[1] Cf. W. Manson, *Jesus the Messiah* (1943), p. 34.

11

MIRACLES IN
THE ACTS OF THE APOSTLES

BY

G. W. H. LAMPE

G. W. H. LAMPE

G. W. H. Lampe, D.D. (Oxon.), HON. D.D. (Edinburgh), F.B.A., is Ely Professor of Divinity in the University of Cambridge, Fellow of Gonville and Caius College, Canon of Ely Cathedral, and Honorary Canon of Birmingham Cathedral. He was educated at Blundell's School and Exeter College, Oxford; trained for the Anglican Ministry at the Queen's College, Birmingham; and was ordained in 1937 to a curacy at Okehampton. He was Assistant Master at King's School, Canterbury, 1938–41; Chaplain to the Forces, 1941–5 (awarded the M.C., 1945); Fellow and Chaplain of St. John's College, Oxford, 1943–53; Professor of Theology at Birmingham University, 1953–9, Dean of the Faculty of Arts, 1955–9, Vice-Principal, 1957–60. He is well known for many publications, including *The Seal of the Spirit* (1951), and as Editor of the *Patristic Greek Lexicon*. He is married and has two children.

MIRACLES IN
THE ACTS OF THE APOSTLES

ONE OF THE most tiresome features of a certain kind of Christian apologetic, common in the Church from the second century onwards, is a tendency to assume that the truth of Christian doctrine may be proved by the ability of believers to perform apparently impossible feats. This assumption colours the more popular literature, such as the apocryphal Gospels and Acts, and not a few of the acts of the martyrs; it is widely prevalent among Church historians (though with important differences) and one might easily gain the impression from Bede that the evangelization of this country was carried out, to no small extent, by a series of conjuring tricks. Thus, when St. Peter, according to the *Acta Petri*, was engaged in his conflict with Simon Magus at Rome, he won his greatest triumph by throwing a sardine into a swimming bath and causing it to swim: and to continue swimming for a long time, lest it should be alleged that he had momentarily deluded the people. Seeing the sardine actually swimming and, so far from being a phantasm, real and solid enough to eat bread thrown to it, many of the people believed in the Lord. It seems probable that the composer of the longer ending of Mark may have shared this assumption about the evidential value of miracles. Did Luke share it too?

Certain features of his second volume suggest, at least at first sight, that his attitude is not very far removed from that of the popular literature of the second and following centuries. 'Signs and wonders' appear in Mark and Matthew only in that part of the Markan Apocalypse which deals with false messiahs and false prophets. The Fourth Gospel does not think well of those who will not believe unless they see signs and wonders. Luke, however, has no hesitation in making *semeia kai terata* a very prominent feature of Acts. When we read, for instance, that 'through the hands of the apostles many signs and wonders took place among the people' and that 'the people magnified them', we may well imagine that we are already on the way to the kind of 'miracle-apologetic' which dominates the apocryphal Acts and so much else in later Christian literature.

Luke's point of view, however, is really somewhat different from this, though it is by no means always easy to draw a clear line of distinction. It is not that of a writer describing the incredible performances of Hellenistic wonder-workers. It is much closer to that of the Old Testament, and especially Deuteronomy, the Deuteronomic Psalms and the prophets. To these writers 'signs and wonders' are the manifest operations of God, his mighty works for the salvation of his people. 'Thou shalt remember . . . the signs and the wonders, and the mighty hand and the stretched out arm, whereby the Lord thy God brought thee out.' 'The Lord brought us out of Egypt with a mighty hand; and the Lord showed signs and wonders, great and sore, upon Egypt, upon Pharaoh, and upon all his house, before our eyes.' 'Signs and wonders' attest the Lordship of Yahweh. They are at the same time the visible modes of his saving work for Israel: mighty works of redemption for his people and of destruction for his enemies. So, too, a prophetic sign, such as Isaiah walking naked and barefoot, is a sign and a wonder upon Egypt (Is. 20. 3). Signs and wonders are thus not external to God's work of salvation and judgment. They are not conjuring tricks, designed to induce belief in God but basically irrelevant to God's saving acts, as Peter's sardine was essentially irrelevant to the gospel (although the competition between Moses and the magicians of Egypt does fall almost, if not quite, into that class). Rather, for the most part, they are focal points at which the continuous activity of God becomes manifest both to his people and to their oppressors. Except in folk-tales, it is perhaps worth noticing, the great and spectacular wonders in which God's judgment and mercy are declared in action are usually assigned to certain supreme turning-points in Israel's history, especially to the remote past of the Exodus and the conquest of Canaan. Luke's conception of the purpose of miracles seems to be largely determined by the Old Testament.

It is never very profitable to consider Acts in isolation from the Third Gospel, but as the latter falls outside the scope of this essay, no more than brief remarks can be made about it here. In his treatment of the birth, calling and ministry of Jesus, Luke lays considerable stress on certain features which are also emphasized, but with scarcely so much consistency, by the other synoptists.

One of these is *dynamis*, with its close association with the concept of the divine Spirit. God had anointed Jesus with Holy Spirit and power. This meant that God was with him and that his ministry could therefore be summed up in terms of beneficence, and of healing those who were under the tyranny of the devil (Acts 10. 38). This reference to the anointing of Jesus looks back to his proclamation in the synagogue at Nazareth which sets the keynote for the whole story contained in Luke-Acts and determines the importance and the significance of the miracles recorded in both volumes. The age of fulfilment is at hand, and its characteristic manifestations are to be the release of captives (like the woman whom Satan had bound for eighteen years), the recovery of sight by the blind, and the liberation of the bruised. In Jesus the power of God is at work; this is attested by his miracles. Jesus is a man attested by God in works of power (*dynameis*, the concrete expression of the *dynamis* that has been bestowed upon him), in wonders and signs. They are God's operation through him: the *dynamis* of God was with him for healing (Lk. 5. 17).

It is the divine *dynamis* which is the source of the authority of Jesus; and Luke lays particular stress on this, especially on the power of his word. 'What is this word? for with authority and power he commandeth the unclean spirits, and they come out' (Lk. 4. 36). On many occasions the power and authority of his word is specially noted by Luke. Thus the fever of Simon's mother-in-law is *rebuked*, like a demon, and the patient *immediately* rises at the word of Jesus, without physical contact with him. The dead man at Nain is raised by the spoken word; the ten lepers find themselves cleansed after Jesus has spoken to them from far off. The centurion never comes face to face with Jesus. Here, other motives help to determine the Lukan form of the story: Jesus does not have direct dealings with Gentiles in the pre-Resurrection period, and it is through the mediation of Jewish elders that communication is established between this Gentile and Jesus in the first instance. Luke seems to have made an artificial reconstruction of the tradition and to have failed to carry it through to the end of the story, for the phrase 'Jesus marvelled at him' ('at him' is not paralleled in Matthew) strongly suggests that at this point the centurion is present in person. One effect of this treatment is to heighten the centurion's confidence in the authority of the uttered word of Jesus, especially if the non-Western textual tradition is right and we should include the words 'wherefore neither did I think myself worthy to come to you' (Lk. 7. 7).

Luke always tends to associate works of healing very closely with the ministry of the word: the teaching of Jesus and his proclamation of the Kingdom. This is shown explicitly in such a passage as 5. 15, where we are told that the crowds came together to hear and be healed, and it is perhaps also implied in Luke's picture of the Gerasene demoniac not merely 'sitting' as in Mark (that is, restored to calm sobriety) but sitting 'at the feet' of Jesus (that is, as a disciple listening to him). Hence Jesus, as the bearer of God's word and as empowered by his Spirit, is a prophet; indeed, the great prophet (cf. 7. 39), like Moses (Lk. 24. 19; cf. Acts 7. 22; 3. 22 ff.; 7. 37), like Elijah (especially in the raising of the widow's son), and like the prophet of Isaiah 61 whose commissioning furnishes the text for his own ministry. The mighty works are a decisive and challenging sign to Israel: thus the healing of the paralytic takes place in the midst of a formal assembly of Pharisees and teachers of the Law gathered from all Galilee, Judaea and Jerusalem. Miracle-stories occasionally supply no more than occasions for pronouncements concerning the narrow legalism of contemporary Judaism which blinds it to the needs of the outcasts. The woman with a spirit of infirmity is a daughter of Abraham, who is, by implication, being treated like an outcast; the man with dropsy affords a text, as it were, for a renewed condemnation of this obstructive legalism; and the story of the ten lepers is also told not so much for the intrinsic importance of the healing as for the implied teaching that an outcast is praised for his response to God's act through Jesus whereas the Jews are condemned for their failure to turn back to God as a result of the ministry of Jesus.

The miracles are sometimes, in anticipation of the second volume, closely associated with the commissioning of the apostles. The miraculous catch of fish is an acted sign which reinforces and illuminates the Markan promise that the disciples will catch men; it also declares Peter's leadership in the apostolic mission. Just as the narrative of Pentecost sums up in a dramatic form the whole story of the Church's mission as this is to be unfolded in the rest of the Book of Acts, so the story of the miraculous catch of fish embodies in a single episode the commissioning of the apostles and their subsequent achievement. It is probably by design that Luke sets the mission of the Twelve, not in Mark's context of the rejection at Nazareth, but directly after the great miracle of resurrection (the raising of Jairus' daughter), at a moment of triumph rather than after a decisive reverse, just as the explanation of Jesus' own mission, given to John's envoys, follows immediately upon the resurrection at Nain.

Yet the divine power is at work, in a sense, only proleptically in the pre-Resurrection ministry of Jesus. In his messianic anointing with Holy Spirit and power, and in the operation of that power in his mighty acts, the age of fulfilment is anticipated; but all this was but a foretaste of what was to follow

M

when Jesus had been 'taken up'. The Johannine saying, 'He who believes in me, the works which I do shall he do also, and greater things than these shall he do, because I am going to the Father', expresses very clearly Luke's conception of the relation of the works done by Jesus in his ministry to the signs and wonders performed in his name after his ascension. It is as concise a summary of a central Lukan theme as is that other Johannine comment, 'Spirit was not yet because Jesus was not yet glorified'. Though Jesus had been attested by God by signs and wonders done publicly, and though he had been proclaimed at his birth to be 'saviour', 'Messiah', and 'Lord', he was made 'Lord' and 'Messiah' when, through suffering, he entered into his glory; thenceforth there is 'salvation' in none else and no other name in which we must be saved.

The true beginning of the new age, in the sense of the time when the fulfilment of the prophetic hopes becomes manifest, is therefore the Ascension and its counterpart at Pentecost. This is the moment for which the apostles had been told to wait: the promised endowment with power, through the coming upon them of the Holy Spirit, for the mission of witness to the end of the earth. The time of the final consummation of the Kingdom rests in the authority of the Father; and Luke always implies that it lies far ahead. But the period of the world-wide mission of the Church is itself part of the last days foretold in the prophecy of Joel. Like the age of the Exodus, the wilderness and the entry into the Promised Land, these are times of God's manifestation of 'signs and wonders, the mighty hand and the stretched out arm'. The divine *dynamis* is mediated through, or perhaps, rather, guaranteed by, the *name* of the exalted Lord. The preaching of the apostolic witnesses, that is the proclamation of repentance and remission of sins, is in his name. To the spoken word there corresponds the visible manifestation of the gospel in 'mighty works, signs and wonders', somewhat in the way in which the prophetic signs in ancient Israel were related to the uttered word of the Lord. God works mightily through the name of Jesus the Messiah. This divine activity, in its powerful impact through word and sign, is the Spirit, the witness to Christ who speaks and acts through the missionaries, proclaiming and attesting the gospel (cf. Lk. 12. 12).

Miracles are, therefore, in Luke's understanding of the matter, part and parcel of the entire mission of witness. The whole is miraculous, in so far as it is a continuous mighty work of God. By the divine power the gospel is preached, converts are made, the Church is established in unity and brotherhood, the opposing powers, whether human or demonic, are conquered, persecution, of which, certainly, much has to be endured, is turned to good account for the furtherance of the gospel, and judgment overtakes the persecutors. The whole mission, as Luke looks back on its early history in the light of his theological interpretation, is seen in terms of miracle: that is to say, as effected by supernatural power, whether in the guidance given to the missionaries, in their dramatic release from prison or deliverance from enemies or shipwreck, or in the signs of healing and raising from the dead which attest the message of the witness given in Christ's name. It is, consequently, difficult to pick out the miraculous from the non-miraculous in Luke's story. Nevertheless, in the course of his impressionistic and 'supernaturalized' account of the progress of the gospel, Luke has selected certain particular mighty works as typical. These are also focal points at which the meaning of the mission and its impact are dramatically summed up and illustrated in concrete form. They are not mere marvels, extraneous to the gospel itself, like the episode of Peter's sardine. They are an integral part of the apostolic witness as Luke understands it, and they are characteristic signs of the new age which the Ascension has inaugurated. Thus Luke's conception of the signs and wonders is essentially similar to that of Paul when he speaks of the things which Christ has wrought through him with a view to obedience on the part of the Gentiles, 'by word and deed, in the power of signs and wonders, in the power of the Spirit' (Rom. 15. 18 f.), or when he claims that the signs of the apostle were wrought among the Corinthians with 'signs and wonders and mighty works' (2 Cor. 12. 12). Hebrews 2. 4 expresses the same attitude.

Nevertheless, Luke's miracle-stories give the impression that the writer is looking back, through the traditions that have come down to him, to events which lie far back in the past. His attitude is not unlike that of the Old Testament historians as they contemplate the mighty works which surrounded the Sinai covenant and the beginnings of their nation. His stories are stylized, and they are impressionistic in the sense that they are signs in which the entire meaning of the gospel and its effect on its hearers, whether for acceptance or rejection, are, as it were, crystallized or embodied in a few dramatic episodes. The healing of the lame man at the Temple gate, with its accompanying discourse, is the point at which the entire proclamation of the gospel to the leaders of Israel in the holy city of Jerusalem finds its focus. So, too, when we read of Peter healing the paralysed and raising the dead, we are inclined to ask, as we do of the stories in the gospels, whether these are dramatic signs and representations of a deeper and wider reality: whether they signify the kind of healing and resurrection which, for example, the writer to the Ephesians indicates when he says that God has made us alive with Christ when we were dead in trespasses and raised us up and made us to sit in the heavenlies in Christ Jesus. One would like to know much more about Paul's own attitude to the signs and wonders which, he evidently believed, were actually accompanying his preaching; and one would like to know how far, if at all, Luke consciously thought of the miraculous focal-points in his story as being in some sense parabolic. It is perhaps worth remarking that there does not appear to be much significant difference between the treatment of miracles in the 'we passages' and in the rest of Acts. It might be suggested that in the former the miracles are less spectacular and marvellous: the cure of the possessed girl at Philippi (it is not entirely clear whether the 'diarist' was still present when this happened) is relatively commonplace; the incident of the snake at Malta is easily rationalized, for the island has no poisonous snakes; the cure of Publius and of other sick people in the same country is, again, not particularly startling. Eutychus at Troas is not said by Paul to have come to life after having died, but rather to be still alive. Yet Luke certainly supposed, and tells us, that Eutychus 'was taken up dead'; and there is little reason to believe that he himself thought that the acts done by God through Paul and recorded in the 'diary' were really on a different and more ordinary level as compared with those in the rest of the book. It is reasonable to hold that in all cases alike Luke believed that the miracles which he recorded were concrete historical events, but that their parabolic significance was such as to entitle him to arrange them in his story, furnish them as it might be appropriate with explanatory speeches, and write them up in the light of parallels both in the Old Testament and in the ministry of Jesus. This is done with the object of showing that the invocation of Christ's name, responded to by faith in him, does enable his followers to bring his mighty word to bear powerfully on men's physical and spiritual infirmities, to punish offenders against the Spirit (like Ananias), to confound those who (like Elymas) try to hinder the gospel, and to find even prison bars to be no obstacle to its progress.

It is central to Luke's understanding of these miracles that they fulfilled the ancient prophetic hope. Joel had prophesied 'wonders' in heaven and earth. Luke adds 'signs' to Joel's 'wonders', and the Western text's omission at Acts 2. 19 of Joel's reference to 'blood and fire and vapour of smoke' is perhaps intended to underline Luke's original point that Joel's prophecy is to find its fulfilment in the signs and wonders done in the name of the exalted Christ through his followers. Soon after the speech in which Peter recalls Joel's words we are told that 'many signs and wonders happened through the apostles' (Acts 2. 43). They are the visible evidence of the new age. The Spirit that was upon Jesus when he was attested by mighty works, signs and wonders is now working through his disciples.

The first detailed account of one of these signs forms the text for the missionaries' appeal to the leaders and the people of Israel. The healing of the lame man at the Temple gate fulfils the prophecy of Isaiah 35. 6, as Luke suggests in his allusion to the man 'leaping'. The episode has a general resemblance to Christ's healing of the paralytic; it also has touches, such as the raising up of the man by Peter, which recall other miracles of Jesus, especially the raising of Jairus' daughter. This physical contact presumably signifies a link between Christ and the patient through the person of Christ's apostle. Restored life is given to the paralytic in the power of the name: that is, by the authority of Jesus the Messiah who, as Acts 3. 13 makes plain, has been glorified by the God of Israel in being enthroned at his right hand. To this authority there corresponds the faith of the paralytic in the present and continuing power of Christ.

This miracle is a major sign to Israel, just as the parallel healing of a paralytic by Paul at Lystra attests the mission to the Gentiles. It is witnessed by all the *laos* (the people of Israel: Acts 3. 9). It is a 'notable sign' (4. 16); and it attests the gospel to Jerusalem in such a way that the people, as opposed to the rulers, enthusiastically accept the sign and the preaching, and glorify God (4. 21 f.). The prayer of the Church (4. 30) sums up this conjunction of word and sign: the word is to be spoken with the stretching out of God's hand for healing and for the doing of signs and wonders through the name of Jesus. The answer to this prayer comes when the apostles testify to the resurrection of Jesus 'with great power' (4. 33).

Another aspect of this power is seen in the story of Ananias and Sapphira: its potency for the judgment of those who sin against the Spirit. Meanwhile, throughout the mission to Jerusalem, the apostolic witness is publicly attested by signs and wonders. The prayer of the Church (4. 30) continues to receive its answer: 'many signs and wonders took place among the people' (5. 12). It seems probable that Luke transfers to Peter the account, which he omits at Mark 6. 56, of the sick being laid out in the villages so that they might touch the garment of Jesus. Certainly Luke has no hesitation in believing that Christ's power can affect the sick through 'overshadowing' by the shadow of Peter. Luke's use of the word 'overshadow' at Luke 1. 35 and 9. 34 suggests that here, too, it is intended to signify the impact of the divine presence and power. This takes effect through Peter, as the leader of the mission to Jerusalem, just as it does through Paul, as the leader of the wider mission to the Gentile world (Acts 19. 12). In the latter instance it operates through another form of extremely indirect personal contact: handkerchiefs and aprons brought to the sick from Paul's person. Acts 5. 16 marks the parallel between the works done by Jesus in his own ministry and those which are carried out in his name: the general healings mentioned here correspond to those recorded in such passages as Luke 4. 40 f. At Acts 5. 19 we first encounter the repeated theme of miraculous deliverance from prison; the mission cannot be obstructed by prisons any more than by sentences of death, which, as in Stephen's case, afford opportunities for the fulfilment of Christ's promise (Lk. 12. 12) that the martyr will be enabled to give his testimony under the immediate inspiration of the Spirit.

Stephen's own preaching was accompanied, like that of the apostles, by signs and wonders done publicly (6. 8). He is described as full of 'grace and power'. So, too, with Philip at Samaria: the word is associated with works, exorcisms, and the healing of the paralysed and the lame, which recall the acts of Jesus as prophesied in Isaiah 35 and which are described as 'signs' and also, perhaps in conscious contrast with the popular acclamation of Simon Magus, as 'the power called great', as 'great powers' (i.e. mighty works).

Another theme that recurs in Acts is to be found in the story of the conversion of Saul. Like Elymas the sorcerer, the enemy of the gospel is struck down and blinded by the power of God,

though in Saul's case he is immediately raised by the Lord's
word. He is restored to sight (as so often in the gospels, physical
and spiritual blindness seem to be interconnected) by Ananias,
who, in fulfilling this commission, is acting as the direct agent
of Jesus. It is as the representative of Jesus, too, that Peter
heals Aeneas. In the latter episode there is a close parallel with
the healing of the paralytic by Jesus (Lk. 5. 18–26), just as there
is between Peter's raising of Tabitha and the raising by Jesus of
Jairus' daughter. The parallel is closer in this last instance to
Mark's version than to Luke's own reproduction of the Markan
story; but it is fairly clear that in Luke's mind this episode
shows that the works of Jesus are reproduced in the apostles'
mission, and that behind both there lie Old Testament foreshadowings, for the echoes here of 1 Kings 17. 19 and 2 Kings
4. 33ff. are strong and point back to Elijah and Elisha. It is odd
that in the story of Tabitha it is nowhere said that Jesus, or God,
or the 'name' effects the miracle. In contrast with the cure of
Aeneas, who is told that Jesus Christ heals him, Peter himself
does this healing; but his action reproduces that of Jesus in
Jairus' house, and it is preceded by prayer.

It seems likely that the extension of the mission to Gentiles at
Antioch, like the earlier move into Samaria, was accompanied
by mighty works, for this is presumably implied by the statement (11. 20) that 'the hand of the Lord was with them'. The
reappearance of the theme of release from prison in the story
of Herod and Peter needs little comment apart from two obvious
points. Luke suggests a parallel with the Passion narrative when
he alludes to the Passover season as the setting of Peter's
imprisonment which Herod meant to be the prelude to his
public execution; and he lays immense stress on the total
impossibility, at the human level, of any escape on Peter's part.
The divine power which delivers Peter in spite of chains, iron
gates, and an extraordinarily numerous guard, is afterwards
manifested negatively, as it were, in the destruction of Peter's
persecutor, whose fate is modelled on those of Antiochus

Epiphanes (2 Macc. 9) and Herod the Great (Josephus, *Ant.* 17. 168–79).

In the Pauline mission the works which attested the preaching of Peter and his associates have their counterpart. In Paul's case the cycle *begins* with the overthrow of an enemy. A Jew who, being a false prophet, is an agent of the devil tries to prevent a representative of the Roman Empire and of the Gentiles, who will hear the gospel while the Jews reject it, from receiving Paul's word. He is worsted by the power of the Spirit (13. 9), just as Peter, less 'miraculously', overcame the false prophet in Samaria. Normally, the 'hand of the Lord' is at work for salvation; here it is exercised in judgment. The temporary blinding of Elymas is like a negative version of a conversion story.

On their mission Paul and Barnabas perform signs and wonders at Iconium, as the apostles had done at Jerusalem (5. 12). The new mission receives the same divine attestation that had been given to the original preaching, as Paul later claims (15. 12). At Lystra the healing of the cripple at the Temple gate by Peter and John is reproduced; Acts 14. 10 echoes Acts 3. 8, and Isaiah 35. 6 is again in the background. The deliverance at Philippi marks the triumph of the gospel in the Gentile lands, as Peter's release was a climax to his work in Jerusalem. Luke's apologetic purpose probably enters into the story of the events at Philippi. Roman authorities beat and imprison the apostles; but they are miraculously set free, and the story ends with the same authorities escorting the missionaries out with humble apologies. Into this dramatic episode Luke has packed a great deal of significant information about what he believes to have been the relationship between the apostolic missionaries and the Roman world. It is possibly worth noticing that Paul does not refer to his experiences at Philippi in anything like the same terms (1 Thess. 2. 2). A non-miraculous counterpart to Luke's story of Philippi appears in the apostle's triumph in a Roman court at Corinth and the abject humiliation of his Jewish opponents.

Acts 19. 11 shows Paul performing mighty works at Ephesus, parallel to those recorded in Acts 5. 15 and also in Luke 8. 44 where the touch of Christ's garment conveys healing power. The episode of the sons of Sceva magnifies Paul's mission, and later, at Troas, he works a great miracle, according to Luke's understanding of the incident of Eutychus. It is parallel to Peter's raising of Tabitha; it echoes at one point the story of Jairus' daughter (Mk. 5. 39: 'Why do you create a commotion and weep? The child is not dead but sleeping'); and it recalls once again the miracles of Elijah and Elisha in 1 Kings 17 and 2 Kings 4.

Finally, at Malta, there are other mighty works. The story of the serpent, which, with the people's conclusion that Paul was a god, looks more like a typical Hellenistic wonder, is presumably intended by Luke as a sign to attest the divine purpose in rescuing Paul from the sea. The healing of Publius and of many others is the last work by which the mission of Paul is confirmed and empowered by God's authority. The way in which Luke ends his miracle-stories may be significant. As the apostolic preaching approaches the capital of the world Luke introduces a story of how a single victim of fever was healed, and follows this with a general description of the cure of many sick folk. Thus, near the close of his second volume, he reproduces the pattern of the first healings, as distinct from exorcism, which he recorded at the beginning of the first volume (Lk. 4. 39 f.).

The ministry of Jesus, exercised through the operation of the Spirit in his own person during the humility of his earthly life, and through the working of the same Spirit, after his exaltation to Lordship, in his apostles, extends, in Luke's perspective, from Galilee to Rome. Though the proclamation of Christ's gospel falls into clearly marked and distinct stages, its progress is continuous and from Galilee and Jerusalem to the centre of the Gentile world its course is the same: in the word of repentance and forgiveness and the expression of that word in signs and wonders and mighty works.

12

'JOHN DID NO MIRACLE'

BY

ERNST BAMMEL

ERNST BAMMEL

Ernst Bammel studied Theology and History in the Universities of Bonn, Göttingen, Tübingen and Vienna. After taking Doctorates in Theology and Philosophy at Bonn he was appointed Lecturer in New Testament and Rabbinics in the University of Erlangen in 1953. He has spent some time doing research in both Oxford and Cambridge and he has been a lecturer at the latter University since 1962. His main interest is in the Jewish background of the New Testament.

'JOHN DID NO MIRACLE'

I

WE ARE puzzled by this statement in John 10. 41. The life of Jesus is surrounded by miracles, and according to the Acts even more those of his apostles. Why not that of his forerunner and main witness too? This is outstanding within the gospels which are, *par excellence*, a 'wonderbook'—even the false prophets are supposed to perform miracles.[1] But it is equally exceptional within the framework of Hellenistic civilization. The *divinatio* of an eminent man is expressed in extraordinary circumstances which accompany his birth and surround his public activity. The signs which bear witness to the excellency of the *homo imperiosus* are a feature especially emphasized in the Augustan era. It was characteristic of the restorative tendency of this period that interest and belief in the supernatural and the miraculous are demonstrated. Perhaps not taken too seriously —there are many nine days' wonders—the miraculous element has become part of the usual stylistic equipment. Disbelief in particular miracles is not unheard of, but to state that someone did no miracle is, as far as I know, unique. Sages and prophets are 'divine persons' (θεῖοι ἀνέρες) more than anybody else; and in their case the miracle is, as has been shown by Ludw. Bieler,[2] a *conditio sine qua non*.

The Jewish world is no exception to this. There is, it is true, a certain tendency to reserve the full measure of the 'signs and wonders' (*otot we-mopatim*) for the time of Moses. But this is not to be taken as a piece of Rabbinic enlightenment.[3] It is only the

---

[1] 2 Thess. 2. 9; Rev.13. 13.   [2] ΘΕΙΟΣ ΑΝΗΡ, I (1935).

[3] A disregard of miracles occurs very occasionally. Is. Heinemann points to certain features in Hellenistic Judaism (*Die Kontroverse über das Wunder im Judentum der hellenistischen Zeit*, Festschrift B. Heller, Budapest (1941), esp. p. 186 ff.). An unknown rabbi declares that the whole story of Job with its miracles is a myth (*BB* 15a). Maimonides explains that Moses was more than a prophet and that not every ordinary prophet is expected to perform miracles (see J. Kramer, *Das Problem des Wunders . . . von Saadja bis Maimuni*, Diss. Strassburg (1903), p. 98).

expression of the rabbis' evaluation of their own time, of their
realization of the difference from the 'wonderland' of the past.
It is with regard to this background that it is said that this era
is a time without prophets, miracles and other gifts of God.[1] The
rabbis are forced by their religious system to take the miracle
seriously;[2] that is the only reason why many of them feel uneasy
about signs of the present age. Realizing this these men waited
all the more for the future when the miracles of the past will be
repeated on a larger scale: 'there will be marvellous things
which I have never done for the fathers'.[3] The lack of the great
miracles of the desert pilgrimage testifies to a state of calamity
which may be relieved by God any minute. This is why the
same period is filled by excited announcements and even procla-
mations of the first eschatological miracles.[4] The latter, a form
of eschatology curved back into the present is more typical of a
kind of apocalyptic activism than of the spirit of the rabbinic
schools. There we encounter a certain tendency to fill history
with miracles. Elijah and Elisha are hailed as the great wonder-
workers, all the biblical miracles from Noah to Esther are
recounted. True, the rabbis emphasized the inferiority of their
own time—the former generations used to be ready to sacrifice
their lives for the sanctity of the name, we . . . not; they deserved
it, we not[5]—but, on the other hand, they make Elijah and
Elisha the great examples of pious men,[6] they extend the normative biblical miracles to include that of the feast of Dedication
(*Chanuka*),[7] and accept the miracle of the divine voice (*Bath Qol*)
for the settling of practical and at times even legal questions.[8]

---

[1] See *Theol. Lit. Zeitg.*, 1954, Sp. 351 f.

[2] Hence the many considerations about the difference between miracle worker,
sorcerer and deceiver.

[3] *Mech.* Ex. 15. 11 (Lauterbach, II. 66). Valuable material is collected by R.
Meyer, *Der Prophet aus Galiläa* (1940).

[4] Jos *Ant.* 20 § 97 f.   [5] *Ber.* 20a.   [6] *Gen. r.* 77. 1 (Berachja's remark).

[7] Its reliability was proved in an extraordinary way; *Shabb.* 21b; *Joma* 29a.

[8] A. Guttmann, *The Significance of Miracles for Talmudic Judaism*, Hebr. Un. Coll.
Ann., 1947, p. 267–74.

Not every rabbi is a miracle worker. But quite a number of the contemporaries of Paul, Ignatius and Justin are reputed to have performed miracles[1] (even more so in Tannaitic than in Amoraic times).[2]

Thus, viewed from every angle of ancient religion, the statement of John 10. 41 sounds equally strange. But is the evangelist likely to have aimed at something completely new? Is he really likely to disclaim the miracle *a priori*? Could his sentence possibly be interpreted as proclaiming that the Baptist's words were true because he did no miracle? We hesitate to do so and ask: is it not possible and worth attempting to give these words, strange as they surely are, a meaning within the accepted religious framework?

II

The first question which arises is that of the historic credibility of the statement. Is it the simple truth, or is it a point which was disputed and is disputable? The gospels do not narrate miracles performed by the Baptist. Not too much should be deduced from this however, as the gospels almost entirely avoid describing details of his life. It is only Luke who reports God's miraculous act in the birth of the Baptist. God's action is an event on a different level; but the narrative is phrased in such

---

[1] There is a certain tendency in research to attempt to establish a difference between rabbi and wonderworker. Ad. Schlatter's book (*Das Wunder in der Synagoge* (1912)) is characteristic of this inclination (similarly, G. Kittel, *Jesus und die Rabbinen* (1914), p. 25: it seems clear, that 'grundsätzlich der älteste echte Rabbiner kein Wundermann war und sein wollte'). But Schlatter is misled by the theological stylization of the rabbinic presentation which frequently conditioned the description of a miracle as being performed by God on the petition of a certain rabbi. But, surely, a rabbi who is in the position to force God to certain things, is a miracle worker himself (valuable remarks in L. Gulkowitsch, *Die Bildung des Begriffes Hasid*, I *Acta et Commentationes Univ. Tartuensis Hum.*, 37 (1935), p. 26). Material in P. Fiebig, *Rabbinische Wundergeschichten d. ntl. Zeitalters* (1911); J. Bergmann, *Legenden der Juden* (1919); L. Ginzberg, *Legends of the Jews* (1911–38); A. Guttmann, op. cit., p. 399 f. For the important figure of Onias see the material assembled by Ad. Büchler, *Types of Jewish-Palestinian Piety* (Jews' Coll. Publ. No. 8, 1922, p. 196 ff.).

[2] Guttmann, p. 404.

a way that similarly mighty deeds are expected of the man who is described as 'great in the eyes of the Lord' (1. 15), to whom will be granted the power of Elijah (1. 17) and who is called 'a prophet' (1. 76), which probably refers to the eschatological prophet described in Deuteronomy 18. 15. This means that his activity is seen surrounded by eschatological, in some way miraculous, deeds, and this view is all the more interesting, if, as has been suggested,[1] the passage is based on a birth narrative, composed and circulating in Baptist communities. True, no mention is made of single miracles, but the position is similar in the Christian christological formulae (apart from Acts 10. 38). There are only a few hints which may possibly throw some further light on the question. Mark 6. 14 gives an interpretation of the person and ministry of Christ in the light of the past. The 'mighty deeds' ($\delta\upsilon\nu\acute{\alpha}\mu\epsilon\iota\varsigma$) of somebody else—John especially is taken into consideration—are operative in him. $\varDelta\upsilon\nu\acute{\alpha}\mu\epsilon\iota\varsigma$ may include miracles (cf. 6. 2; 5).[2] In this case it may not be impossible that the Baptist's activity too was seen in miraculous colours. This is a possible, although not a cogent, interpretation of the Mark-Matthew stream of tradition—Luke, whose report is to be preferred, does not contain anything similar. Secondly, Mark 11. 27 ff.: 'You are doing these things' ($\tau\alpha\hat{\upsilon}\tau\alpha$ $\pi o\iota\epsilon\hat{\iota}\varsigma$) may include miracles, and Jesus' evasive reference to John may presuppose similar deeds done by the Baptist. Thus, the existence of a side-line of tradition interested in certain miraculous aspects of the life of John cannot be ruled out.

The scanty Baptist sources we still have add to the birth story reports about their hero's miraculous end: he was raised to heaven by Hivil Ziva.[3] Apart from this they contain very

---

[1] See R. Bultmann, *History of the Synoptic Tradition* (1963), p. 294 f.; C. H. Kraeling, *John the Baptist* (1951), p. 16.

[2] Cf. Lk. 24. 19: 'a prophet, mighty in deed and word', a statement which implies that a prophet performs miracles normally. The sy[sin] text of Mk. 6. 30, which reads $\acute{\epsilon}\pi o\acute{\iota}\eta\sigma\epsilon\nu$, includes miracles in his activity.

[3] *Ginza R.* 192–6; H. Petermann, *Reisen im Orient*, II (1861), p. 455; E. S. Drower, *The Mandaeans of Iraq and Iran* (1937), p. 280.

few miraculous features. He is prophet—that is maintained again and again;[1] but details are not given. 'At the sound of his proclamation the house of the people shakes, the temple and the priest's dome quake',[2] but this may be a rhetorical phrase—similarly the other which speaks of Mirjai's 'wondrous voice' which makes the fishes gather out of the sea and the birds from the mouth of the Euphrates.[3] This silence is symptomatic, although it could be over-estimated.

The Mandaean texts are Gnostic documents. In general, Gnosticism, especially in its developed form, is reserved in its attitude towards miracles. The *Pistis Sophia*, although half-Christian, goes so far as to state that raising of the dead and healing of the sick are works of the 'rulers' ($\check{\alpha}\rho\chi o\nu\tau\epsilon\varsigma$), that is, devils.[4] It is in keeping with this that the same text, when it speaks of Jesus' power implanted in Elizabeth, describes it as a power which will enable the child, 'to preach before me, to prepare my way and to baptize with the water of forgiveness of sins'. Nothing more is said. Thus, Mandeism too was interested neither in the invention of miraculous scenes nor in handing down traditions possibly already existing.

The later Christian traditions centred in Syria and Egypt do not lead much further. The Garshuni life of John the Baptist claims in an appendix that the dead body of the holy Mar John the Baptist wrought miracles, prodigies and wonders of healing among the people of the Lord Jesus Christ'[5] but it does not

[1] *Johannesbuch*, ed. by M. Lidzbarsky, II (1915), pp. 87 ff., 93 ff., 96, 101 ff., 112 ff., 119 ff.
[2] *Johannesbuch*, p. 93 (96); E.T. in G. R. S. Mead, *The Gnostic John the Baptizer* (1924), p. 48. [3] *Johannesbuch*, p. 139 (134); cf. Mead, p. 67.
[4] *Pistis Sophia*, p. 281 (p. 182 in Schmidt's 1954 translation); cf. C. Schmidt, *Gnostische Schriften in koptischer Sprache* (1892), p. 420.
[5] 7 Ed. by A. Mingana, *Woodbroke Studies*, I (1927), p. 235 ff., esp. 257 ff. On the origin of the Alexandrian traditions on the Baptist see Th. Innitzer, *Johannes der Täufer* (1908), p. 394 f. W. C. Till, *Mitteilungen d. Dt. Archäolog. Inst. Abteilg Kairo*, XVI (1958), p. 310 ff., gives a survey of the Coptic material dealing with the Baptist. Add the sermon edited by K. H. Kuhn, *Muséon*, 1963, pp. 55–77.

N

recount any miracle of his lifetime. According to a Syrian legend the Baptist reveals himself in a church in Edessa which is named after him, and heals a man who is suffering from a disease of the eyes, admonishing him not to invoke him further in that church, because he is no longer there, as it had been taken by the Chalcedonians.[1] This is all the relevant material. The reason for this restraint is found in the close correspondence of these traditions with the New Testament reports. Although these legends are meant to fill gaps, this task is not performed by adding or inventing stories, but mainly by embellishing those traits which are envisaged already in canonical tradition.

The anti-Baptist passages in Christian literature are short remarks, interested solely in the doctrinal aspects of the difference between the two movements. The only passage worth citing is that of Ps.-Clem. *Hom.* 2. 24, according to which Simon Magus, who was considered to be John's disciple, was abroad studying magic when his master was killed—implying in this way that the full blame for magical activities is not to be laid at the feet of the Baptist himself.

Josephus, a 'neutral' witness, portrays John[2] in a different manner from the miracle-promising claimants to Messiahship he mentions several times. The Slavonic text of the *Jewish War* adds the story of the interpretation of Philip's(!) dream given by the Baptist.[3] This may be a rejudaized Christian legend.[4]

The sources, varied as they are, give no real justification for a picture of a wonder-working Baptist or claims with respect to this made by his followers. Even the very scanty quotations we find are late and do not substantiate the theory that the hints of Luke 1 were developed to a blossoming miraculous tree.

---

[1] *Patr. Orient.*, VIII, 157 f. Cp. J. Tomajean, 'Le culte et les fêtes de St. Jean-Baptiste', *L'Orient Syrien*, pp. 309–16.

[2] *Ant.* 18. 117–19.   [3] After *Bell.* 2. 9. 1.

[4] Philip is prominent in the Christian legends dealing with the Baptist. It is his wife, who misleads Herod (*Patr. Orient.*, IX, 135–9; *MPW*, 132, p. 1062); this tradition is linked with the other known from the gospels in Mingana's text.

True, the sources do not exclude, or rather they admit, the fact that such ideas may have been entertained, but their relevance is of such a small degree that it seems unreasonable to suppose that this may have influenced the wording of John 10. 41. Hence, the theory of some scholars, that the verse is to be understood solely as a tendentious polemic against the truth and that a wonder-working activity of the Baptist can be deduced from this (*e negativo*),[1] does not really match the facts. On the other hand, it is much more likely that the lack of signs became an embarrassment within the Baptist communities, and it may even be that statements palliating the lack of signs circulated in these communities, which had not yet moved to the Gnostic habit of disregarding and even despising miracles.

It should perhaps be mentioned in passing that a very different solution was advanced by Rich. Reitzenstein. He presumed that John's disciples had claimed miracles, even the Messianic miracles of Trito-Isaiah for their master, but transposed them into the spiritual sphere. The author of the Fourth Gospel, directing himself against such claims, makes the multitude confess that the Baptist was not able to perform miracles, just as Luke 7. 22 levelled down Jesus' answer to the material sphere.[2] John and his first followers already are forced into a Gnostic framework by Reitzenstein and that is what makes his solution, attractive as it may sound, impossible.

To summarize: the context of the parallel material dealing with the Baptist does not solve the problem completely. Probably, the statement of John 10. 41 is in agreement with the facts; but the parallels give no hint which explains why the lack of miracles is stated here so solemnly and why this is done in connexion with statements about his pronouncements.

[1] W. Baldensperger, *Der Prolog des vierten Evangeliums* (1898), p. 89: 'es wäre gegen alle Analogie, wenn die Johannesjünger ihrem Meister keine Wundertaten zugeschrieben hätten. . . . Mit Joh. 10. 41 wird eine andere Ansicht negiert'. B. is seconded by R. Bultmann, *Synoptic Tradition*, p. 24.302; *Johannesevangelium*, p. 300, and R. Meyer, *Der Prophet aus Galiläa* (1940), p. 40. 115.

[2] *Die Vorgeschichte der christlichen Taufe* (1929), p. 61 f.

And this is the other problem raised by the passage. Both statements are linked in one sentence. This fact makes it likely that there is an inner connexion. The Greek text with its μέν-δέ formulation only hints at this,[1] whereas in parts of the textual tradition the connexion indicated in the Greek is obliterated and the statement split into two disconnected entities.[2] Is it, nevertheless, possible to trace the underlying conjunction and union of the two parts?

III

The passage presupposes as normal a relationship between 'sign' (σημεῖον) and pronouncements which differs from that implied in this particular case. The one envisaged as normal must be a more positive relationship. What is it exactly that is implied?

One instance of such a relation is well known: the life and deeds of the Messiah surrounded by miracles.[3] This was already an Old Testament notion and is emphasized very often in the New Testament. Less developed, but not less interesting, is the related idea where the Messiah offers a miracle to convince disbelievers of his vocation. *Pes. R.* 36 describes the scene where the Messiah, standing on the pinnacle of the temple,[4] offers a sign in order to convince those who do not believe.[5] This element of legitimization is, of course, not foreign to the many

---

[1] μέν is omitted in part of the MS. tradition. The old Latin text renders the Greek faithfully (*quia/quoniam* translates ὅτι; cf. H. Rönsch, *Itala und Vulgata* (1875), p. 402).

[2] in the Arabic Diatessaron (Pott-Preuschen, p. 180).

[3] Innitzer, p. 390, calls his Wunderwirksamkeit 'das messianische Merkmal κατ' ἐξοχήν'.

[4] Strack-Billerbeck, Kommentar III, 9f.: cf. Hegesippus' report on the death of James the Righteous (Eusebius, *H.E.* 2. 23).

[5] The passage occurs in a chapter of *Pes. R.* which contains a collection of old material. The sentence itself is introduced by *teno rabbanan* and therefore certainly tannaitic in character.

passages which boast the miraculous aspect of the Messianic era.[1] It is interesting, however, to note that here (in *Pes. R.* 36) the miracle is envisaged as inaugurating[2] and even constituting the Messianic career and period.

That this passage is not an isolated statement may be demonstrated by the fact that the same principle and scheme are applied to prophetic pronouncements. *S. Dt.* 18. 19 stated that if a prophet who starts to prophesy gives evidence by signs and miracles he is to be heeded; if not, he is not to be followed. This particular statement is anonymous, but it can be given a *terminus ante quem* by a discussion between Jose ha-Gelili and Akiba which presupposes the existence and validity of a statement like the one just cited (*Sanh.* 90a; *S. Dt.* 13. 3). Both men are faced with the problem of defining and circumscribing the validity of practical advice[3] given by a prophet. It was an established principle that a temporary dispensation from certain prescriptions of the Torah either by the Highpriest or a prophet was permissible: 'if the hour demands it'.[4] Both rabbis agree that such advice from a prophet is to be followed, except in one instance, namely, when it demands idolatry. Then, his advice is to be disregarded, even if he were supported by the miracle

---

[1] Cf. R. Bultmann, *Johannesevangelium*, p. 231, n. 5.

[2] It is disputed whether the miracle belongs only to the grandeur of the Messianic age (thus Bultmann in the preceding footnote) or is thought of as legitimizing a Messiah (for the latter opinion see E. Schürer, *Geschichte des jüd. Volkes*, III, 621). Jewish scholars used to point to the example of Bar Kochba, who had not performed any miracles and who, nevertheless, was proclaimed as Messiah. Maimonides concluded from this, that the Messiah is under no obligation to do miracles and J. Klausner followed his footsteps (*Die messianischen Vorstellungen im Zeitalter der Tannaiten* (1904), p. 108; *The Messianic Idea*, p. 395). But this impression is wrong. *Threni R. ad Lam.* 2. 2—in an appendix?—narrated the story of the miraculous strength displayed by Bar Kochba and that it was this miracle which caused Akiba to hail him as Messiah. The story was incorporated (and invented?) in order to satisfy an established scheme.

[3] That a prophet or a *Bath Qol* had no say in halakhic matters had already been stated during the council of Jamnia (*BM* 59b and cf. *N.T.S.*, 1959/60, p. 318).

[4] Material in E. Stauffer, *Jerusalem und Rom* (1957), p. 159, n. 76.

of the sun stopping in its course.[1] This question was certainly
of practical importance at a time when all sorts of concessions
were made to save the Jewish people from martyrdom.[2] Jose
refuses flatly to extend the concessions to (casual) idolatry. The
miracle of the sun—it is the most powerful nature miracle and
its possible occurrence therefore a most tantalizing theological
problem—is nothing, he says, but a miracle of Yahweh to test
the people's love of himself (thus *S. Dt.* 13. 3—an appropriate
exegesis of the text itself). Akiba agrees with him in the main,
but he solves the problem of the miracle differently. It is a real
miracle of God, according to him, and it has a straightforward
positive meaning, but the prophet whom it was to legitimize
has gone astray since. The fact that the miracle is said to precede
the invitation to idolatry enabled Akiba to establish a temporal
interval during which the prophet is thought to have turned
from good to evil. Thus, the inaugural miracle and prophetic
vocation are two aspects of the same thing. Akiba knew that it
did not suffice to legitimize the whole career of a messenger,
but he shared the view that the miracle was evidence for the
fact that the man concerned was a prophet chosen by God.
And indeed, this is the principle which is expressed in the
anonymous statement of *S. Dt.* 18. 19. It is formulated there
without qualification. As it was the intention of both Jose and
Akiba to circumscribe the value of the miracle, it must be
concluded that the formulation of *S. Dt.* is even older than the
rabbis' discussion, and that it therefore goes back at least to the
first century A.D. It seems therefore that it represents a still
unproblematic relationship between inaugural miracle and
prophetic activity. And the zest and cunning with which the
rabbis defined the limits of meaning and validity of a miracle
indicates that these played a more prominent role in the preceding period and that a sign was considered decisive for the

---

[1] The parallel version in *S. Dt.* 13. 3 adds: sun and moon, stars and zodiac.
[2] Some material in N. N. Glatzer, *Geschichte der talmudischen Zeit* (1937), p. 45 f.

recognition of a prophet, of 'a trustworthy prophet' (προφήτης πιστός, 1 Macc. 14. 41), in pre-Jamnian times.[1,2]

Whereas here the miracle is meant to sponsor a prophet's career, we know of another scene where a miracle takes place to support a *single* statement made by a rabbi. Jose b. Qisma[3] is asked in *Sanh.* 98a how soon the Messiah can be expected, and it is by a miracle that the correctness of his answer is attested.[4]

This last passage is the most closely related to our text. Indeed, the Baptist's witness in respect to Jesus—it was a statement of an eschatological nature like that of Jose b. Qisma—is nowhere more emphasized than in the Gospel of St. John. And it was natural to expect the statement to be supported by a sign. All the more so, we are inclined to say, if John was not a prophet himself (as the Fourth Gospel, contrary to the Synoptics, attempts to maintain).

The dispute mentioned above is only part of a tendency of second-century Judaism to restrict the value of a miracle in certain respects. It might be tempting to escape the solution towards which we have advanced so far, by describing John 10. 41 as an early witness of this tendency, by giving it its place within the magnetic field of a Judaism which maintained a critical attitude towards miracles. But this would lead us astray. The praise of a man of God who did *not* perform miracles was completely unknown in Jewish sources. The criticism of the rabbis amounts to no more than the denial of the validity of miracles for settling legal questions, the recognition of the

---

[1] Similarly, *j. Sanh.* 18 (p. 30c in the Krakau ed., p. 57b in the Wilna ed.): if a prophet starts to prophesy and he gives a sign . . . he is to be heeded.

[2] This does not mean that a prophet without signs deserves death (thus G. Dalman, *Jesus-Jeschua* (1922), p. 49; corrected in *Ergänzungen und Berichtigungen zu Jesus-Jeschua* (1929), p. 4).

[3] J. was far from any eschatological fervour; see *Ab. z.* 18a.

[4] Cf. *j. Sanh.* XI. 5, where the story of Hananjah's death (Jer. 28. 16) is reinterpreted: his death is not any longer the punishment for his own false prophecy but the miracle for which he had asked Jeremiah, to prove that the latter's prophecy is right.

practical difficulty of verifying them and confining their meaning.[1] A world, even an age, without miracles was unimaginable to the rabbis.

If our deductions are right, the passage shows a Jewish background. It is to be understood as pointing to a case which is strange enough in relation to this Jewish scheme—the case of John whose pronouncements, that is the claim, are trustworthy, although he performed no miracle. This implies that the formulation is likely to have had its setting in a world which believed in that scheme; in other words, it is likely to have derived from a Jewish-Christian controversy.

Perhaps the sentence not only admits an anomaly but also gives two criteria which may support the Baptist's pronouncements. It is 'many' who testify to the truth of John's statements and who draw the consequences for themselves. Just as it was the outstanding feature of the desert era, that the whole nation was aware of the act of revelation and that Moses' miracles were performed publicly in front of friend and enemy,[2] so it is important for the evaluation of a prophet, that his miracle should be performed openly, so that a *consensus omnium* results from it.[3] It may be, in the light of this principle, that the mentioning of the 'many' is not just a missionary boast but a necessary piece of argument. 'Was true' ($'A\lambda\eta\theta\tilde{\eta}\ \tilde{\eta}\nu$)[4],[5] means that something which was maintained turned out to be true in the course of historical events. This is the principle given in

---

[1] Perhaps for this reason the revenge is left in the hands of God (*Sanh.* XI. 6).

[2] J. Albo, *Ikkarim*, I. 18. Similarly S. ibn Verga emphasizes that the revelation on Sinai took place with accompanying miracles and in the presence of six hundred thousand men (*Schevet Jehuda* ed. M. Wiener, Hannover, 1855+, p. 18; German transl., p. 34).

[3] Emphasized by Abraham ibn Daud, *Emunah Ramah*, 80 f. (German transl. by S. Weil (1852), p. 101 f.). Cf. J. Kramer, op. cit., p. 63 f.

[4] Omitted in part of the MS. tradition.

[5] A different interpretation is given by R. Reitzenstein, op. cit., p. 61: 'ist Wahrheit' = 'beruht auf Gottesoffenbarung'. He interprets the $\tilde{\eta}\nu$ as if it were the present tense. And the truth is not left to be tested historically but is of such a nature as to convince the people by itself.

Deuteronomy 18. 22 for the recognition of a false prophet: his predictions do not come true.[1] The formulation is phrased in the negative, from which we may conclude that a correct prediction does not necessarily imply that the announcer was sent by God.[2] Similarly here.[3] The ratification by subsequent events is an imperfect one. Nevertheless, the sentence's last words moderate the tension which exists between the two statements, otherwise so very different and poles apart.

IV

The passage is to be found at a very conspicuous point in the otherwise even flow of the gospel. Chapter 11—the whole of the pericope and not only the end of it—is already a foreshadowing of passion and resurrection.[4] It is therefore necessary to view the section as it stands within the gospel.

It could be argued that the evangelist takes this opportunity to summarize the relation of John the Baptist to Jesus. The picture of the ministry of Jesus is somehow overshadowed and influenced by that of the Baptist and demands an interpretation in relation to him whereas the passion is entirely Jesus' own way. It is a natural consequence of taking such a view to interpret 10. 40–42 in the light of the relevant passages of the first, third, fourth and fifth chapters. These passages recognize and restrict the position of the Baptist, they value and take away at the same time. In the same way, 10. 41 f. seems to contain (a) a

---

[1] Circumscribed in Jer. 9: 28. it may be that the prediction of a disaster does not materialize, because the nation has improved; therefore, only positive announcements are a real test. For an interpretation of the passage see G. Quell, *Wahre und falsche Propheten* (1952), p. 150 ff.

[2] The medieval commentators discuss the possibility that he may have stolen his knowledge from a true prophet or that he was informed by demonic powers; cf. D. Hoffmann, *Das Buch Deuteronomium* (1913), p. 176 f.

[3] If we try to verify the statement, it is possible that the tradition underlying John 10. 41 refers to the Lamb (ἀμνός)-saying of the Baptist, that is the announcement that Jesus will die as a martyr. And indeed, the truth of this was to be proved.

[4] The case is similar to that of ch. 2 (*v.* 24 f. and 20–22), but on an enlarged scale.

negative[1] and (*b*) a positive side, both in keeping with the
evaluation of the Baptist by the evangelist. Thus, the verse
appears to be nothing but a 'dogmatic scheme'. There is a
certain force in this argument; that explains its popularity up
to the recent books of C. H. Dodd[2] and W. G. Kümmel.[3]

But there are certain points which may possibly conflict with
this theory. (1) Is it likely that the evangelist, who in his own
words has already drawn the conclusion in John 3. 29 f., should
repeat himself in chapter 10? The reference to the Baptist in
John 5 is so worded as to suggest that Jesus is speaking of the
past. But the past becomes present in John 10; Jesus is confronted[4] with people who had been influenced by the Baptist's
movement and who judge by comparison. (2) The theory presupposes that it is implied that John is inferior to Jesus, who
did perform miracles. But why is this not stated explicitly? Why
is the Baptist not represented as having announced the miracles
of Christ? (3) His witness was right—but why does it need the
support lent by the crowd, which is unknown in the first chapters? (4) The connexion between the two parts of the sentence
is destroyed by interpreting it in this way. It is, in fact, nothing
but a variation of the theory of the two separate clauses, which
already seemed so unlikely at the end of part II.

The distinctive word in our small passage is 'sign' ($\sigma\eta\mu\epsilon\hat{\iota}ov$).
This term is equally the key-word for a whole complex within
the gospel.[5] The fact that it is one complex can easily be sub-
stantiated by the observation that the term is replaced by

---

[1] 'He performed not a single miracle' is the translation which is favoured. The
NEB, surprisingly, paraphrases: 'John gave us(!) no miraculous sign'.

[2] *Historical Tradition in the Fourth Gospel* (1963), pp. 249, 278.

[3] *Einleitung in das Neue Testament* (1964), p. 158. Cf. E. Hirsch, *Das vierte Evangelium* (1936), p. 273.

[4] The Arabic Diatessaron even adds: 'and they said *to him*'.

[5] It is interesting to note, that the Paris MS. of the Gospel of John tries to reduce
the frequency of the term $\sigma\eta\mu\epsilon\hat{\iota}ov$: it reads (in J. A. Thilo, *Codex Apocryphus N.T.*
1832, pp. 861 ff.) $\theta a\acute{v}\mu a\tau a$ in 3. 2, $\iota a\tau\rho\acute{\iota}a\varsigma$ in 6. 2, $\delta\iota\grave{a}$ $\tau\grave{\eta}v$ $\dot{a}\lambda\acute{\eta}\theta\epsilon\iota a v$ in 6. 26, it omits
$\sigma\eta\mu\epsilon\hat{\iota}ov$ in 4. 48; 6. 14; 7. 31 and leaves out the whole passage 2. 15–23.

'deed' (ἔργον) in other parts of the gospel. It seems that σημεῖον has its place in the environment of miracle reports whereas ἔργον figures within speeches.[1] We have reason to suppose that such a document which is characteristically marked by the fact that it describes a number of miracles (although it may have contained other material too) was one of the sources which were used by the evangelist.[2] We can compare this text with Q: both sources see the ministry of Jesus from one angle and it is likely that the σημεῖα source (=Z) existed without a developed passion and resurrection story in the same way as Q almost certainly did.[3] Is it probable that 10. 40 ff. belonged to this document and if so what was its meaning and function within this framework?

Following this line of investigation we have to differentiate again. It is not only the chain of six or seven miracles, the first two of which are expressly named as σημεῖα,[4] which we find in the gospel, but also a number of summaries which sum up the wonder-working activity of Jesus. These summaries which speak of many miracles performed by Jesus do not really fit the miracle-stories. This becomes obvious as soon as 2. 23, where the summary speaks of a plurality of miracles although only

[1] H. H. Wendt used this observation as a basis for the division of the gospel into two different layers: the speech or ἔργον level, which he considered older and the historical or miraculous level, which is a deviation to the pattern of Gemeinde-theologie (*The Gospel acc. to St. John* (1902); *Die Schichten im vierten Evangelium* (1911)). His criticism, epoch-making as it was in his time, is too rough to be useful as a master key for the solution of the Johannine problem. He had assumed in his former work, that 10. 40, in substance at least, belongs to a source, whereas he linked our whole passage with the redactionary stratum in his second book.

[2] For the evaluation of the σημεῖα [Z]-source see Al. Faure, 'Die alttestamentl. Zitate im 4. Evangelium u.d. Quellenscheidungshypothese', *Z.N.W.*, 1922, esp. p. 107 ff.; R. Bultmann, *Das Evangelium des Johannes* (1940), p. 78 f., etc.; W. Hartke, *Die vier urchristlichen Parteien u. ihre Vereinigung z. apostol. Kirche*, I (1961), p. 129 ff.

[3] A different opinion is held by E. Hirsch, *Frühgeschichte des Evangeliums*, II². (1951), p. 342, and H. Helmbold, *Vorsynoptische Evangelien* (1953), p. 62 ff.

[4] Discussed recently, in an unconvincing way by S. Temple, *J.B.L.*, 1962, p. 169 ff.

one event of this kind had been mentioned before. The same
occurs again in 3. 2. The stories are chosen with a definite
purpose, part of which is to answer the question of 2. 18; the
summaries are vague and pretentious. The stories build up a
fixed series of miracles, the summaries embellish certain speeches
(with the exception of 12. 37 and 20. 29). And these last two
instances where the formula occurs are even more perplexing.
12. 37 states the unbelief in spite of 'so many signs' (τοσαῦτα . . .
σημεῖα) and adds a bold pronouncement on the hardening of
men. 20. 31 looks back to 'many other signs also', performed in
private. Certainly, this is a conception of miracle which is not
in keeping with 2. 11: 'and he manifested his glory' (καὶ
ἐφανέρωσεν τὴν δόξαν αὐτοῦ). This is what makes it likely that at
least some of the summaries have a *Sitz im Leben*, which differs
from that of the miracle stories.

In saying this, I venture to deviate from a position held by
R. Bultmann. He made himself the champion of a theory first
put forward by A. Faure and claimed that 12. 37 and 20. 30—
these two verses were originally consecutive—form the end of
Z.[1] I agree with Bultmann in so far as I admit the existence of
such a miracle book and I see insufficient reason to disclaim
the numbering of the miracles for the earliest stratum (as does
J. Wellhausen).[2] But I do maintain that the miracle-summaries
reflect an interest in a miraculous view of the ministry of Jesus
which is as different from the theological direction of Z as it is
from the sophisticating tendency of the soliloquies.

What view are we to take of the argumentative 'sign' (σημεῖα)-
passages? Although they do not necessarily belong to the stories,
questions and demands like those of 2. 18 and 6. 30 arose almost
inevitably. Hence, it is very likely, that explanations, which
give an interpretation and evaluation of the miracles were
added very early. But what was the situation, which demanded
these explanations?

[1] Faure, p. 108; Bultmann, p. 541.   [2] *Das Evangelium Johannis* (1908), p. 24.

Not all these σημεῖα-passages are closely connected with a miracle (2. 18; 7. 31; 6. 30[?]). But at least one of them, 7. 31, is part of a controversy in which the interlocutors are the same as in chapter 9. And this may lead us further. The questions are put forward in both cases by Pharisees.[1] These discussions with the Pharisees are of particular interest.[2] They develop Jewish issues, they reflect real disputes. Quite different are the controversies with the Jews ('Ιουδαῖοι), which are intended to set out the differences and to demonstrate the wickedness of the Jews, to establish a rift which is unbridgeable. The levels are completely unalike and give evidence for different underlying sources. The Jews ('Ιουδαῖοι)-level is later. Not only is this demonstrated by the theological scheme but it also becomes obvious from the insertion of a Jews-passage into a Pharisees-context: 9. 18–23.[3] The Pharisees-passages reflect controversies between the Christian community and shades of opinion within the Jewish world.[4] They represent old valuable tradition.[5] It was unavoidable that the sign question should arise in such discussions (cf. the Synoptics). It may be suggested that these Pharisees-texts were combined with Z at a very early stage. I am thinking especially of 7. 10,[6] 22–32, 40–52; 8. 12–20; 9. 1–3 (3b altered?), 6–17, 24–34, 39–41. The theme of the legitimacy of Jesus' claims is indeed predominant in these disputes; his descent, the basis of his witness (μαρτυρία) and even his signs are the main topics. The case is different with the summaries in the

---

[1] In 6. 30, as it seems by 'the crowd' (ὄχλος), in 2. 18 by 'the Jews' ('Ιουδαῖοι) (but 'Ιουδαῖοι has here not the acute meaning, which is otherwise so characteristic of the Gospel).

[2] Not so the mentioning of the Pharisees in 3. 1; 12. 42—this is redaction level.

[3] Cf. W. Bauer, *Das Johannesevangelium* (1933), p. 137 and Wellhausen, p. 46. Bultmann, p. 250, n. 2; 254, n. 6, decides differently.

[4] 9. 40 is unique within the Gospel; this points to an old layer.

[5] W. Bousset, on the contrary, thinks that all the σημεῖα-passages are secondary: 'das könne "der Kritik als Leitfaden dienen" ' (*Theol. Rundsch.*, 1909, p. 58). Is Bultmann, p. 59, influenced by Bousset?

[6] Introduction to the miracle of ch. 5? Cf. Bultmann, p. 217, n. 1.

true sense of the word: 2. 23; 3. 2; 6. 2, 14 (?); 12. 18, 37; 20. 30 seem to belong to the latest, the redactionary level.[1, 2]

It is in keeping with the theme of interest on the discussion level that the problem of signs and words of command is tackled in 10. 40 ff. But why is it that the name of the Baptist is mentioned here? His name does not occur in the passages discussed so far. But have we covered the whole Z material already?

Faure had already stated that 2. 1 is unlikely to be the beginning of the source and Bultmann is inclined to see its beginning in 1. 35-49.[3] There is some truth in that, in so far as the persons mentioned in chapter 2 had to be introduced somehow; nevertheless, 1. 35 ff. is scarcely a suitable beginning. Representatives of the older generation who spoke of a Johannine *Grundschrift*[4] were prepared to include in this text the other parts of 1. 19 ff. too or even the Baptist verses in the prologue.[5] Undoubtedly, this would make a most suitable opening for a gospel book. But this theory, attractive as it seems, is unlikely to be correct. We have to be content with stating that the

---

[1] Ed. Schwartz (*Aporien im vierten Evagelium. Nachr. d. Gött. Ges. d. Wiss.*, 1908, p. 121) presents valuable observations: 'Die Wundertätigkeit Jesu wird zu einzelnen scharf herausgehobenen ἀρεταὶ θεοῦ "Heldentaten des Gottes", um antik zu reden kondensiert: sie werden gezählt, wenigstens am Anfang (2. 11; 454) und dazu passt das unbestimmte Gerede von den "vielen Zeichen" nicht; wo es vorkommt, bleibt es immer schattenhaft und ist verdächtig. . . . Es ist zu beachten dass die vielen Zeichen nur in Reden und Motivierungen oder in dem eingelegten Räsonnement 12. 37 vorkommen, niemals in der Erzählung selbst, wie oft bei den Synoptikern. . . . Sie . . . gehören in die festgeschlossene . . . Mirakelreihe des vierten Evangeliums nicht hinein' (similarly W. Bousset, *Theol. Rundsch.*, 1909, p. 50, n. 1). It is only that Schwartz does not differentiate between the usage of the word in the summaries and on the discussion level.

[2] Already Faure, p. 111, admits the possibility of different levels within what he likes to call βιβλίον σημείων Ἰησοῦ and tones down thereby the rigour of his own theory.   [3] p. 78.

[4] This line of approach is revived by W. Wilkens, *Die Entstehungsgeschichte des vierten Evangeliums* (1958). 10. 40-42 belongs according to him to the 'Grundevangelium' (p. 55). Similarly, already Spitta, 230, 414 f. and C. Clemen, *Die Entstehung d. Johannesevgls.* (1912), p. 203,

[5] Fr. Spitta, *Das Johannesevangelium als Quelle der Geschichte Jesu* (1910), p. 48 ff. J. A. T. Robinson (*N.T.S.*, 1962/3, p. 120 ff.) reproduced Spitta's thesis in a less convincing form.

source may have included some of the material of chapter 1. That means, the Baptist was already mentioned in the Z source, as in Q[1] and the other gospels.[2] How he was pictured there we do not know.

This observation could be turned against the suggestion, made above that 10. 41 f. should be interpreted independently. But a closer look reveals differences in kind between the first chapters and 10. 41 f. (1) The Baptist of the beginning answers the questions of one or two deputations,[3] he speaks, as it seems, to his disciples about Jesus and he sends these followers of his to Jesus. The Baptist of chapter 10 made known his view to 'many'. (2) John, in chapter 1, speaks of Jesus in so far only as he points to the Lamb—in chapter 10 he is said to have voiced several pronouncements which are envisaged by the word 'all'. (3) It is true that the John of the first chapters states Jesus' superiority, but he does so by speaking of himself, by emphasizing his own inferiority again and again. The John of 10. 41 f. is not reported to have spoken of himself. Lastly, people realize in the light of the events that John had spoken of Jesus. That means, he himself must have employed more indirect language, he is supposed merely to have pronounced a messianic statement.[4] The witness of the introductory chapters is more than direct; there is not room for a test by facts as in chapter 10. The comparison shows that 10. 40–42 displays a picture of John which is much more akin

---

[1] Q is to be split into two sources. One of them, which contained besides speeches quite a few reports (Mt. 3. 1–6; Lk. 3. 7–9, 16–17; Mt. 3. 13–17; Lk. 4. 1–13, 14–16a; 6. 17–49; 7. 1–10, 18–23, 24–35; 9.10b–17; 10. 13–15, 21–24, may have belonged to this source), is keenly interested in the Baptist and the relation of his message to that of Jesus. This is all the more surprising as the second part of Q does not even mention the Baptist.

[2] With the exception of the special source used by Matthew (Mt. 17. 13 is redactionary).

[3] For an interpretation of this passage see E. Stauffer, *Jerusalem und Rom* (1957), p. 92.

[4] Is the Syriac text here nearer to the original wording? Sy[sin] renders a text, which differs from the Greek MS. tradition (about five words are lacking, thus it is impossible to trace the exact meaning of the Syriac text).

to that of the Synoptics. On the other hand, the features we noticed as characteristic for the beginning of the gospel are developed and emphasized by the evangelist. Several theological explanations, which clearly derive from his pen, mark this tendency. That means, the references to the Baptist which are likely already to have been part of the Z source were thoroughly revised by the evangelist, whereas 10. 41 f., so different in character from this redaction, escaped such transformation.[1]

Many scholars agreed in the assumption, more or less strongly worded, that the first verse of the passage (10. 40) may derive from old tradition. The most recent of these statements are those of E. Stauffer[2] and C. H. Dodd.[3] This observation is certainly right. But *vv.* 41 and 42 are equally likely to be an ancient fragment of tradition which represents the source's view of the Baptist more faithfully than does the present text-form of the introductory chapters. Its contents, based on a Jewish scheme, reflect the Christian-Jewish discussion rather than the Christian-Baptist one.[4] The fact, that John was not reputed to have done miracles may have been used as a charge against the Christians, who claimed the Baptist as a witness for their Messiah.

It is a bit speculative to try to find out the meaning of the story within the whole concept of the enlarged signs ($\sigma\eta\mu\epsilon\hat{\iota}\alpha$)-source. Therefore, two considerations only. (1) The miracle-stories in John's gospel normally conclude with some words which mention the belief of the disciples, of the family of the

---

[1] It was misleading to allege that the interpretation was directed by the polemical bias of the first chapters and the passage was given a meaning derogatory to the Baptist (e.g. W. Bauer, p. 17: 'er kann [!] nicht ein einziges Wunder tun').

[2] 'Historische Elemente im vierten Evangelium' (in *Bekenntnis zur Kirche*, Festschrift E. Sommerlath, 1960), p. 39 and n. 78.   [3] p. 241 f.

[4] The *Catena* presents a thoroughly Christianized interpretation: John did no miracle that his testimony to Christ might not be overshadowed by this (J. A. Cramer, II. 306).

centurion, of the hearers. The case is different in chapter 9 (and 5), where the animosity of the Pharisees comes into the open. Is 10. 41 or 42 (1–39 did not belong to the source) a substitute for this standing phrase? (2) Chapter 11 leads to trial and death. This is all the more true if 10. 42 has its original consequence in 11. 7 ff.: 'let us go to Judaea again'.[1] That means, 10. 40 ff. is climax and summary of the report on the ministry of Jesus.

This is overshadowed somewhat in the gospel as it stands now.[2] Its main dividing line is at the end of chapter 12, between a part describing the public ministry and another section dealing with Jesus' private teaching (cf. Mk. 8. 27–29, 50). Except for this line of division the evangelist lends colours to his picture only by inserting the feast journeys. But he has not really obliterated the centres of gravity of his source. And in this case, the evangelist, who had shifted the healing of the blind man from Bethsaida to Jerusalem[3] and who had terminated Jesus' stay by a flight from the holy city, is given by this passage the opportunity to move Christ to a place where he is to receive the call to set out for Bethany and the events of the passion story.

From a literary point of view the passage can be compared with the transfiguration story. There Jesus' disciples are invigorated by two special witnesses. Here, the followers (and the readers) are reassured by being reminded of a witness of the beginning.[4] It was a witness without external attestation.[5] The fact that it deviates so very much from the Jewish scheme points

---

[1] Thus Faure p. 114; a different opinion is held by Bultmann, p. 303, n. 6.

[2] Hirsch, p. 273, may overstate his case when saying: 'der kleine Absatz . . . (ist) für den Aufbau des Gesamtwerks bestimmend'.   [3] Cf. Mk. 8. 22.

[4] The Johannine Christ, of course, cannot be reassured as it happens in Mk. 9. 7.

[5] It is not self-evident that the Church continued to reproduce such a witness. A fully gnosticized Christianity developed a different attitude. The hitherto unpublished text No. 19 of Nag-Hammadi launches a startling attack on the Baptist who is called the 'archon of the multitude' (see J. Doresse, *Secret Books* (1960), p. 219 f. and cf. H. Jonas, *Journ. of Rel.*, 1962, p. 265).

O

—that can be said now with certainty—to the trustworthiness
of the tradition.[1] Being a witness without a sign it testifies to the
greater miracle that, nevertheless, its message was to come true.

[1] H. L. de Wette stated in 1837: 'Merkwürdig und für die Reinheit der Über-
lieferung zeugend ist der Umstand, dass von dem Täufer kein Wunder erzählt
wird' (*Kurzgefasstes exegetisches Handbuch z. N.T.*, I, 3, p. 138). His reasoning shows
a romantic approach. Nevertheless, this essay leads to a conclusion which is not
dissimilar from that reached by the first scholarly commentator of the gospels.

13

MIRACLES AND EARLY CHRISTIAN APOLOGETIC

BY

G. W. H. LAMPE

G. W. H. LAMPE

G. W. H. Lampe, D.D. (Oxon.), HON. D.D. (Edinburgh),
F.B.A., is Ely Professor of Divinity in the University of
Cambridge, Fellow of Gonville and Caius College, Canon
of Ely Cathedral, and Honorary Canon of Birmingham
Cathedral. He was educated at Blundell's School and
Exeter College, Oxford; trained for the Anglican Ministry
at the Queen's College, Birmingham; and was ordained
in 1937 to a curacy at Okehampton. He was Assistant
Master at King's School, Canterbury, 1938–41; Chaplain to the Forces, 1941–5 (awarded the M.C., 1945);
Fellow and Chaplain of St. John's College, Oxford,
1943–53; Professor of Theology at Birmingham University, 1953–9, Dean of the Faculty of Arts, 1955–9, Vice-
Principal, 1957–60. He is well known for many publications, including *The Seal of the Spirit* (1951), and as Editor
of the *Patristic Greek Lexicon*. He is married and has two
children.

MIRACLES AND EARLY
CHRISTIAN APOLOGETIC

THIS ESSAY is restricted to those writings which, during the period between, roughly speaking, the close of the New Testament and the Council of Nicea, were directed explicitly towards the commendation of the Christian Faith to unbelievers and its defence against opponents. It must, therefore, be taken as no more than an introduction to the survey which Mr. Wiles is to make of the role of miracles in the thought of the early Fathers as a whole. The limitation of my theme is very arbitrary. Apologetic is not necessarily confined to set-piece apologies; many sermons and commentaries are bound to include material directed towards the confutation of heathen or Jews and the commendation of Christianity to them; and there is no real reason why the early fourth century should be treated for this purpose as though it were the end of an epoch. The Constantinian era did not mean the end of the need for apologetic, as such a work as the *City of God* was to show.

There are several ways in which an apologist can appeal to miracle. It is conceivable that if he is a preacher confronting the heathen and endeavouring to convert them he may introduce an argument from miracle in the most direct and practical way possible by performing one. This is how the popular romances of the period represented the apostolic missionaries as having acted when they went about their labours of evangelism. This direct use of miracles can take two or three somewhat different forms. Miracles can be performed by a preacher to convince his audience that his preaching has divine authority, and sometimes to frighten them into conversion. Thus St. John (*Acts of John* 39 ff.) stands on a high pedestal at Ephesus, addresses the people, accuses them of being godless, and challenges them to call upon Artemis to strike him dead. If they should prove unsuccessful, he proposes to call on the Christian God to cause every one of them to die. They cry out: 'Slay us not thus; we know that you can do it'. Whereupon he prays that the evil spirit may be put to flight. The altar and image of Artemis are thrown down and the temple roof collapses on her priest. Every one then acclaims the God of St. John.

Miracles may be introduced to support the testimony of the martyr. So in the *Acts of Paul* Thecla is successively delivered from fire and beasts in the arena, and the divine intervention brings about the confusion or conversion of her persecutors. Where the Christian preacher is faced by strong opposition, especially from heathen magicians, the appeal to miracle takes the form of a competition in wonder-working on the lines of the contest between Moses and the magicians of Egypt. Such is the struggle between St. Peter and Simon Magus as described in the *Acts of Peter*.

All this belongs essentially to the realm of popular fiction. Such stories are normally set in the remote past. They concern the holy apostles themselves or their associates: people who could plausibly be represented as missionaries who could do marvels in order to gain credence for their words. The miracle-stories in Acts ought not, as I think, to be read in this sense; but they readily lent themselves to an 'evidential' interpretation, and they seem to have been generally understood in this way in the post-New Testament literature and thus to have been taken as some kind of warrant for the marvels ascribed to apostles and their companions in the second and later centuries. Such tales are generally found in the popular romances, where they served as a sort of equivalent to science fiction, and they plainly belong to the sphere of fantasy.

Serious authors pay little attention to all this, but Eusebius (*H.E.* 1. 13) reproduces the legend of Abgar, king of Edessa, with its account of how Thaddaeus the apostle prefaced his preaching at Edessa with the healing of Abgar without the use of medicine or herbs but simply in the name of Jesus, with the cure of one Abdu who suffered from gout, and with unspecified healings of many of the citizens. Arnobius is unusual among serious apologists in quoting such legends. He speaks (2. 12) of the Romans hastening to give up their ancestral religion because they had seen the chariot of Simon Magus and his fiery car blown to pieces by the mouth of St. Peter, and vanish at his pronouncement of the name of Christ.

Competition in the miraculous is represented, outside the romances, mainly by the tendency of pagans to assert that the miracles of Christ and the apostles are no more remarkable than the wonders ascribed to gods and heroes, and the apologists' reply that they are indeed much more marvellous, and that the character of the miracles and of those who performed them shows that they are divine, whereas the heathen miracles are, as many Christian writers from Athenagoras onwards insisted, the work of devils. Apologists are thus beginning to change the ground of their argument when faced with this kind of counter-attack; and in the end they are forced into the position, not so much of supporting the doctrine with miracles, as of appealing to the doctrine, or the character of its teachers, to lend credence to the miracles.

The early acts of martyrs, again, when these are of a serious character and stand wholly apart from the apocryphal romances, are remarkably free from the miraculous features which are so characteristic of popular legends. Even the story of Polycarp (whether or not one accepts the text which makes a dove come out of his body) is restrained; the martyr's testimony is sealed by death, and not, as so often in the late martyr-legends, by a series of fantastic deliverances from death. We are mainly concerned, therefore, with the more sober appeal to the miraculous which is made in the rational arguments of the apologists. This may take the form of an appeal to the mighty works of Christ, to those of the apostles as recorded, or hinted at, in the New Testament, or to miracles which an author alleges to be taking place at the present time.

Christ's own miracles naturally take a prominent place in the arguments of the apologists. The line which these arguments take is generally similar to that of St. Peter's speech on the day of Pentecost: 'Jesus, a man attested of God by mighty works and wonders and signs'. These guarantee the truth of his teaching and manifest his divinity. The argument can be used naïvely, as by Arnobius (2. 11): Christians believe in Christ because his miracles are not human works but manifestations of a divine power. The pagan philosophers, admittedly, are praiseworthy; their moral teaching is sound, their learning and eloquence are admirable; their logic is impressive; but was any of them capable of checking a storm with a word, restoring sight to the blind, reviving the dead, or even (which is much easier) healing by one word of rebuke, a boil or a thorn in the skin? The good teacher is he who accompanies his promises with the guarantee which good works furnish.

Athanasius presses these arguments further in the *De Incarnatione*. The Logos met men in their own situation. If they worshipped nature, Christ's nature-miracles were there to convince them that he is the Lord of nature. If they worshipped men as gods, his works marked him out for them as being uniquely the Son of God. If they worshipped demons, he gave them proof that he was the master of the demons; or heroes, the Resurrection proved him to be greater than any (*Inc.* 15). His miracles demonstrate that he is God (18). No marvels attributed to gods or men can compare with what he has done; for Athanasius ascribes to the Logos, who is Christ, the formation of his own body from the Virgin and the raising of it from the dead, as well as the healing of diseases and the cure of one who was actually born blind. By contrast, the gods and heroes are feeble. Asclepius discovered herbal remedies; but he did not create the herbs. Heracles fought with men and beasts; but not against diseases and demons (49).

Arnobius, again, lays stress on the superiority of Christ's works over those which were ascribed to the gods. The gods may have ordered medicines or special diets for the sick, poultices and the like, but any good doctor can do as much, and, in any case, the healing properties are in the drugs, not in those who prescribe them. But Christ, unlike any heathen deity, could heal by a word and restore men to complete health (1. 48).

The argument, however, had to meet two objections. It could be alleged that the miracle-stories were fictitious. These things had not happened. Alternatively, their truth could be admitted, but, just as at the time they were ascribed to Beelzebub, so now it can be maintained that they were done by sorcery.

To the former objection Quadratus, probably the earliest apologist, was prepared, according to Eusebius (*H.E.* 4. 3. 2), to point to first-hand testimony. Those who had been healed or raised from the dead by the Saviour, he says, were not only present when Christ was on earth but lived for a considerable time after his departure, so that some of them survived 'even to our own day'. It may be significant that, even so, Quadratus neither offered more detailed information about these people nor claimed to have personal knowledge of any of them. In any case this was a line of defence which was already losing its effectiveness when Quadratus was writing: had he been able to say that someone who had benefited from Christ's works was actually alive in the contemporary world, he could have carried more conviction. In the next generation it would be altogether too late to carry on the argument in this fashion, and as time went on the Christian tradition itself became vulnerable to Arnobius' attack on pagan legends: 'antiquity is the most fertile source of errors' (1. 57).

Faced by this situation, apologists appealed to the moral character of those who originated the tradition. This is the usual answer given by Christians to the charge that the records of miracles are untrue. Eusebius develops it at length in the *Demonstratio Evangelica* (3. 4–6). He gives a list of the miracles, including both healings and nature-miracles, leading up to Christ's Death (which was marvellous in that it was voluntary;

he gave up the spirit when he so willed), Resurrection and
Ascension. Resurrection and Ascension are regarded by Eusebius, as by Athanasius, as being Christ's own deed. All these
are 'marvels of virtue' and 'evidence of the divinity within him'.
Heathens, indeed, disbelieve the records; but Christ's moral
teaching was such that the disciples who were attracted by it
could not subsequently have devoted themselves to the fabrica-
tion of false testimony. The numbers which would have had to
become involved in a conspiracy of that kind would have been
improbably large (twelve apostles plus the seventy). Indeed,
so large a number of witnesses itself merits credence, for instead
of a mere two or three witnesses we have no less than eighty-two,
and these men, moreover, gave their testimony at the cost of
suffering and death. If the record were false, what inducement
could the disciples have had to incur hardship and suffering
as evangelists? Why should they actually deny and forsake
Jesus during his earthly life, only to deify him after he had died
a shameful death? Why, after his death, should they incur
death themselves, just in order to provide him with a false
posthumous reputation? They might have been able to bam-
boozle peasants in their own country, but they could not have
hoped, on this basis, to evangelize the whole world from Persia
to Britain. Such a conspiracy would have had to be most complicated, involving agreement between all the disciples to pre-
fabricate the same tale. They would have had to show extraordinary loyalty in continuing unitedly to stick to their story
even after some of their number had been put to death. Moreover, the character of each apostle, as recorded in the New
Testament, guarantees their reliability as a group. If they
invented the miracles, why should they go out of their way to
record such embarrassments to their cause as Christ's distress
at Gethsemane or Peter's denial? Why did they not invent
stories about some terrible divine vengeance immediately over-
taking Judas or Caiaphas or those who mocked Jesus?

Arnobius followed a similar line (1. 54 ff.). How could the whole world be persuaded of a falsehood? The self-sacrifice of the witnesses attests their reliability. It is no argument to say that they were uneducated or that they wrote abominable Greek. Nor will it do to argue that no divine being could have been put to death; therefore Jesus was not divine; therefore he could have done no miracles. What hung on the Cross was only the human form which the divine being had put on. If brigands were to kill the Sibyl while she was prophesying, that would not mean that Apollo had died. Arnobius has been counter-attacked at a weak point in his theology.

The argument that the miracles, though genuine, were done by magic gave the apologists more trouble. Cyprian touches on the belief that Christ was regarded by the Jews as a magician and put to death on that account (*quod idola dii non sint*, 13). Celsus accepted Christ's miracles as historical, but believed that he had acquired magical powers in Egypt (*Contra Celsum* 1. 28). Why, then, asks Origen, did Christ bother about ethical teaching? What has that to do with a magician? (1. 38). He who reformed men morally cannot have been a sorcerer (1. 68).

At *Contra Celsum* 2. 48, Origen embarks on a fairly full discussion which includes the debate about whether Christ was a sorcerer. It leads him on to a line of argument which could easily, if pursued, end in a purely 'parabolic' interpretation of the miracle-stories and a consequent abandonment of the traditional appeal to the miraculous altogether. Celsus claims that Christians believe Jesus to be Son of God because he did healings and raised the dead. Origen says he certainly did heal men. That he would do so had been prophesied in Isaiah 35. 5 f. He also raised the dead. The truth of this is guaranteed by the fewness of the raisings attributed to him. Fiction would not have been content with three, nor would it have allowed those who were raised to be people who had only recently, or relatively recently died; they would have been men who had died and been buried long ago. In fact, only those were raised whom

the Logos knew to be suitable for resurrection, and it was done
in order that Christ's act might symbolize certain truths and
lead many to the wonderful teaching of the gospel.

In Origen's view, unlike that of most apologists, the miracles
are but signs and foreshadowings of the 'greater works' which
Christ promised should be done by his disciples. These works
are greater than any physical miracle. The eyes of the spiritually
blind are always being opened; the ears of those who are deaf
to any talk of virtue now hear eagerly about God. Those who
were lame in the feet of the inner man and who have been
healed by the Logos do not now merely leap but leap as an
hart, an animal which kills serpents, so that the spiritually lame
can trample on the serpents and scorpions of evil.

After this spiritualization of miracles, which leaves the Gospel
stories intact but reduces their meaning to the status of parables,
Origen has to deal with the question of magic. Celsus asserts
that Jesus warned people against evil men who would one day
come and perform similar miracles to his own. But since these
evil men are sorcerers, this implies that his own works were of
a similar kind to those of sorcerers and that he did not really
regard them as divine. Origen rightly points out that the passages
where Christ warns his followers about coming false prophets,
contain nothing about sorcery; false prophets are not the same
as magicians. Moreover, if someone could claim to be the Christ
and do similar works to those of Jesus, this would really be an
argument for Jesus' divine power. The Egyptians did similar
works to those of Moses; they did them by trickery, he by the
power of God. So, too, the miracles of false prophets will be lies,
aimed at deception, whereas Christ's miracles led to salvation.
The wolf is not a dog, even though it may look and bark like
one. When something bad pretends to be something good, this
is an argument for the existence of that good something which
is the antithesis of the bad. Hence the existence of sorcery
implies the reality of divine miracles. In every case, Origen
goes on to say, the criterion is the moral character of the people

concerned and the effects of the miracle. The works of Moses and Jesus are divine. They can be recognized as such because the former created a nation and the latter introduced the life which is in accordance with the gospel. The proof of the miracle of the Resurrection is ultimately the behaviour of Christ's disciples.

Eusebius deals with the matter rather more simply. Sorcery is incompatible with Christ's moral character. Magicians always aim at securing money, fame, or sensual pleasure; but Christ was truly *philosophos* and *eusebes*. His followers, too, invariably shun all magical practices; no Christian goes in for such things. Therefore Christ could not have taught his disciples magic. Moreover, if he were a magician where did he learn the art? If it was from the Egyptians, why do we hear nothing about these extraordinary magicians in Egypt who, since they could instruct Jesus, must have actually excelled him in the art? Not only Christ's character, but the achievements of his followers in evangelizing the world and, in the process, abolishing magic everywhere, render the whole notion absurd. Sorcerers, further-more, always use incense and libations, and invoke demons. It is well known that Christians prefer to die rather than do any of these things. On the contrary, Christians repel the workings of demons through the name of Jesus and prayer. Even now every demon fears the name of Jesus, just as in the days of his ministry. Jesus, therefore, did his works through divine power, for scripture attests him as God's Word and Power dwelling in flesh. The works of the apostles, too, prove that the power of the risen and living Christ is truly divine.

Thus Christ's miracles demonstrate the victory of God over demons, and even, as Arnobius (1. 47) claims, over fate itself; for his healings released people from sufferings which had been brought upon them in accordance with fate's decrees.

Christian apologetic found that the appeal to miracles was by no means a trump card to play. It involved arguments which could be turned back upon those who used them, and it was often necessary to take up a defensive position in respect of the miracles which were so prominent in the Gospels. Christians discovered that they could not rest their case simply on miracle-stories. If these were to win credence they themselves needed the support of Christ's recorded teaching and, above all, of the recorded impression of his character. Miracles might commend Christ, but Christ was first needed to commend the miracles. It was not enough to ask men to believe in Christ's divinity because of the miracles; they had to be asked to believe the miracle-stories because they first accepted his divinity. His divine character had to be appealed to in order to vindicate the authenticity and the divinity of the miracles, at least in a world where the idea that *theioi andres* can work marvels was familiar and where there was no disposition to regard Christ's works as unique.

The tradition also spoke of similar miracles being done by Christ's disciples. Eusebius (*H.E.* 2. 3. 2) remarks that the initial success of the gospel was due to Christ's power, displayed both in his disciples' teaching and in their works. These miraculous deeds seem to have been regarded as an extension, as it were, of Christ's own. The latter attested his divinity; the disciples' works guaranteed that divinity was inherent in the proclamation of the gospel, enabling it to spread through the entire world. Without the aid of this divine power, says Origen (*Contra Celsum* 1. 38), the disciples would not have possessed the necessary confidence to undertake their mission. Yet, once again, they were not magicians; their own teaching forbade all sorcery. It was, says Arnobius a proof of Christ's marvellous power that men who were only unskilled peasants could do such wonderful works without any material aids. These were necessary in the apostolic age, as Eusebius maintained. Without miracles, as Origen remarks (*Contra Celsum* 1. 46), men could not have been persuaded to accept totally new teaching.

The early apologists do not explicitly say, like Chrysostom and other later writers, that the age of miracles belongs essentially to the past; that they were part of the initial proclamation, intended by God to cease after a short time; that their purpose was to enable the gospel to get off the ground, as it were, and that they have now, as a general rule, ceased since the Church can make its own way without their aid. Yet there are hints of something approaching this point of view. Irenaeus indeed, in a well-known passage (*Haer.* 2. 48–9) argues directly from the presence of miracles in the contemporary Church, claiming that these include exorcisms, healings, and actually a few raisings from the dead. Eusebius, however, quoting him, says only that miraculous gifts were still granted to fit persons, even until the times in question, i.e. the times of Irenaeus, not of Eusebius himself. Karl Holl pointed out that neither Montanus nor his prophets claimed to work miracles; and on the whole the attitude of Christian apologetic to contemporary miracles is cagey. Eusebius (*Dem. Ev.* 3. 4) alludes to 'some small measure' of the Lord's power which he still allows to be manifested in the Church. Origen says that according to the will of the Logos Christians still exorcize, perform cures, and discern future events; but he chiefly emphasizes the marvellous way in which many people are converted by means of visions, whether by night or day (*Contra Celsum* 1. 46), and he is mainly interested in 'spiritual' miracles in the contemporary Church. Tatian (*Orat.* 16) speaks of healings and exorcisms taking place; and Tertullian and Eusebius both make general allusions to miracles and occasionally even to particular events such as the episode of the 'Thundering Legion'. For the most part, however, these writers tell us little that is either very detailed or specially marvellous.

The one form of contemporary miracle, if that is the right word for it, which figures prominently in apologetic is exorcism. I find it hard to pin-point the difference between the New Testament's ideas of exorcism and those of the later Church; but I think there is a considerable difference between them. When Judaism ceased to be the main enemy and Christians found themselves confronted, as they are already beginning to be in the time of the Apocalypse, by the organized force of the pagan State linked inseparably with the worship of gods whom they believed to be demons, the Christian life became a continual conflict with devils. Christians were surrounded on all sides by a civilization which devils controlled and inspired. It can scarcely be supposed that everyone imagined a sane pagan to be in the same condition as a person actually possessed by demons, in the manner of those from whom Jesus expelled unclean spirits. Yet everyone, it was held, who belonged to the heathen world needed to be exorcized, frequently and thoroughly, before he could receive baptism. This fact may indicate the difference that I have in mind.

The allusions to exorcism are sometimes specific, but more often they are general. In either case it is often a heathen deity who is adjured and overthrown, or compelled to reveal his true character as a demon. Thus Eusebius (*H.E.* 7. 17) tells of Astyrius, a converted senator, who overthrew the demon-deity at Paneas by the force of prayer. That Christians compel the demons to confess their true nature is asserted by Theophilus (*Autol.* 2. 8) and Minucius Felix, who says (27. 3) that the demons afflict people with diseases and torments so as to induce them to offer sacrifices; they then release the sufferers from the bonds that they have themselves imposed on them, so that they may gain credit for curing them. Tertullian similarly (*Apol.* 23) says that when any Christian commands a possessed person to speak he, or rather the spirit in him, will declare itself to be a demon. Thus Christian exorcism reveals the true nature of the pagan gods. Lactantius also believes (*Inst.* 2. 16) that exorcism compels the demons to declare themselves and even to reveal their true names. Cyprian suggests the same idea (*quod idola dii non sint*, 13), and asserts that the way in which the Christians torment the demons in exorcism reveals the weakness of the gods (*Ad Demetr.* 15).

Tertullian also claims that Christians benefit society because they expel demons (*Apol.* 37); that the Christians' exorcisms, and their prayers for rain, have impressed the heathen greatly (*Ad Scap.* 4); that a Christian who served as a soldier would be defending the demons he has conquered in exorcism (*De Corona Mil.* 5. 11); and that to trade in incense would be inconsistent with the Christian profession, for the Christian exorcizes the demons to whom it is offered (*De Idol.* 7. 12).

Exorcism is a standing proof of the Resurrection, since it exhibits Christ's present power over idols and demons (Athanasius, *Inc.* 30). A briefer expression of the same idea is found as early as Justin (*Dial.* 30), who also says that the work of exorcists, including their exploits at Rome, proves the truth of Christian belief about Christ (2 *Apol.* 6), and that the defeat of demons throughout the world testifies to his Messiahship (*Dial.* 121). Thus it is much less to miracles of healing that apologists point as evidence, within the contemporary scene, for the truth of Christianity than to exorcisms which demonstrate the present activity of Christ's power and the efficacy of his Name. Exorcism, however, does not seem to be normally regarded as especially marvellous. It is a part, only, of the constant and universal struggle against a pagan, and therefore demonic, environment.

It might be added that miracles are occasionally invoked in a kind of negative apologetic: not as proofs for the unbeliever, but as warnings to Christian backsliders. Thus Cyprian tells of horrifying occurrences which support his policy towards the lapsed: such as the story that the eucharistic bread has changed to ashes when the lapsed have presumed to receive Communion without being reconciled (*Laps.* 24–6). Less often in the pre-Nicene Church do we meet that familiar phenomenon of later times: the story of a miracle which vindicates orthodoxy against heresy. We have, however, the tale of the heretical Roman bishop, Natalius, who was beaten by angels and so compelled to recant and to submit to Bishop Zephyrinus (Eusebius, *H.E.* 5. 28. 12), and Firmilian's story of how a woman who had

P

claimed to prophesy and had celebrated the sacraments was exorcized and thus revealed as being possessed of a demon when she did these things (*Epistle* ap. Cypr. *Ep.* 75. 10).

These developments, however, lie beyond the scope of apologetic proper. Of the latter, during this period, it can be said that the appeal to miracle is made at different levels, but, among the more serious Christians, with more sense and restraint than at some later stages of Church history; and that, in the hands of the sophisticated, the argument from miracles proves to be double-edged weapon, to be used in a supporting role only.

14

MIRACLES IN THE EARLY CHURCH

BY
M. F. WILES

M. F. WILES

Maurice Wiles was a scholar of Christ's College, Cambridge; trained for the Anglican Ministry at Ridley Hall; served a curacy at Stockport; and came back to Ridley Hall as Chaplain, 1952–5. He was a Lecturer in University College, Ibadan, Nigeria, 1955–9, and then returned to Cambridge again as a University Lecturer in Divinity and Fellow and Dean of Clare College. He is married and has three children.

MIRACLES IN THE EARLY CHURCH

THE THEME of Professor Lampe's paper[1] was the nature of the appeal to miracle in the apologetic work of the second and third centuries. I want to try and build upon this in two main directions. In the first place, I shall say something fairly briefly about the shift in approach occasioned by difficulties in the historical appeal to miracle, which arose mainly in the later part of that period and in the century following. I shall then go on to consider at slightly greater length the more philosophical type of argument about the possibility of miracle in the writings of the early period in general. This will lead to a few brief remarks in conclusion about the connexion between miracle and the idea of God as creator.

I take up first of all therefore the historical appeal. The primary difficulty which begins to make itself felt in the third and ensuing centuries was that the really evidentially impressive miracles were getting steadily further away in time. On one occasion, when trying to show the superiority of Christian over pagan miracle stories, Arnobius asserts that, whereas the pagans argue for the greater trustworthiness of their miracle stories on the ground that they are more ancient than the Christian stories, in actual fact 'antiquity is the most fertile source of errors'.[2] But to a more sensitive soul, like that of Origen, it was evident that reasoning of this kind could be something of an embarrassment to the Christian case. The time had long gone by when Quadratus, as mentioned by Professor Lampe, had been able to speak of people healed or raised by the Saviour as surviving to his own day (though it is perhaps worth noting that even he doesn't appear to claim to have known any such personally).[3] In his Commentary on St. John, Origen frankly admits that

---

[1] That is, No. 13.   [2] Arnobius, *Contra Gentes*, 1. 57.   [3] Eusebius, *H.E.* 4. 3. 2.

while the τεράστιοι δυνάμεις of Christ, his stupendous miracles, were able to bring his own contemporaries to faith, they have lost their demonstrative power with the lapse of time and have begun to be regarded as mere tales (μῦθοι).[1] And what applied to the miracles of Jesus, applied in lesser degree also to the miracles of his followers. Irenaeus (to recall another passage mentioned in Professor Lampe's paper) had been able to speak of raisings from the dead as experiences of the Christian community (though again the wording does not suggest any claim to personal experience of such events).[2] But Origen, while continuing to claim that there are traces of miraculous powers still in a few people whose souls have been purified by the Logos, admits that they have become steadily less numerous with the passage of time.[3]

What then was to happen to the appeal to miracle as lapse of time modified the immediacy and therefore the effectiveness of it as a ground of appeal?

In the first instance it could be propped up by being linked in with some other form of argument rather than being required to stand fairly and squarely upon its own feet. Thus in the passage just quoted from the Commentary on John, where Origen explicitly admits that the sheer evidential value of the miracles of Jesus is a diminishing asset, he goes on to argue that their credibility and consequent evidential value are greatly reinforced by the fact that they were foretold in Old Testament prophecy. Tertullian follows a similar line of argument against Marcion. He points out that according to the New Testament false Christs will do signs and wonders. It is signs and wonders which have been foretold that are important, because (among other things) they do not lack 'the evidences of that antiquity which wins the assent of faith'. Tertullian's argument here is very close to that which Arnobius so vigorously rejected.[4] More

---

[1] Origen, *Com. Jn.* 2. 34.   [2] Irenaeus, *Haer.* 2. 32. 4.
[3] Origen, *Contra Celsum*, 7. 8.   [4] *Adversus Marcionem*, 3. 3.

frequently (as was stressed throughout Professor Lampe's paper) the argument is used that the credibility of the miracle-stories is strongly enhanced by the dedicated quality of life of those who recorded them.[1]

But these are only palliatives. They tend to involve either so radical a shift of argument that the argument really becomes primarily an argument from prophecy rather than miracle, or else to leave virtually untouched the hard core of the problem— namely that the appeal to ancient miracles is not very convincing. They do not really deal with the objection that in such matters antiquity is a fertile source of errors.

There was one way, however, which could claim to be a continuing appeal to miracle and at the same time appear at least to escape from this difficulty. I referred a moment ago to the fact stressed by Professor Lampe that the transformed life was frequently appealed to as supporting evidence for the credibility of the miracle-stories. But it is easily possible to shift the balance of the argument and to make the moral and spiritual transformation of human lives not just supporting evidence but the substance of the appeal, and at the same time to treat this as still essentially an appeal to miracle. The miracles that are really important, it will then be claimed, are not the 'stupendous miracles' ($\tau\epsilon\rho\acute{a}\sigma\tau\iota o\iota$ $\delta\upsilon\nu\acute{a}\mu\epsilon\iota\varsigma$) of Jesus literally understood; they are the changed lives which he effects. This line of development flows very naturally and impressively from the allegorical pen of Origen.

> I might say that according to the promise of Jesus the disciples have done greater works than the physical miracles which Jesus did. For the eyes of people blind in soul are always being opened, and the ears of those who were deaf to any talk of virtue eagerly hear about God and the blessed life with him; and many too who were lame in the feet of their inner man, as the Bible calls it, but have now been healed by the Logos, do not just leap, but leap as a hart, an animal hostile to serpents and superior to all the poison of vipers. In fact, these lame people who have been healed

[1] E.g. Origen, *Contra Celsum*, 5. 57; Arnobius, *Contra Gentes*, 1. 55.

receive from Jesus power to walk on their feet, where before they
were lame, over all the serpents and scorpions of evil, and in
general over all the power of the enemy, and on their walk
they do nothing wrong; for they have even become superior to all
evil and the poison of daemons.[1]

But this line of approach was not limited to radical allegorizers
such as Origen. Athanasius speaks of it as a great sign ($\sigma\eta\mu\epsilon\hat{\iota}o\nu$)
to make a damsel live as a virgin, and a young man live in
continence, and an idolater come to know Christ.[2] John Chrysostom argues that the spiritual sight of the redeemed Christian
is a better sign than the physical healing of the blind man. The
latter is open to suspicion (even if unjustifiable suspicion in the
case of the Christian miracles) and may (as in the case of
Simon Magus) give rise to no more than a desire to get the
same power for oneself. It is a better sign to be ready to die for
one's faith than to be able to raise the dead; to despise money
as grass than to be able to turn grass into money.[3]

Nevertheless, this line of argument was not carried through
with the thoroughness that would have been required if it were
to do away altogether with what we may call the problem of
miracle. The same Chrysostom who stresses the greater value
of the miracle of the holy life has no doubts about the historicity
of the miracles of Jesus; they were outward and visible signs
appropriate to the start of a great spiritual movement. The
early miracles were needed to give rise to a faith which makes
further miracles unnecessary. But the reality and the importance
of the early miracles remain for Chrysostom.[4] So also with
Athanasius: it is the same Athanasius who extols the $\sigma\eta\mu\epsilon\hat{\iota}a$ of
continence and conversion, who in the *De Incarnatione* uses the
miracles of Jesus as evidence of his divinity.[5] Origen might have
been an exception, but most emphatically he is not. He was

---

[1] *Contra Celsum*, 2. 48.   [2] Athanasius, *Ep.* 49. 7.
[3] Chrysostom, *Hom. in Matt.* 32. 11; 46. 3.
[4] Chrysostom, *Hom. in Matt.* 12. 2; 14. 3; *Hom. in Jn.* 12. 3; *Hom. in* 1 *Cor.* 6. 2.
Cf. F. H. Chase, *Chrysostom*, pp. 127–9.   [5] Athanasius, *De Inc.* 18.

prepared to use the allegorical method to get rid of historical embarrassments from the New Testament as well as from the Old. He does so in the case of historical conflict between the different gospel accounts. He could have done so in the case of miracle. He could have used the allegorical method with the same vigour as some to-day would use a subjectivist approach to history so as to remove the crude and embarrassing problem of the gospel miracles altogether. But emphatically he does not do so. In the very same section of the *Contra Celsum* (2. 48) in which he speaks of the greater spiritual works of the disciples, he argues on historical grounds that 'Christ really did raise the dead and this is not a fiction of the writers of the gospels'.

So I would conclude this stage of the inquiry by saying that while there was a shift of emphasis from the increasingly more distant physical miracles of Jesus to the continuing miracles of conversion and continence, the problem of miracle in its outward physical form still remained. And this raised philosophical difficulties from which there was no escape and to which I want shortly to turn.

But before I go on to take up these more philosophical issues, I want to spend a few moments in a kind of limbo or no-man's land which belongs to the realm of neither strictly historical nor philosophical appeal.

There is a certain level of naïve appeal to miracle at which all the difficulties with which we are concerned are simply ignored. In Christian literature this kind of approach is represented by the apocryphal Acts and later hagiographical writings. I do not want to discuss this aspect of miracle in the early church beyond pointing out that such an appeal to miracle continued all the time alongside a more serious grappling with philosophical difficulties. That it should have done so need not necessarily have caused any serious embarrassment either to enlightened pagan or Christian. There is an Arabic fragment of Galen's commentary on Plato's Republic which reads: 'Most

people are unable to follow any demonstrative argument con-
secutively; hence they need parables and benefit from them—
just as now we see the people called Christians drawing their
faith from parables and miracles and yet sometimes acting in
the same way as those who philosophize'.[1] Strabo speaks similarly of how religious awe, which is necessary for the unphilo-
sophical multitude, cannot be produced without myths and
miraculous tales.[2] When this is compared with the double truth
theory of writers like Clement and Origen, it is clear that
some at least of the intelligentsia on both sides could have
accepted a popular appeal to miracle of a naïve kind, at the
same time as carrying on serious debate at another level about
the real possibility of miracle.

In so far as the naïve appeal ever concerned itself to justify
the reality of the miracles to which it appealed, it would do so
by the simple affirmation that God is omnipotent and can do
anything. Jesus had said 'with God all things are possible' and
the Christian *simpliciores* gladly quoted him to that effect.

But as soon as any attempt to justify miracle is made, the age
of innocence is gone. The concept of divine omnipotence at
once raises philosophical questions and was a well-worn issue of
contemporary philosophical debate. There were philosophers
who were ready to support that same view that God can do
anything. For the most part these seem to have been Stoics for
whom God was identical with the cosmos. In asserting that God
can do anything therefore they were asserting not so much a
superiority of religion over science, of God over the world, as
the infinite variety of potential experience. As one of their
critics puts it, their real belief was that matter, which is the
source and substance of everything that is, is so flexible and
mutable that there is nothing which the divine providence,

---

[1] R. Walzer, *Galen on Jews and Christians*, pp. 15 and 57. There is some doubt
about the authenticity of the words 'and miracles' in the original text (op. cit.,
p. 57, n. 4), but as the ensuing quotation from Strabo shows myths and miracles
often go together in this kind of context.   [2] Ibid., p. 70.

which moulds the world, could not produce from it even instantaneously.[1]

But the main line of philosophic thought (of Platonic ethos) would have none of this. On occasion the idea is held up to ridicule, as illustrated by the remark: 'The Stoics say that God can do anything. In that case would that he had made the Stoics wiser than to believe everything with such meticulous superstition.'[2] In developing more substantial attacks of this kind, opponents of the Stoic view frequently compile lists of things that God cannot do. Most of these are logical absurdities such as making the diagonal of a parallelogram equal in length to the side. These were not, of course, intended to deny the idea of divine omnipotence, but only to express it more accurately. Not all of the examples in such lists however would appear to us to have the same measure of logical contradiction. Thus Pliny asserts that God cannot die, give mortals immortality, or recall the dead, change the past, or make twice ten unequal to twenty.[3]

The inclusion of 'recalling the dead' is significant, because it was on this question in particular that the issue arose sharply for Christians. For they maintained not only that this had happened to Christ and a few others whom he or his immediate disciples had raised in the past, but that it would ultimately happen to every one of us in receiving the resurrection of the body. The proclamation of the resurrection had been the chief rock of offence to Paul's Areopagite audience, and it remained a great stone of stumbling (especially in the form of the expected universal resurrection of the body) for thoughtful non-Christians in the succeeding centuries. Most early Christian writers would seem to fall back ultimately on the straightforward affirmation that God can do everything.[4] Celsus therefore was not being wilfully perverse

---

[1] Cicero, *De Nat. Deorum*, III. 92. On this whole question see R. Walzer, op. cit., pp. 26–32; R. M. Grant, *Miracle and Natural Law*, Ch. 9.
[2] Cicero, *De Div.* 2, 41, 86.   [3] *N.H.* 2. 27.
[4] E.g. 1 Clement 27. 2; Athenagoras, *De Res. Mort.* 9. See H. Chadwick, 'Origen, Celsus and the Resurrection of the Body', *H.T.R.* (41) 1948, p. 84.

in claiming that on this topic of the resurrection of the body Christians relied upon the philosophically unrespectable affirmation of an unqualified divine omnipotence.[1] Origen is highly sensitive on this point. He fully admits the strength of Celsus' objection but claims that he misrepresents the Christian view. Origen readily agrees that God cannot do what is shameful or what is contrary to nature. The problem, however, is to know what is contrary to nature, and Origen still argues that miraculous events which may commonly be regarded as contrary to nature may in fact be a matter of transcending nature.[2] Indeed, so strongly did Origen feel on this whole question that he turns upon the *simpliciores* precisely the arguments that Celsus raises against Christianity in general and taunts them in just the same way with taking refuge in the cry that all things are possible with God and then quoting in their support words of scripture which might seem to support their case when taken literally.[3]

But in order to escape fully from the force of Celsus' objection (and indeed from the difficulties about the whole notion which he felt for himself), Origen in fact developed a view of the resurrection body which involved at least ultimately the elimination of fleshly substance altogether.[4] Perhaps there is no midway position between that and a crude form of the argument from divine omnipotence. Certainly Augustine, whom no one could accuse of naïveté, does not seem able to escape from the dilemma. From the earliest times Christians had been taxed with the question of how the bodies of those who had been eaten by animals, or still worse by cannibals, would be reassembled and resurrected. Athenagoras had tried to deal with the objection by arguing that man cannot eat man; it is unnatural and if, under pressure of famine, one were to try to do

---

[1] Origen, *Contra Celsum*, 5. 14.   [2] Ibid. 5. 23.
[3] *Sel. in Ps.* 1. 5 (*P.G.* 12, 1092).
[4] The exact nature of Origen's teaching on this question is not easy to determine, but I believe the statement made above to be a fair summary of his position.

so, one would in fact be unable to digest it.[1] But Augustine is less sanguine; not only ancient stories but recent experience show that it does happen. The conclusion of his argument is worthy of quotation.

> The flesh of the famished man that hunger consumed is exhaled into the air, and thence (as we said before) the Creator can fetch it again. This flesh therefore of the man that was eaten shall return to the first owner, of whom the famished man does but as it were borrow it and so must repay it again. And his own flesh which famine dried up into air shall be re-collected and restored into some convenient place of his body; and even if it were so consumed that no part thereof remained in nature, yet God could fetch it again in an instant and when he would himself.[2]

To claim that God can fetch again in an instant what does not even remain in nature is indeed to base one's case on the divine omnipotence in the most complete and drastic manner.

But even if on the particular question of the resurrection of the body there seemed to be no resting place between spiritualizing the idea away (with Origen) or falling back into the sheer affirmation of omnipotence (with in effect the rest of the Church), it would be totally misleading to suggest that, in general approach to the question of miracle, Origen was the only scholar to be free of the sheer naïveté of the *simpliciores*. Other writers, if less sensitive to the difficulties involved in falling back when hard pressed on to the argument of sheer omnipotence, did not regard the words 'God can do anything' as a panacea which left nothing more needing to be said. It is clear that they were working with a conception of miracle which was closely linked with their understanding of God as Creator, and that it was one which did not have simply to be presented as deserving of belief because it was impossible, but about which certain things could be said which would help to enhance its intelligibility and credibility.

---

[1] Athenagoras, *De Res.* 4–6.
[2] Augustine, *De Civitate Dei*, XXII. 20. On this whole question see H. Chadwick art. cit. and R. M. Grant, op. cit., Ch. 15.

This link between miracle and the notion of God as Creator comes out very early with relation to Marcion. Sheer miracle by itself was used by Marcion to suggest the idea of Christ as superior to and in conflict with the Creator-God. This was attacked by Tertullian, not simply on the ground (already mentioned) that the miracles were foretold in the Old Testament, but also on the ground that they were foreshadowed by similar types in Old Testament history. Indeed Tertullian stresses the superiority of the Old Testament type—e.g. Christ fed 5,000 on one occasion on the inferior food of bread and fish: the Creator-God of the Old Testament fed 600,000 for forty years on the manna of heaven.[1] It was also attacked by placing an emphasis on Christ's use of physical means in the performing of his miracles. This is a characteristic emphasis in the writings of Irenaeus. The use of clay in the healing of the man born blind is seen as an echo of Genesis 2. 7 in the creation story.[2] Indeed this idea of illustrating oneness with the Creator becomes a standard first point in commentary on many of the miracles (such as the turning of water into wine)[3] in almost all subsequent patristic exegesis. This anti-Marcionite emphasis tends to conflict with the more obvious emphases of apologetic. Against Marcion the magnitude of the miracles of Christ is played down for fear they may give rise to faith in a docetic Christ; against Marcion the use of physical means is stressed whereas at other times it was played down or conveniently forgotten in answering the charge of magic or sorcery.[4] Perhaps the fact that most of the early apologists were also involved on the anti-Marcionite front may have something to do with the relative restraint of their appeal to miracle.

Yet this restraint was not overdone. What I have called the apologetic emphasis was still needed both for apologetic purposes and for the determination of Christian doctrine. If the

---

[1] Tertullian, *Adv. Marc.* 4, 20–1.   [2] Irenaeus, *Haer.* 5. 15. 2.
[3] Ibid. 3. 11. 5. Cf. Origen, *Comm. Jn.* (ed. Brooke) *Frag.* 30; Athanasius, *De Inc.* 18; Chrysostom, *Hom. in Jn.* 22, 1–2.   [4] E.g. Arnobius, *Contra Gentes*, 1. 48.

miracles were in danger of suggesting a docetic Christ, the sufferings were in danger of suggesting an Ebionite one. What in the long run therefore was forthcoming was not a playing down of the consideration of miracle in understanding the person of Christ, but rather a keeping of it in proper balance with the consideration of his sufferings. So in all discussion of the two natures of Christ the miracles are treated as the primary illustration of his divinity just as the sufferings are of his humanity. 'The evidence for his divinity comes through the miracles' (ἡ τῆς θεότητος μαρτυρία διὰ τῶν θαυμάτων ἐστί), says Gregory of Nyssa.[1]

The way in which this argument from the miracles could be developed is well brought out by a fuller quotation from Gregory of Nyssa's *Catechetical Oration*. The emphases which he makes in this passage are the exact opposite of those which mark the anti-Marcionite writings of Tertullian and Irenaeus.

Now unquestionably in not one of those who had lived in history from the beginning of the world had he (i.e. the Devil) been conscious of any such circumstances as he observed to surround him who then manifested himself, i.e. conception without sexual union, . . . motherhood with virginity, . . . the healing of natural disease without the use of means and of an extraordinary character proceeding from him by the mere utterance of a word and exercise of his will, the restoration of the dead to life, . . . his walking through the sea not by waters separating on either side and, as in the case of Moses' miraculous power, making bare its depth for those who passed through, but by the surface of the water presenting solid ground for his feet and by a firm and hard resistance supporting his steps; then his disregard for food as long as it pleased him to abstain, his abundant banquets in the wilderness whereby many thousands were fully fed (though neither did the heavens pour down manna on them, nor was their need supplied by the earth producing corn for them in the natural way, but that instance of munificence came out of the ineffable store-houses of his divine power), the bread ready in the hands of those who distributed it, as if they were actually reaping it, and becoming more the more the eaters were filled.[2]

[1] *Catechetical Oration* 34.   [2] Ibid. 23.

It is difficult not to feel that we have here lapsed back in
practice into the docetism of Marcion. The main differences
from Marcion's view would seem to be two. In the first place,
this is not all that Gregory would want to say about Christ. It
would be balanced by statements about the reality of the
sufferings in terms of his human nature. Consistent docetism is
replaced by the paradox of orthodox Christology, which is
some advance but no solution. In the second place, Gregory
does not see these miracles as contrary to nature and thereby
representing conflict with the Creator. He prefers to describe
them in words reminiscent of Origen as 'greater than nature'
($\mu\epsilon\hat{\iota}\zeta\omega$ $\tau\hat{\eta}s$ $\phi\acute{v}\sigma\epsilon\omega s$).[1] Hilary of Poitiers develops what is essentially
the same idea when he says that, being divine, Christ had a
heavenly body and that for that body to walk on the water or
to enter a closed house is in accordance with its proper nature.[2]
I suspect that to-day we are inclined on occasion to use an
argument of this kind with reference to the resurrection of
Jesus, but that we probably feel a little unhappy about Hilary's
more extensive use of it in relation to the pre-Resurrection
miracles—and with good reason. Hilary's Christ is surely indis-
tinguishable in the end from Clement's Christ, whose body was
of a superior nature so that it did not *need* food and drink, but
only took them in order to confound the docetists.

The inescapable problem appears to be: Can one use miracle
to show the divinity of Christ (in the full anti-Arian sense
insisted upon by Gregory and Hilary) and escape from having
to use the sheer unqualified affirmation of divine omnipotence
as the *deus ex machina* to rescue one from the ensuing difficulties
in argumentation and imaginative description? I do not think
that Gregory or Hilary succeed in doing so. Hilary indeed ends
his account of the feeding of the 5,000 with the direct affirmation: 'What we see passes our understanding: our only resource
is faith in God's omnipotence'.[3]

[1] Ibid. 13. Cf. Origen, *Contra Celsum*, 5. 23.   [2] Hilary, *De Trinitate*, 10. 23.
[3] Ibid. 3. 6.

Yet, all the time, the patristic writers are *trying* to escape from this dilemma. They want to stress the absolute transcendent nature of the miracle that it may make its point, but at the same time they want to show its congruity with other aspects of experience so that the Christ of faith may be seen to be in harmony with the God of creation, and also so that it may be intelligible to their audience or readers. This is a part at least of what is implied in calling the miracles beyond and not contrary to nature. In so far as this can be done in any more positive way it is done by the use of analogies with nature. Even that lover of paradox, Tertullian, uses this kind of reasoning. In the *De Resurrectione Carnis* he appeals to the admittedly faint and obvious image of resurrection in nature as a whole, and ends with the (to him) far more impressive illustration of the phoenix dying and returning to life again on its birthday— an illustration which he even claims to find explicitly indicated in scripture in the words of Psalm 92. 12: 'The righteous shall flourish like the phoenix'.[1] But the most common example of this kind is appeal to the miracle of human birth—the fact that a small drop of human seed can be formed into bones, sinews and flesh. For Justin this is evidence of the rationality of the miracle of the resurrection of the flesh;[2] for Gregory of Nyssa it is evidence of the rationality of the claim that a drop of water in baptism can perform the miracle of second birth.[3] Similar examples could be drawn from almost every patristic writer.

It may be that remarks of this kind ought to be dismissed as no more than common-places of proverbial wisdom. I would at least offer the suggestion that they ought perhaps to be valued a little more highly. The early Christians were trying to

---

[1] *De Res. Carn.* 12–13. Christian writers vary as to whether they treat this as history or fable. Tertullian treats it as history. Whether he seriously regarded it as such is perhaps another matter. Similarly, it is very likely that he knew that *phoenix* really means a palm-tree in Psalm 92. If so, it only serves to illustrate the unscrupulous debating nature of his writing and emphasizes how much he wanted to find arguments of the kind I am discussing.

[2] *Apol.* 1. 19.   [3] *Catechetical Oration* 33.

describe a unity of divine and human in the person of Christ and we know how difficult they found it. It is within that context that they saw the issue of miracle, when they were concerned with the Christian understanding of it, rather than simply with its use in apologetic. In the more historical and philosophical treatment of the issue they run into great difficulties—the miracles either prove too little (and ultimately disappear as miracle altogether), or they prove too much (and leave us with a docetic Christ and a superstitious kind of faith in divine omnipotence). I do not think that this linking of the historical miracles with the idea of a sacramental universe, with a sense of wonder in relation to life as a whole, *solves* any of the other problems. But I do think that it is at least healthily consonant with the best thought of the Fathers—to wit, that the miracles are signs of the Creator-God, who acted in Christ uniquely yet in a way fully consistent and harmonious with his total activity towards and within the world of his creation.

EXCURSUS I

THE VOCABULARY OF MIRACLE

BY

C. F. D. MOULE

IT IS FREQUENTLY said that one of the striking facts about the vocabulary of miracle in the New Testament is the extreme rarity of any word that, in fact, corresponds to the word 'miracle'; for, broadly speaking, the words most used are not *thaumasion* ('marvel'), but *dunamis* ('power') and *semeion* ('sign') —the latter mainly in St. John's Gospel.[1] This is true; but the matter is not an entirely simple one, and a sweeping generalization of this sort may give an exaggerated impression of single-mindedness in the choice of words and lead to rash conclusions about the writers' intentions.

In an attempt at rather closer definition, we may begin from the fact that so disconcertingly 'pagan' a word as *teras* (usually translated 'portent', Vulgate, *portentum*) is used with approval in the Acts, in the Pauline epistles, and in the Epistle to the Hebrews. In the Gospels, it is true, its rare occurrences are in contexts of disapproval: Mk. 13. 22, Mt. 24. 24 (false Messiahs and false prophets using *semeia* and *terata* to deceive); Jn. 4. 49, 'Unless you see *semeia* and *terata*, you will not believe'. So also once in the Pauline corpus in 2 Thess. 2. 9, it is the rival to the Messiah who will use every sort of false *dunamis* and *semeion* and *teras*. But, elsewhere *teras* is used with approval, as follows: *terata* and *semeia*: Acts 2. 22, 43; 5. 12; 6. 8; 7. 36; 14. 3; *semeia* and *terata*: Acts 4. 30; 15. 12; Rom. 15. 19; 2 Cor. 12. 12; Heb. 2. 4.

The article τέρας by K. H. Rengstorf in *T.W.N.T.*[2] helps to explain the position of *teras* in the New Testament. He shows

---

[1] *Semeion* is also (so G. MacRae, above, p. 143) 'by far the more common word [as compared with *paradoxon*] for the miraculous in Josephus'.

[2] viii (1965), 113 ff.

that *teras*, which may have meant, at first, a mythological and purely irrational 'portent' (which was often a 'monstrosity') was gradually brought under religious control—as when, in Homer, it is regularly associated with Zeus. But it then passed largely out of use, except in the *Hebrew-based* parts of the Septuagint. *Teras* has no place in the world of Polybius; it is practically lacking in the non-literary papyri; and it is virtually absent from the purely Greek books even of the Septuagint. In the Hebrew-based parts of the Septuagint, however, it frequently stands for the Hebrew *mopheth*. Now this word, too, is, in the Bible, always connected by context with God's direct dealing with the world so as to achieve his purposes. It is thus more than a mere portent or monstrosity, and is a vehicle for revelation. *Mopheth* is frequently parallel with the word *'oth* (which then always precedes it), for which *semeion* ('sign') is the normal rendering; and *semeia* and *terata* becomes a standing phrase for the marvellous happenings of the Exodus, regarded as, *par excellence*, God's revelation of himself in his dealings with his people and in his achieving of his purposes. In the same way, in the rather rare occurrences of *teras* in Philo, the word is theologically handled and subordinated to the activity of God.

Thus it seems reasonable to regard the occurrences of the word in the New Testament as a kind of archaic survival, after the word had been largely dropped by contemporary Greek. Here, in the New Testament, it survived, but only as part of a cliché (and *teras* never occurs without *semeion*) borrowed from the Exodus-idea and applied either to signal manifestations of God or to malicious rivalry by his opponent. Thus, this originally pagan word has been brought inside a cliché which has become fastened to a distinctively religious notion of God's manifest action. Whether there is any significance in the way in which the order varies in the New Testament (see the analysis above) is questionable. Wisd. 10. 16, 19 seems to be the only Septuagintal exception to the order *semeion* and *teras*.

The presence of *teras* having been thus acknowledged and the word having been shown to be, as it were, baptized into a religious connotation, it may now, with the more confidence, be observed that, in fact, the rarity in the New Testament of words denoting mere surprisingness or portentousness is striking. In the Septuagint, 'a marvel', *thaumasion* (= Hebrew *pele'*) frequently occurs; but from the New Testament such words have almost vanished in descriptions of what we (despite this!) still persist in calling 'miracles'. The crowds and onlookers are, it is true, described as expressing mere surprise at what is done, and so, sometimes, are even the disciples; but the actual happenings are described by the Evangelists not as wonders, but as signs of God's power. *Dunamis* and *semeion*—'power' and 'sign'—are the usual terms. Only once is the actual word *thaumasion*, 'a marvel', used in the New Testament for such a deed (Mt. 21. 15). Only once does *paradoxon*, 'a surprising thing, contrary to expectation',[1] occur (Lk. 5. 26)—and then only in the onlookers' exclamation. It is true that *dunamis* is sometimes found in this sense also in pagan writers; it is true, also, that, as we have seen, both *dunamis* and *semeion* are sometimes used in the New Testament in derogatory contexts. But, in the main, the use of terms seems to be significant.

The facts, then, although not patient of a tidy classification, seem to point fairly conclusively to the beginnings of a distinctive outlook on the part of the New Testament. 'Miracle' (*thaumasion*, etc.) is, on very rare occasions, applied by Christian writers to something done by Jesus or by Christians; conversely, both *dunamis* (2 Thess. 2. 9) and *semeion* sometimes apply to what Christians would repudiate as alien; while *teras* lives on, albeit in a limited existence, to show that a word which originally, it seems, denotes the unnatural and monstrous can still be applied by New Testament writers to what they recognize as the deeds of God. But *thaumasion* is so rare as to be nearly extinct in the

---

[1] See G. MacRae's essay (above, p. 143) for the fact that Josephus also makes only very sparing use of this, 'which was a common term in Hellinistic Judaism'.

New Testament vocabulary; and the prevailing usage undoubtedly leans so heavily in the direction of a vocabulary denoting *significant manifestations of power*, as to mark a striking advance, even over the Old Testament, towards concern with the realm of personal relations.[1]

One additional observation is perhaps worth making, namely, that there seems to be in the New Testament, and, indeed, in the whole Bible, a lack of specific words for *omens*—that is, signs *presaging future* events. *Semeion* in Mt. 24. 3 is used thus; and, in the Hebrew of the Old Testament, *'oth* sometimes relates to the future (as in Is. 7. 11, 14; 38. 7, Septuagint, *semeion*): and there are, indeed, in the apocalyptic passages of the New Testament, references to events which are going to indicate a crisis. But there seems to be no actual word in the Hebrew or Greek Bible exactly equivalent to portent. (In the Vulgate, both *portentum* and *prodigium* are used for *teras*.) If there is any significance in this, it is, perhaps, that the Bible is more interested in signs of God at work then and there than in signs which foretell the future.

---

[1] In all fairness to non-Christian Judaism, G. MacRae's remark (already quoted, n. 1, p. 235) about Josephus' use of *semeion* must, however, be borne in mind. And Josephus' use of *epiphaneia* and *emphaneia* (ibid., pp. 145 f.) is striking.

EXCURSUS 2

THE CLASSIFICATION OF MIRACLE STORIES

BY
C. F. D. MOULE

WHAT FOLLOWS is nothing more than a few observations on classifications involved in the comparative study of miracle stories. Such a study, if it ranged freely over many literatures, could fill many life-times, and would require the most complicated system to bring it into anything like coherence. I am concerned only to sketch out some considerations about methods of approach within the very narrow field of such material as is easily available to me.

First of all, it is obviously of value—indeed, probably a necessity—to group the miracle-stories under consideration into categories. The type of classification most widely recognized at present is that used by the techniques of so-called 'form criticism', by which each miracle-story is classified as far as possible (some may think sometimes further than possible) in terms of its apparent stage in its evolution in the course of transmission. The theory is that transmission via the oral tradition of a community causes stories of this type to evolve according to a fairly uniform process: each assumes at first a standard minimum pattern, and this becomes elaborated in the process of transmission. This principle, however plausible theoretically, seldom keeps abreast of the complexities of actual circumstances, and it tends to be too simple and mechanical by far. It is probably better, therefore, although at first sight less scientific, to start, after all, by classifications according to content rather than according to form or pattern.

One very obvious category of content, however, has already been recognized as unsatisfactory in one or two of the essays in this collection: I mean that of the so-called 'nature-miracle'. Nature-miracles are often contrasted with miracles in the personal realm: the stilling of a storm is contrasted with the cure of a leper or, still more, with a 'psychological' cure like exorcism. But it is not only difficult sometimes to know where to draw the line even in a category so defined—is the virgin birth strictly a 'personal' or a nature-miracle, for instance? The category is an unsatisfactory one also because it implies—as I shall observe at greater length in the last section of this note— that there is an order of regularity and consistency in it different from that which obtains in the personal realm. It suggests an *a priori* assumption that you could not alter the weather but you might change a personality; and this is an arbitrary assumption.

On the other hand, a category which does seem to be worth singling out is concerned with content in a very specific way— namely, that of raising from the dead. Although it is perfectly possible for two stories of raisings to belong in opposite categories by the criterion of their *moral* significance and, possibly, of their literary *genre*, nevertheless raisings, as such, do present a category which can be treated as a distinguishable one in its own right. And something might be gained, I think, by asking whatever literatures are under investigation such questions about this particular category as the following: (*a*) How are these stories distributed? For instance, within the Bible, note the extreme paucity of raisings in the Old Testament; and, within the New Testament, note the frequency of mere allusions to them in contrast to the paucity of circumstantial descriptions; note, too, the paucity of such stories outside the Gospels; and, outside the Bible, the rapid diminution until a much later date; and so forth. (*b*) What are the characteristics of the subjects—young or old, male or female, recently or long deceased? (*c*) In the Christian literature, what is the distinction between the raisings attributed to Jesus, and the rising from death of Jesus himself?

Wherein do the 'Resurrection'-narratives differ from narratives of 'raisings'?

Another reasonably well-defined category of content is exorcism, and I cannot help thinking that the last word has not yet been said about many of the questions which it poses. Why— to ask the familiar question—has the Fourth Gospel no instance, although it contains references to demon-possession? Why, in the Synoptic Gospels, is exorcism almost confined to the material shared by all three? Why is there virtually none in the Old Testament (unless it be in the story of Saul)? Why does it come back again in the post-New Testament period?[1]

Yet a third category of content might be 'second sight'.

So much, for the moment, for categorization by content. Another mode of approach to comparative study might be through the examination of degrees of credulity (or credence) and scepticism. As we have already seen, there are ancient literatures where miracles seem simply not to be believed in, or, at least, not taken into account (e.g. 1 Macc.) and others (e.g. 2 Macc.) where they are recounted in plenty; and R. M. Grant quotes instances from antiquity of expressed incredulity. But there is a slightly different and more subtle aspect of the same question to be noticed, when one asks what indications are there in a given literature of the attitude of the writer's audience —or of the witnesses present, or alleged to have been present, in the story? For instance, in Jn. 9. 32 the onlookers are made to declare that the opening of the eyes of a man born blind was something that had never been heard of before; the Christians, fervently praying for Peter's release, tell Rhoda (Acts 12. 15) that she is mad, as soon as she announces that the prayer is answered—and so on; whereas, in other instances, the miracle may be accepted as almost commonplace, but the means are questioned—is it by Beelzebub, or by the finger of God? Does this apply only to exorcisms? A further aspect of the same line of inquiry might, of course, concern itself with the presence of

[1] See pp. 215 ff. above.

rationalizations. Luke has a sort of rationalization (though demonstrably misconceived), Lk. 23. 45, where the 'supernatural' darkness at the crucifixion is decribed as due to an eclipse of the sun. R. M. Grant has examples from antiquity, and Mr. Sweet's essay considers that extremely interesting example from Wisdom.

Once again, one might usefully classify according to the degree of reticence: contrast all the Gospel Resurrection-narratives with (e.g.) the apocryphal Petrine tradition.

Further, the distribution of miracle-stories over the whole of the literature under consideration, or within sections of it, might obviously be significant. Miracles in Mark, for instance, as has been noted,[1] decrease in frequency from the beginning to the end of the Gospel. The distribution of different categories is equally something to be watched: reference has already been made to the distribution of raisings and exorcisms.

The presence or absence of miracle stories in the stories of outstanding persons is again, a matter for comparative observation. 'John did no miracle . . .' (Jn. 10. 41) is a most striking pronouncement. The patriarchs, I think, have no miracle stories attaching to them in the Old Testament, though Moses and many of the prophets have. No miracles are attributed to the infant or child Jesus in the canonical Gospels.

All such observations, and many more, may help to organize the material for consideration. But, on reflection, it seems to me that the only categories that are ultimately significant are those which take into account what character is implied for God by the stories under consideration. One might, perhaps, speak of stories of destructive miracles over against restorative or creative ones; and, again, of miracles with no apparent moral content over against those with a moral significance. In the hierarchy of classification, this, it would seem, is the only comprehensive one, over and above the purely literary types

[1] See p. 159

of classification—which, of course, are endless—and classifications of content. The literary and narrative form of a miracle story may vary considerably; the content is, as has been said, another criterion; and in a comparative study these are obviously important. But it is the theological implications of the content that matter most.

The infancy narratives of Thomas, for instance, are full of sheer conjuring-tricks without moral content—or, in some cases, with an immoral content. So in the Old Testament, there are the 'conjuring-tricks' of Moses and Aaron (Exod. 7. 8–12), and a good many 'destructive' miracles. Even in the New Testament there is the seemingly 'amoral' turning of water into wine (Jn. 2. 1–11), if it is not actually meant as an allegory; and certain 'destructive' miracles—in the Gospels, the swine (Mk. 5. 13) and the fig-tree (Mk. 11. 20); in the Acts, Ananias and Sapphira (Acts 5) and Elymas (Acts 13. 11); in the Revelation (but only in vision), what the two witnesses can do (Rev. 11. 5). But the bulk of the New Testament miracles are constructive and manifestly moral in the sense that they exhibit motives compatible with the character of Christ as we know it by other evidence, and the dealings of God with his children as full persons. The 'conjuring-tricks' of immunity in Mk. 16. 17 f. (cf. Acts 28. 5) might possibly be defended as at least symbols of the immunity of God's witnesses from harm until their commission is complete, in the same sort of way in which stories of release from prison (Acts 12, etc.) might be viewed. On the other hand many or all of these, in the light of authenticity tests, fall more naturally into the category of the symbolic, like the story of the burning fiery furnace in Daniel.

BIBLIOGRAPHY

THE FOLLOWING bibliography makes no attempt to be exhaustive. It simply exhibits, without necessarily recommending, books and articles that have come to hand or been noticed in the course of this investigation.[1]

BERTRAM, G., article θαῦμα, etc., *Theologisches Wörterbuch zum Neuen Testament*, ed. G. Kittel, vol. iii (Stuttgart, Kohlhammer, 1938), 27 ff.

BURKILL, T. A., *Mysterious Revelation* (Cornell Univ. Press, 1963).

CAIRNS, D. S., *The Faith that Rebels* (S.C.M., 1928; 3rd ed., 1929).

DELLING, G., 'Josephus und das Wunderbare', *Novum Testamentum*, 2 (1957–8), 291 ff.

DELLING, G., *Wunder-Allegorie-Mythus bei Philon von Alexandreia*, Wiss. Zeitschr. der Martin-Luther-Universität, Halle-Wittenberg, Ges.-Sprachw. VI/5 (1957), 713 ff.

DODD, C. H., 'Miracles in the Gospels', *Expository Times*, 44 (1932–3), 504 ff.

FARMER, H. H., *The World and God* (Nisbet, 1935, revised ed., 1936), Chh. IX, X.

FIEBIG, P., *Die Umwelt des Neuen Testamentes* (Göttingen, 1926).

FIEBIG, P., *Rabbinische Wundergeschichten*, Kleine Texte, ed. H. Lietzmann, 78 (Bonn, 1911). *Antike Wundergeschichten*, Kleine Texte, ed. H. Lietzmann, 79 (Bonn, 1911).

FRIDRICHSEN, A., *Le Problème du Miracle* (Strasbourg, 1925).

FULLER, R. H., *Interpreting the Miracles* (S.C.M., 1963).

GOODWIN, J., *Why Miracles?* (Simeon Booklets No. 10, S.P.C.K., 1964).

GRANT, R. M., *Miracle and Natural Law in Graeco-Roman and Early Christian Thought* (Amsterdam, 1952).

GRUNDMANN, W., article δύναμαι, etc., *Theologisches Wörterbuch zum Neuen Testament*, ed. G. Kittel, ii (Stuttgart, Kohlhammer, 1935), 286 ff.

GUTTMANN, A., 'The Significance of Miracles for Talmudic Judaism', *Hebr. Un. Coll. Ann.* 20 (1947), 363 ff.

KALLAS, J., *The Significance of the Synoptic Miracles* (S.P.C.K., 1961).

LAWTON, J. S., *Miracles and Revelation* (Lutterworth, 1959).

LOHSE, E., article χείρ, in *Theologisches Wörterbuch zum Neuen Testament*, ed. G. Kittel and G. Friedrich, viii (Stuttgart, Kohlhammer, forthcoming).

---

[1] References to further and more specialized works occur in the essays.

LEWIS, C. S., *Miracles: a Preliminary Study* (London, Geoffrey Bles, 1947).

McCASLAND, S. V., *By the Finger of God* (New York, 1951).

McCASLAND, S. V., article 'Miracle' in *The Interpreter's Dictionary of the Bible* (Abingdon, 1962), iii, 392ᵇ ff.

MARTIN, B., *The Healing Ministry of the Church* (Lutterworth, 1960).

NEIL, W., 'Expository Problems: the Nature Miracles', *Expository Times*, 67 (1955–6), 369 ff.

PRITCHARD, J. B., 'Motifs of O.T. Miracles', *Crozer Quarterly*, 27 (1959), 97 ff.

RENGSTORF, K. H., article τέρας, *Theologisches Wörterbuch zum Neuen Testament*, ed. G. Kittel and G. Friedrich, viii (Stuttgart, Kohlhammer, 1965), 113 ff.

RICHARDSON, A., *The Miracle Stories of the Gospels* (London, S.C.M., 1941).

SMITH, MORTON, 'A Comparison of Early Christian and Early Rabbinic Tradition', *Journal of Biblical Literature*, 82 (1963), 169 ff. (esp. 173).

SMITH, MORTON, *Tannaitic Parallels to the Gospels* (*Journal of Biblical Literature*, Monograph Series, VI, Philadelphia, 1951).

SCHLATTER, A., *Das Wunder in der Synagoge* (Beitr. z. Förd. Chr. Theol. 16. 5 (1912)), 49 ff.

S.P.C.K. Theological Collections, *The Miracles and the Resurrection: some recent studies by I. T. Ramsey, G. H. Boobyer, F. N. Davey, M. C. Perry, Henry J. Cadbury* (S.P.C.K., 1964).

TAYLOR, A. E., *David Hume and the Miraculous* (Cambridge, 1927).

VAN DER LOOS, H., *The Miracles of Jesus* (Leiden, Brill, 1965).

WILDER, A. N., *Early Christian Rhetoric* (London, S.C.M., 1964), 68 ff.